MW00564187

GOLD RUSH

GOLD RUSH

How Mr. Prospector
Became Racing's Billion Dollar Sire

BY AVALYN HUNTER

Lexington, Kentucky

Copyright © 2007 Blood-Horse Publications

All rights reserved. No part of this book may be reproduced in any
form by any means, including photocopying, audio recording, or
any information storage or retrieval
system, without the permission in writing from the copyright holder.
Inquiries should be addressed to Publisher, Blood-Horse
Publications, Box 919003, Lexington, KY 40591-9003.

Library of Congress Cataloging-in-Publication Data

Hunter, Avalyn.
    Gold rush : how Mr. Prospector became racing's billion-dollar sire
    / by Avalyn Hunter.
—1st ed.
        p. cm.
    ISBN-13: 978-1-58150-173-5 (hardcover)
    1. Mr. Prospector (Race horse) 2. Race horses—United States—
    Biography.
I. Title.
    SF355.M7H86 2007
    798.40092'9—dc22
    [B]

                                                    2007015132

Printed in the United States of America
First Edition: 2007

a division of
Blood-Horse Publications
PUBLISHERS SINCE 1916

Contents

Introduction

A Champion That Never Was

A small crowd filled the Gulfstream Park winner's circle —
beaming owners, track dignitaries, photographers. And, of course,
the winning horse: veins popped on the silken near-black coat, nostrils
flared, eyes bright, a blanket of orchids draped over the sweat-slick neck
and shoulders.

But one person was missing — the trainer. "I have to go
saddle the big horse," said Jimmy Croll as he excused himself from the
ceremonies.

The big horse? A horse that excited Croll more than
Royal and Regal, his newly minted winner of the 1973 Florida Derby?
The next race was only an allowance for non-winners of three races
worth $3,100 or more to the winner since the previous October 15
other than maiden or claiming. The Florida Derby had been the
feature race on the card; this was just a routine six-furlong sprint.

Except that it wasn't routine. A bay streak whipped through the
first quarter in :21 3/5, seizing the lead by half a length. At the half
he was on top by five in :43 2/5, which meant he'd run his second
quarter in :21 4/5. Most seasoned stakes horses can't keep that kind
of pace going; they're done by the stretch call, gasping and being
passed by one late runner after another. The bay colt couldn't quite

keep that pace either, but he didn't need to. He'd run his nine rivals dizzy, sauntering his last quarter in :24 2/5 and stopping the teletimer in 1:07 4/5.

It was a new track record. Jimmy Croll's "big horse" had just clipped three-fifths of a second off the Gulfstream Park track record, had just missed tying Grey Papa's world record for the distance by only two-fifths of a second. And he hadn't been pushed in the least; he'd been in hand at the finish, winning as jockey Walter Blum pleased. Nine and one-half lengths separated him from second-place Son of Glut, a colt that already had a stakes win to his credit.

Small wonder that the name on everyone's lips the next morning wasn't "Royal and Regal."

It was "Mr. Prospector."

The making of a champion racehorse takes many things. It takes a trainer with the ability to see talent and develop it both mentally and physically at the horse's pace. It takes an owner's dreams and ambitions in putting money into an unraced yearling or two-year-old, or perhaps buying a broodmare, breeding her, and waiting the long months and years for the foal to be born and grow into a racehorse. It takes grooms, whose daily care helps keep the horse healthy and happy, and equipment that fits properly and is suited to the animal. It takes a huge dollop of luck. And, of course, it takes those factors that lie within the racehorse itself: speed, stamina, courage, soundness, the desire to run.

Mr. Prospector was one of those horses that seemed to have it all. Born of the finest of Thoroughbred parentage, he was a colt that even an inexperienced eye would have picked out as something more than ordinary from the first. A sales-topping yearling, he had been placed in the hands of a veteran trainer with a fine reputation for developing young horses. The colt had speed and desire, and on March 31, 1973, it all came together in a breathtaking performance at Gulfstream Park.

Yet the promise Mr. Prospector had shown on a spring day in Florida was never fully realized. There would be no trophies from major stakes races on his owner's mantelpiece, no championship speeches made in his honor. With legs battered by repeated injuries, he would limp away from racing to a modest place as a stallion at his owner's Florida farm.

Repeated injuries always raise the question of unsoundness, and indeed, there is cause to believe that part of the fault lay within Mr. Prospector's makeup. Yet, unsoundness seldom arises in isolation; it is most often an interaction between a horse's innate level of fragility and the tasks it is asked to do. For some, the basic demands of racing are too much. For others, unsoundness results when an animal is asked to do more than its level of maturity or fitness can handle. And many horses walk a hair-thin line between racing fitness and unsoundness, the balance depending on the skill of the trainer in managing their physical limitations and placing them where they can be competitive without being overstressed. Sometimes, too, the owner must be managed with delicate skill: too much rigidity on the trainer's part and he loses the horse to another barn, but too much unchecked ambition on the owner's part, and the horse may pay a bitter price as it is pushed beyond limitations the owner may be unable or unwilling to see.

Potential, promise, dreams, and fragility — this is the world of the Thoroughbred racehorse: a world in which the difference between a great champion and just another name in the records may be a single crucial decision.

Potential, promise, dreams, and fragility — this was Mr. Prospector, a champion that never was.

Two Men And A Horse

1

Warren A. "Jimmy" Croll Jr. was already a thirty-year veteran of the racetracks by the time Mr. Prospector came into his life, though Croll hadn't originally planned on a career as a racehorse trainer. Yet horses were in his blood from an early age. Born in Pennsylvania in 1920, he had grown up in the Eastern hunt country, riding in foxhunts and hunt-meeting flat races and sometimes helping with a string of cheap horses his uncle raced in Maryland.

Croll knew from early on that his future would involve horses, so following high school, he enrolled in the University of Pennsylvania with veterinary medicine as his long-term goal. But he loved hands-on horse work too much to stay away from it. Arranging his classes so that they didn't start before 10 a.m., he would drive daily to his friend Morris Dixon's farm to gallop horses for him from six to nine in the morning. He also made rounds with veterinarian R.D. Connolley, who taught the young Croll practical skills in managing equine injuries.

Croll could have made a good veterinarian, but he was restless in the classroom; it was the actual work with the animals that he enjoyed. Also, the strain of galloping horses for three hours every morning while still carrying a full schedule of classes was getting to him. As he later confessed to the *Daily Racing Form*, he became so preoccupied one morning that he snapped back to alertness to find himself driving the wrong way down a one-way street. It was quickly becoming apparent he could either become a veterinarian or immerse himself in the life of a hands-on horseman, but he could not do both.

So after a year and a half at the university, he made his choice. He left school and began earning his daily bread by wintering horses and breaking yearlings in Pennsylvania over the winter of 1939–40. By the spring of 1940, he had his trainer's license and was working with a string of claimers for Dr. Jack Deubler at the Havre de Grace meeting in Maryland.

He'd also picked up a filly by the English import *Pick of the Circus for a mere $50, and that year at Delaware Park she rewarded him by becoming his first winner. All told, Circus Wings won five races as a three-year-old in 1940 and eventually wound up winning twenty-three races and $21,687 from 142 starts. Fifteen years later Croll still pegged Circus Wings as his best business venture ever.

A stint in the Army — cavalry, naturally — interrupted Croll's training career, but he got right back to the track the day after he left the military service. He began training horses for Blue Stone Farm, the *nom de course* of his uncle, W. Ellis Johnson. For Johnson, Croll trained the speedy stakes winner War Phar, who set a track record of 1:03 2/5 for 5 1/2 furlongs at Gulfstream Park in 1953, and Scimitar, a $5,000 claim who ended up winning two stakes and $88,000.

Scimitar was a tricky horse to manage. Although gifted with natural speed, he was constantly beset by minor injuries and required careful management. At that, he was probably sounder than Sharpsburg, an *Alibhai colt whom Croll bought from Calumet Farm on behalf of Roy Faircloth for a mere $2,500. The price reflected Jimmy Jones' belief that Sharpsburg was a hopeless cripple, but the sale proved to be one of

Jones' rare errors in judgment. Sharpsburg was never terribly sound — in the words of the *Daily Racing Form*, he had "an amazing list of infirmities" — but under Croll's care he developed into a nice handicap horse at five, winning four 1958 stakes and running second by three-quarters of a length to the great Bold Ruler in that year's Monmouth Handicap. Sharpsburg eventually earned $200,056.

Croll was, in fact, developing quite a reputation for his ability to make runners out of horses that other trainers had given up on, and his experience with such horses as Scimitar and Sharpsburg stood him in good stead a few years later when he was training Parka for Rachel Carpenter's Pelican Stable. Having been claimed out of a $10,000 race at Atlantic City in 1961, Parka began showing stakes-level ability as a four-year-old in 1962 and won seven turf stakes for Croll and Mrs. Carpenter in 1963–64. But the gelding chipped a sesamoid in February 1965 in the Hialeah Turf Cup, and Mrs. Carpenter ordered him retired to a life of ease rather than risk a breakdown.

She meant well, but she hadn't quite reckoned on the bond between Parka and his trainer. Wanting to care for Parka personally and fearing the horse would fret away from his familiar surroundings, Croll asked for and received permission to keep him with the racing string rather than send him to the farm. After having the loose sesamoid chip removed and giving the horse sixty days of stall rest, Croll began walking Parka along the shed row. That touch of racetrack routine seemed to perk up the gelding's interest in life; further, he was walking sound. So the veterinarians were called in. After examining Parka, they told Croll the horse was fit to resume training. And so he was: By the end of the year, Parka had won four more good turf stakes, including the $125,000 United Nations Handicap at Atlantic City, and had been crowned the nation's champion turf horse.

Parka put some extra change in Croll's pockets, too. Always known as a generous owner, a delighted Mrs. Carpenter gave bonuses to both Croll and jockey Walter Blum on top of the normal 10 percent of the purse each received after the gelding won the United Nations. Croll certainly didn't mind the extra money, but it left him at something of a loss, which he resolved in the manner of a born horseman. He went shopping at the Timonium sales in Maryland and came home with four yearlings.

Croll was not exactly playing at the top end of the market. His four purchases totaled $18,200, with the most expensive of the lot being a $6,500 filly by Pied d'Or. Three of the youngsters were quickly resold at cost to some of the owners Croll trained for, but no one offered for the Pied d'Or filly. A year later, racing in the colors of Croll's wife, Bobbi, Like a Charm won all three of her starts, including the Sorority Stakes, boosting her value to a lot more than $6,500. As if that were not enough, she later produced grade III stakes winner Herecomesthebride, winner of six stakes and $174,368 for the partnership of Mrs. Croll and Mrs. Carpenter, as well as three other stakes winners.

Herecomesthebride was sired by another of Croll's bargain purchases, a gray colt by The Axe II whom the trainer had picked up for $14,000 on Mrs. Carpenter's behalf at the 1967 Keeneland summer yearling sale. (According to legend, Mrs. Carpenter — who had a noted predilection for grays — specifically told Croll prior to the sale that she wanted him to buy her a dapple-gray colt within a specific budget, but Croll has always denied being given such orders.) Named Al Hattab, the attractive youngster — a shorter-legged, more compact version of his Epsom Derby-winning grandsire *Mahmoud — went on to win ten stakes and $452,913 before becoming a successful sire.

It rapidly was becoming apparent that Croll was every bit as gifted at spotting young talent at modest prices as he was at rehabilitating other trainers' rejects. In addition to Al Hattab, his purchases at the 1967 Keeneland sale included a bay son of Never Bend for $21,000. Named Prevailing, the colt won four stakes and $147,007 before going to stud in Florida. (He eventually was sold for stud duty in Ireland.)

Prevailing was the first good horse Croll trained for Abraham "Butch" Savin who only had gotten into racing a few years earlier. The first racehorse to carry Savin's silks was Needles' Count, a colt Savin had bought for $10,000 at the 1964 Hialeah sale of two-year-olds in training. As Savin later confessed to Joe Hirsch of the *Daily Racing Form*, the purchase was more whimsical than planned. He hadn't particularly intended to buy a horse when he went to the sale, but the chance to pick up a nice-looking son of Needles at a bargain price was a little too tempting to resist, especially when a glance at the sale catalog revealed the colt and Savin shared a March 1 birthday. As a racing fan, Savin had thought a lot of Needles, the co-champion juvenile male of 1955 and champion three-year-old of 1956, and when he saw the bidding moving slowly on the colt out of Countess Tecla because of a slight cut on one hind leg, Savin waded in and found himself with a racehorse.

Savin put his new purchase into training with Les Lear, a former professional football player and coach who had previously trained the brilliant juvenile Sadair. In a fictional racing story, Needles' Count would doubtless have gone on to be a Kentucky Derby winner. In the real world, the truth was more prosaic but still pretty nice for Savin's newly formed Aisco Stable, as the colt developed into a solid allowance runner and eventually bankrolled $84,227. It was a good experience for the first-time owner, if not exactly the stuff Hollywood scripts are made of.

Even before Needles' Count showed what he was made of, however, Savin had moved ahead with his Thoroughbred interests. In the summer of 1964, he bought more young horses at the Saratoga summer sales. Then, in 1965, Savin made two key purchases: 450 acres of undeveloped land near Ocala, Florida, and a two-year-old filly by Native Dancer, one of seven young horses that Savin purchased at the Hialeah sale of two-year-olds in training. By the end of the following year, Native Street had won the Kentucky Oaks and the tract of land had become Aisco Farm, where Savin would breed Thoroughbreds for nearly two decades.

Although Savin came into the Thoroughbred game already past sixty when he bought Needles' Count, horses had been part of his life ever since he worked with draft horses on his father's farm as a young boy in New London, Connecticut.

World War I found the young Savin employed in helping to build gun emplacements for the Army Corps of Engineers on Fishers Island, a narrow strip of land in Long Island Sound. From there, Savin worked for other construction outfits and then struck out on his own, forming the Abraham I. Savin Construction Company, or Aisco, in 1928. He prospered immensely, playing major roles in the construction of New York's Idlewild Airport, the New Jersey Turnpike, and Pittsburgh's Conemaugh Dam, among other major projects. Although he sold Aisco in the early 1960s, he soon purchased another firm, the Balf Quarry Company, and continued contracting major construction projects.

With his business, his memberships in numerous professional and civic organizations, his family, and his hobbies of aviation and golf, Savin was a busy man. He never forgot his boyhood love of horses, however, and always kept several saddle horses at his Connecticut estate.

He was also an enthusiastic racing fan when time permitted. And so it was natural enough that when the moment came, he tackled his venture into the Thoroughbreds with the same combination of enthusiasm and business sense that had made him one of the country's leading contractors.

Named after Savin's original construction company (as was-Savin's *nom de course*, Aisco Stable), Aisco Farm soon became a showplace. Its most unique feature was a twenty-seven stall oval-shaped barn built around a massive oak tree. In the surrounding pastures a growing broodmare band grazed, with Native Street the star of the herd after her retirement in 1967. And by the early 1970s, several stallions had taken up residence in the stud barn, headed by Prevailing (whose first foals were born in 1972) and a son of Round Table named Around Two Turns. Both were well bred: Prevailing could claim as his granddam a full sister to 1941 Triple Crown winner Whirlaway while Around Two Turns was a half brother to 1959 Horse of the Year Sword Dancer. Other members of the Aisco Farm stallion roster included Amazing, an unraced son of Bold Ruler out of the War Admiral mare Striking, and 1968 Widener Handicap winner Sette Bello, a son of *Ribot.

Not one of these stallions was the kind someone could build a farm around, however, and Savin knew it. He was not so wealthy that he could afford to buy a top-class stallion even if one were available for sale, nor was a first-flight racehorse within his means to buy as a stallion prospect. His options were limited: He could try to breed a first-class colt himself, or he could try to spot a good prospect in the yearling market at a price he could afford.

Savin did meet with success in breeding; in fact, his very first homebred winner proved to be a champion. The only hitch was that it was a filly. Named Forward Gal, the chestnut filly by Native Charger out of Forward Thrust won the Sorority Stakes at Monmouth Park, the Spinaway Stakes at Saratoga, and the Frizette Stakes at Belmont to claim the 1970 champion two-year-old filly title for Savin and Jimmy Croll.

The year 1970 also saw the birth of Native Street's third foal. Her first foal, a 1968 son of Nashua, had been a hulking disappointment who at Croll's recommendation was sold before he ever raced; named Dependable, he eventually broke his maiden in a $7,500 claimer. Her second foal, a 1969 son of Buckpasser named Native Admiral, was more promising (he would go on to place in stakes at two and three), but this third foal, a neatly made son of *Vaguely Noble, looked like he could possibly be something special. By the colt's first birthday, Savin was already fielding offers for the youngster, whom he had named Royal and Regal.

But as good as Royal and Regal looked, Savin didn't want to pin all of his hopes on the colt panning out as either a racehorse or a sire. So when the catalog for the 1971 Keeneland July yearling sale came out, Savin looked through it, then asked Croll to come help him pick out a horse.

After underlining the names of some fifteen to twenty colts that Savin and Croll thought might have good pedigrees for prospective sires, the two traveled to Lexington where pre-sale inspection of the youngsters pared the list down to one. This was Spendthrift Farm's handsome bay colt by Raise a Native out of Gold Digger, foaled on January 28, 1970. Of medium size, the colt was a well-built, masculine individual with an unusually straight and powerful hind leg.

The colt's pedigree was certainly everything Savin could have hoped for. His sire, Raise a Native, was undefeated in four starts at two and had been the co-champion two-year-old male of 1963 before settling down to a successful stallion career at Spendthrift Farm. He had all the blinding speed of his sire, the great Native Dancer, and had already proven he could sire a staying runner by getting Majestic Prince, winner of the 1969 Kentucky Derby and Preakness Stakes.

Raise a Native's one question mark was soundness — a bowed tendon had ended his career — but his mate, Gold Digger, amply compensated. A daughter of the iron-sound Nashua, Horse of the Year in 1955, Gold Digger had won ten of her thirty-five starts. Five of her victories had come in stakes, and she boasted as good a family as any other mare in the country. Her dam, Sequence, was a stakes-winning daughter of 1943 Triple Crown winner Count Fleet out of the Kentucky Oaks winner Miss Dogwood, who was herself a daughter of the excellent sire *Bull Dog and Myrtlewood, the American champion sprinter of 1936.

The problem for Savin and Croll was that just about everyone else at the sale could see the colt's potential, too. As *The Blood-Horse's* Kent Hollingsworth put it, the colt's conformation was exciting "nothing but praise and admiration." Further, the colt's full brother Search for Gold, an $80,000 purchase for leading Canadian owner-breeder E.P. Taylor at the previous year's Keeneland July sale, had just finished second in the National Stallion Stakes at Belmont Park.

For Croll, the auction proved a nerve-wracking experience. "I'd bought horses before, of course," he recalled during a 2006 interview. "But it was mostly like $10,000 or $15,000 for a horse. I really had no idea what this colt might be worth. So the bidding kept going up, and Mr. Savin kept looking at me and I'd say 'yes' for each bid he wanted to make. But when the price got up over $100,000, I started getting nervous, and I slowed down. At $150,000 I just dropped my head and from then on Mr. Savin did the bidding without me. And, of course, he got the horse for $220,000, which was a lot of money back then. He used to rib me for years after that about my looking at my shoes instead of him and mumbling

'I don't know' when he asked me if he should keep bidding.

"Anyway, there was another problem, though I didn't find out about it until later. You see, Mr. Savin didn't have enough ready cash to pay for the colt. So he went to Mr. Combs [Leslie Combs II, the colt's breeder and consignor], unbeknownst to me, and talked him into spreading the payments over six months. And that's how we got Mr. Prospector."

For the moment Savin could bask in the limelight. He had just purchased the most expensive horse in the entire sale. But in the back of his mind, the thought that he had just taken a $220,000 gamble on the future of his Thoroughbred business had to be lurking. After all, the horse was at least four times more expensive than any of his previous yearling purchases — according to grandson Scott Savin when interviewed by Gene McLean of the Lexington *Herald-Leader* in 1987, Butch Savin had never spent more than about $45,000 for a youngster before. Would the new colt pan out, or would he be one of Thoroughbred racing's long list of expensive disappointments?

Only time would tell.

Derby Fever

2

Derby fever is a strange malady. It intoxicates doting owners with dreams of roses and makes them believe their otherwise ordinary colts have suddenly grown the wings of Pegasus. Hundreds of these owners pay rich fees to make their horses eligible for American racing's magnificent obsession — the Kentucky Derby.

For most of the young horses involved, no real harm is done; cold reality, in the form of mediocre racing performances, soon brings the owners back to earth. For a fortunate few three-year-olds everything comes together in the months leading to the Derby: talent, performance, maturity, and good racing health. But for the yet immature or inexperienced colts that have shown evidence of raw talent, the road to Churchill Downs is fraught with peril; for too many, it becomes a dead end.

For Mr. Prospector, of course, such considerations were still well in the future. Like many other young horses, he was busy transitioning from the pampered, relatively inactive life of a yearling destined for the major sales to the more rigorous life of a two-year-old in training. Under Croll's watchful eye, he would learn to accept saddle, bridle, and rider and begin the arduous process of physical and mental conditioning needed to turn an unbroken youngster into a racehorse.

Horses are individuals, and no two are alike in how they train in the long months leading to their first race. Some are eager, some are downright reluctant, and some are merely going along with what is asked of them. Most of the intelligent ones learn everything quickly; those that are dim-witted or high strung require endless patience and repetition to learn the basics. Like big, growthy teenagers, some young horses require extra time to develop coordination; a few have everything come together early only to burn out later as their slower-maturing peers come into their own.

With Mr. Prospector, Jimmy Croll knew early he had a runner — "from day one," as he later put it. The colt was proving a trainer's dream: easy to handle around the barn and eager, yet businesslike, on the track. And then there was the way he moved: easy, fluid, powerful.

Like all young Thoroughbreds, however, Mr. Prospector was having to adapt to the new demands being put on his body — demands that proved just a little too much for a growing horse. He developed shin splints. A common ailment among two-year-olds, shin splints result when the sheath covering the front of the cannon bones becomes inflamed, usually a result of too much stress on the animal's forelegs as bone development struggles to catch up with the need for greater strength and density imposed by training. The condition is not usually considered serious and is treated by hosing the legs with cold water, administering anti-inflammatory medication, and backing off training until the inflammation subsides.

Many horsemen of decades past also used firing (repeatedly jabbing a heated pin or probe into the inflamed area) as part of the treatment. While undoubtedly painful for the horse, firing was believed to speed healing by encouraging blood flow to the inflamed area. Some horsemen still use this method to treat chronic inflammations that have not responded to other treatments (though sedation and local anesthesia now generally are used).

Croll, believing Mr. Prospector might benefit from the procedure, went ahead and had the area fired. However, at about the same time, he also spotted something he didn't like: a small irregularity in the right front cannon that didn't respond to the firing; if anything, it seemed to be getting ever so slightly larger as the colt resumed training. Still, it was a small blemish, and the colt seemed to be moving without discomfort as his shin splints cleared up.

Croll decided to take the colt along with the rest of the string he was shipping from Belmont Park to Saratoga. The colt was shaping up nicely for a possible debut at the quickly approaching meet, but the little knot on his right foreleg niggled at the trainer. He called in the track veterinarian, who took X-rays and found nothing.

Despite the veterinary reassurance, however, Croll still wasn't quite satisfied and kept a close eye on the youngster. When the time came for Mr. Prospector's first breeze over the Saratoga surface, Croll watched keenly.

"When he came back, I asked the rider how he felt," Croll recalled. "And the rider said, 'He felt a little off pulling up.' So I had X-rays taken again, and this time they found a tiny crack, maybe a quarter-inch long, in his right front cannon. We had to stop on him until Hialeah. If we hadn't found it, we were going to run him at Saratoga some time that week."

Years later Croll told author Ed Bowen he regretted not being able to run Mr. Prospector as a two-year-old. Yet the trainer's acumen may have been the difference between Mr. Prospector's having a racing career and his being just another fine prospect that broke down early.

* * *

The months slipped by, and with the winter Croll's stable shipped to Florida. Like all Northern Hemisphere-born Thoroughbreds of 1970, Mr. Prospector and Royal and Regal both officially turned three on January 1, 1973.

Still, Croll took his time with Mr. Prospector, and the colt was responding. Working in the mornings with Royal and Regal and the older Second Bar — a proven runner with five stakes wins under his belt — Mr. Prospector was more than holding his own. Jaws were clacking around the backstretch about the speedy Raise a Native colt, more so after Royal and Regal proved his own quality with scores in the grade III Dade Turf Handicap on January 6 and in the grade III Bahamas Stakes on January 31.

At long last Croll was satisfied Mr. Prospector was 100 percent fit to make his long-awaited debut. He entered the colt in a six-furlong maiden special weight at Hialeah on February 6.

The race was the first on the card, and Mr. Prospector opened the day's racing with a flourish. Under the handling of jockey Walter Blum, the colt broke alertly, prompted the pace of Imposer for a quarter-mile, then drew off steadily to win by twelve lengths. Despite Blum's taking the colt in hand down the stretch, Mr. Prospector's time of 1:09 4/5 was just one second off the track record set eleven years earlier by Beau Admiral. The next day, Fred Gallant, writing for the *Daily Racing Form*, opined that had Blum not applied the brakes during the final sixteenth of a mile, Mr. Prospector would surely have set a track record — and this while carrying 122 pounds against the 110 that the four-year-old Beau Admiral had carried.

Many a maiden has debuted impressively only never to be heard from again. Mr. Prospector was, after all, expected to win; he had gone to the post as a heavy favorite. Nor was the field he defeated distinguished, though one of the also-rans, Billy Come Lately, would mature well enough to win the historic Massachusetts Handicap, a grade II event, at four. But the style in which Mr. Prospector won was something else. The buzz that had begun with his impressive pre-race works was doubled and redoubled: This colt just might be something special — very special.

On February 2 Mr. Prospector did nothing to disappoint his backers in his second start, a seven-furlong allowance for non-winners of a race other than maiden or claiming. Again away alertly, Mr. Prospector hustled right to the front and stayed there throughout, winning by 5 3/4 lengths in a solid time of 1:23 2/5. Two races later a quick colt named Shecky Greene — already winner of the rich Arlington-Washington Futurity the year before — captured the Carl G. Rose Memorial Handicap at the same distance in 1:22 3/5 while under intermittent urging.

Jimmy Croll was never one to rush a horse, and it is a measure of his confidence in Mr. Prospector that the colt's next target was the seven-furlong Hutcheson Stakes at Gulfstream Park, a grade III sprint for which Shecky Greene also was being pointed. But on March 4, three days before the Hutcheson, Mr. Prospector began running a fever. Although not serious, the illness left Croll with no choice but to scratch the colt from the Hutcheson. In his absence, Shecky Greene started as the odds-on favorite and won by 3 1/4 lengths from Forego while equaling the track record of 1:20 4/5.

Mr. Prospector quickly shook off the fever and was soon demanding his feed as vigorously as ever. Nonetheless, Croll, ever cautious, chose a relatively easy spot for the colt's return to racing: a six-furlong allowance on the Florida Derby undercard.

On March 31, 1973, Mr. Prospector went to the post in the day's tenth race at Gulfstream Park. A jaw-dropping 1:07 4/5 later, Jimmy Croll had a big problem: Butch Savin had Derby fever.

***

Immediately following the Florida Derby card, Croll made it clear to the press that no decision had been made regarding Mr. Prospector's status as a Kentucky Derby prospect. Two days later, when questioned as to whether the colt would run for the roses, Croll was noncommittal. "A possibility, but remote," was all he would say.

But behind the scenes, the pressure was building rapidly, as Croll recalled during a 2006 interview. "After the race [Mr. Prospector's Gulfstream win], Mr. Savin and his sons, Herb and Peter, were all pushing for me to get the horse ready for the Kentucky Derby — especially Peter, who liked to gamble. I told them I couldn't get the horse ready to go 1 1/4 miles in just a month off a couple of six-furlong races.

"They said, 'If you don't, we'll find someone who will.' And I couldn't afford to quit."

When interviewed by Gene McLean of the Lexington *Herald-Leader* in 1987, Butch Savin's grandson Scott also recalled an increasingly heated situation. "There's no doubt," he said. "We all had Triple Crown fever. He [Mr. Prospector] was the fastest horse I have ever seen."

By April 4 the matter was settled: Mr. Prospector was going to Kentucky along with Royal and Regal. Publicly, Croll was positive about the trip. "He is a lot of horse, and I felt he deserved the chance to show what he can do," the trainer told Marvin Gay Jr. of the

Louisville *Courier-Journal*. However, Croll admitted that the colt's lack of experience and seasoning worried him.

And in private Croll still voiced his concern with the Savins' decision. He would not buck the owner to the point of losing his job; he would prepare the colt to the best of his ability. Nonetheless, he still hoped to persuade Butch Savin that a Derby run was not in Mr. Prospector's best interests.

Although the colt unquestionably had looked impressive in his three victories and had hung up fast times, he had faced only modest opposition. He also had never gone farther than seven furlongs in competition. Trying to ready him to go 1 1/4 miles with only five weeks between his dazzling six-furlong victory and the Kentucky Derby would be a daunting task even for a savvy veteran like Croll. Even though Walter Blum had opined after Mr. Prospector's Gulfstream victory that the colt "could have gone around again," the fact remained that the colt was completely unproven around two turns while most of his prospective rivals had already won over 1 1/16 miles or more.

Savin's optimism regarding Mr. Prospector would not have been terribly logical even in an ordinary year. And 1973 was not an ordinary year. The heavy favorite for the Kentucky Derby was a chestnut rocket named Secretariat, who had already shown such overwhelming talent he had been voted Horse of the Year as a mere two-year-old in 1972. Sharp wins in the grade III Bay Shore Stakes and the grade II Gotham Stakes indicated the big red colt had not lost a step between two and three, and his maturity was as unquestionable as his talent. The second choice was Sham, a rangy son of Pretense who had been only a modest runner at two but had announced his arrival on the Derby scene with powerful wins in the Santa Catalina Stakes and grade I

Santa Anita Derby; excepting Secretariat, he had turned in more impressive performances in his pre-Derby races than any other colt on the Derby trail.

Logic, however, has never played much of a role in Derby fever. Mr. Prospector, along with Royal and Regal, shipped to Lexington with a possible start in the Blue Grass Stakes in mind. But behind the scenes, Croll continued to try to cool the fever down.

"I kept working and working at Mr. Savin, telling him that the horse wasn't ready to go two turns," he recalled. "There was a seven-furlong allowance coming up and a mile and one-sixteenth one. Mr. Prospector could have won the seven-furlong one easy, but that wouldn't have proved anything. I finally talked Mr. Savin into letting me put Mr. Prospector into the mile and one-sixteenth race and dropping Royal and Regal into the seven-furlong race instead."

Fans crowded five and six deep around the Keeneland walking ring to get a look as Mr. Prospector entered for the Calumet Purse on April 17. Led by his groom, Brian Hutcheson, the colt made a splendid appearance. So good did he look, and so greatly had the races he had run in Florida impressed the crowd, that he was made a 2-5 favorite over Our Native, already winner of the grade I Flamingo Stakes, and three other rivals.

Had the race been judged on pre-race reputations, Mr. Prospector would have won nicely. But races are won and lost on the track. When the gate opened, Mr. Prospector bounded to the lead, bowling through six furlongs in 1:10 4/5 with apparent ease. But when Our Native challenged him at the stretch call, the tank came up empty. Mr. Prospector struggled home a tired third behind Starkers, the longest shot on the board, who overhauled Our Native in the final yards but was stripped of the victory in favor of Our Native after bearing in and impeding the latter colt in the drive.

Publicly, Croll blamed the loss on a Keeneland surface that was "tiring" although officially rated fast. Privately, however, he continued to argue against Mr. Prospector's going in either the Blue Grass or the Derby. Two days after the Calumet, Royal and Regal just got up in the final strides to win the Forerunner Purse, helping Croll's case by making it quite likely that Savin would have at least one Derby starter regardless of what else happened.

Savin finally gave in, at least in part. When the horses went to the post for the Blue Grass Stakes on April 26, Mr. Prospector was not among them. Only Royal and Regal went to the post under the Aisco Stable colors, and he struggled home a dismal seventh behind the winner, My Gallant.

That performance cooled the *Vaguely Noble's colt's stock considerably, and Savin must have realized that Royal and Regal probably had little chance to win the Kentucky Derby. But Mr. Prospector might yet carry the banner — if he could win the Derby Trial on May 1, just four days before the big race.

Going into the race, Croll actually felt fairly good about the Derby Trial. The distance, a flat mile, was right for trying to develop the colt's stamina gradually, and the trainer knew that even if the colt won, he might well be able to buy time by persuading Savin that the Preakness, two weeks after the Derby, was a more realistic target. The crowd agreed with the veteran trainer's assessment of Mr. Prospector's chances, once again making the colt an odds-on favorite.

But the race was a disaster. "[It] was a fiasco," said Walter Blum, reminiscing about the 1973 Derby Trial in 2006. "The start was very rough, with horses on each side banging into him severely enough to cost him the race."

Thrown off balance by the body slams, Mr. Prospector stumbled badly — "out to his knees," said Croll. Once in stride, the colt rushed up to take the lead by the half-mile point, but the effort was costly; though he responded willingly when challenged by Settecento, he had too little left to stave off his rival and ended up 1 1/4 lengths back in second place.

For Mr. Prospector, the Derby trail had ended — one race too late. He came back lame from his game effort in the Trial; X-rays revealed a chip at the end of his pastern. He was done for the year.

Four days later Royal and Regal finished a tired eighth behind Secretariat in the Derby.

What Might Have Been

3

The summer and fall of 1973 slipped by. While Secretariat stirred the nation with his Triple Crown heroics, Mr. Prospector faded into the shadows, the brilliant promise he had shown in March all but forgotten.

Yet, slowly, his injury healed. And, slowly, Croll began preparing him to return to the racetrack. Never again would there be pressure to have Mr. Prospector ready for a particular race; time, once Croll's enemy, was now his friend in getting the colt sound and fit once more.

When the Gulfstream meeting opened, a well-prepared Mr. Prospector was entered in a six-furlong allowance race on February 13, 1974. As had been the case in every one of his other races, he was an odds-on favorite, and he delivered like one. Breaking cleanly under the handling of his old friend Walter Blum, Mr. Prospector seized command by the end of the first quarter, widened his margin thereafter, and came home an easy five lengths in front. The time was a brisk 1:08 1/5, just two-fifths of a second off his own track record.

Cautious as ever, Croll wanted to keep Mr. Prospector sprinting for the time being, but no suitable sprint stakes were coming up at Gulfstream. The trainer decided instead to send Mr. Prospector north to run in Aqueduct's six-furlong Paumonok Handicap, a grade III race, carded for February 25.

Run since 1906, the Paumonok has been won by some first-rate horses, among them 1923 Kentucky Derby winner Zev, two-time handicap champion

Devil Diver, and champion sprinter White Skies. Mr. Prospector, however, was not to add his name to that list. Sent off once again as an odds-on choice, the colt prompted the early pace of Dawn Flight before taking the lead at the half-mile pole, only to fade to third behind Torsion and Infuriator.

Following the Paumonok, Mr. Prospector returned to the friendly haven of South Florida, but perhaps the tiring effort sandwiched between two long van rides had dulled his edge. Sent after Hialeah's Royal Poinciana Handicap on March 5, he lacked his usual early speed and chased the eventual winner, Lonetree, all the way through the seven furlongs. The victor did set a track record of 1:21 flat for the distance, but Mr. Prospector was beaten by 2 1/4 lengths and barely saved second by a nose over the late-running Governor Max.

Available records do not indicate whether Mr. Prospector suffered from some minor illness or injury or was simply tired, but he did not reappear under silks until April 20, when he went postward for the six-furlong Whirlaway Handicap at Garden State Park. For the first time in his racing career, he did not start odds-on, but he was the favorite and ran like one. Setting sharp early fractions of :22 flat for the quarter and :44 2/5 for the half over a track that had been deep and tiring all meeting, the colt was ridden out to a four-length victory in 1:08 3/5, clipping a fifth of a second from the track record set by I Appeal in 1955 and matched by champion Tosmah in 1964 and Tumiga in 1968.

With the long-sought first stakes win finally on Mr. Prospector's record, the next logical move was to seek a graded stakes victory to enhance the colt's stud value. That made Belmont's seven-furlong Carter Handicap, a grade II event, a suitable target. The Carter would not take place until May 18, however, so in the meantime, Mr. Prospector won the High Gun Purse, an allowance event at Aqueduct on May 9, spinning the six furlongs in 1:09 flat while ridden out.

May 18 dawned clear and bright for what was to be the biggest test of Mr. Prospector's career. There was no question that he was fit and ready, and with two sharp wins under his belt, he was in top form. But, for the first time in his career, he was not the favorite — and with good reason. Forego was in the race.

A hulking son of the Argentine champion *Forli, Forego was a member of Secretariat's crop, as was Mr. Prospector. He had been slow to come into his own, not winning his first stakes until November 24, 1973. That day he had taken Aqueduct's Roamer Handicap by five lengths. He followed up by winning the Discovery Handicap on December 8 under a solid 127 pounds. So good was his late-season form that *The Blood-Horse*'s Free Handicap (compiled by veteran racing secretary and handicapper Jimmy Kilroe) co-rated Forego with Sham at 127 pounds among American three-year-olds, second only to Secretariat's rating of 136 pounds.

Since then, Forego had opened 1974 with victories in the grade III Donn Handicap, the grade II Gulfstream Park Handicap, and the grade I Widener Handicap. His task in the Carter would not be easy; he was dropping back from ten furlongs to seven, and he was carrying 129 pounds. Mr. Prospector, at 124 pounds, was the second highweight; the rest of the field carried from the 122 pounds assigned to Forage down to the 113 carried by Timeless Moment. Nonetheless, the crowd had faith that Forego was more than equal to the task and bet him down to 7-5. Mr. Prospector was second choice at 9-2.

The race went just as the crowd had predicted. Sent to the front by Walter Blum when the gates popped open, Mr. Prospector carved out opening fractions of :22 1/5 and :45 flat while maintaining a daylight lead over Lonetree; Forego, unhurried early, was sixth after a half-mile. But the giant gelding was on the move and picking up ground with every stride. Mr. Prospector kept the lead until the field straightened away for home, but that was all. Once clear of the turn, Forego kicked in. Mr. Prospector dug in gamely, but to no avail. Forego swept by without effort and went on to win by 2 1/4 widening lengths, stopping the clock in a quick 1:22 1/5. Mr. Prospector held on for second, a length ahead of Timeless Moment.

Although Mr. Prospector had been defeated, it was perhaps the finest race of his career. He had met a truly great horse and, while beaten, had not been disgraced. That effort must have made his next race all the more disappointing. Sent out to try 1 1/16 miles for only the second time in his career — the Solicitor II Purse, a turf allowance on June 7 — Mr. Prospector prompted the early pace and had the lead by six furlongs, clicking off the distance in 1:10 flat, but retreated rapidly thereafter and ended up a well-beaten fourth.

The Solicitor marked the end of Mr. Prospector and Walter Blum's partnership. The jockey had ridden the colt throughout his career but now had to part ways with him due to other riding obligations. When Mr. Prospector went to the post for the Gravesend Handicap, twelve days after the Solicitor, Jacinto Vasquez was in the irons. The pair got off to an auspicious start as Mr. Prospector showed a new dimension in the Gravesend. Running patiently in second as Lonetree flew off to a long lead, the colt responded strongly when Vasquez asked for his best, catching Lonetree by the stretch call and drawing off to win by five lengths. His time of 1:09 flat was just two-fifths of a second off the Belmont track record.

The next stakes sprint on the New York schedule was the seven-furlong Nassau County Handicap, a grade III event slated for June 26 at Aqueduct. When the entries were dropped in the box, however, Mr. Prospector's name was not among them. Forego was in the race, and even though the eventual Horse of the Year was loaded up with 132 pounds, Croll wanted no further part of him at any distance. (Ironically, Forego ended up losing the race to Timeless Moment, who had finished behind Mr. Prospector in the Carter.) Instead, Croll shipped Mr. Prospector to Liberty Bell Park in Pennsylvania with the intention of running him in the grade III Firecracker Handicap on July 4.

Croll was confident in spite of Mr. Prospector's 128-pound weight assignment, which required him to concede from nine to seventeen pounds to his seven rivals. The colt was in top shape, and Jacinto Vasquez, who had ridden the horse so well in the Gravesend, had agreed to come down and ride Mr. Prospector in the Firecracker as Blum was still not available.

But the day was hot — about 100 degrees Fahrenheit — and Vasquez was not content to sit around in the jockeys' room and wait for the Firecracker, the eighth race on the card. It wasn't often that one of the top New York jockeys came down to ride at Liberty Bell, and Vasquez found himself asked to take several mounts in the earlier races of the day. He accepted — and, according to Croll's estimation, lost some six pounds of sweat before riding to the post for the Firecracker. Vasquez' dehydration may have cost Mr. Prospector dearly; on top by a length at the stretch call, the colt was nosed out on a head bob by the late-running Barbizon Streak.

"[Vasquez] was weak and couldn't ride as strongly as he needed to," Croll recalled when reminiscing about the race in 2006. "I felt the horse lost the race because of the ride he was given."

Mr. Prospector never received a chance for redemption in a graded stakes, or for that matter in any other race. On July 19, while breezing over a heavy track at Monmouth Park, Mr. Prospector fractured a sesamoid and was retired.

* * *

On the surface Mr. Prospector's racing career seemed fairly modest. In fourteen starts he won seven times and placed in six more, earning $112,171 — a shade more than half his purchase price. He won two six-furlong stakes, placed in three graded sprints, and set two track records, both at six furlongs.

The colt's speed was never in question. In all but one of his wins, he came within a second of the track record. Although he did not win a graded stakes, he was competitive with horses that had won grade II and grade III events, and one must take into account the fact that graded stakes for sprinters were nowhere near as common in 1974 as they are today.

Mr. Prospector never won beyond seven furlongs, yet one can argue that he never got a fair opportunity to display his ability beyond sprint distances. Still quite green when he made his first attempt at a distance beyond a mile, he was collared by a grade I stakes winner and a horse strongly bred for stamina; a rough start and injury compromised him in the Derby Trial. His one race beyond a mile at four followed a taxing effort in the Carter Handicap and may have indicated a lack of aptitude for turf racing just as much as a lack of stamina.

Certainly, Jimmy Croll did not feel the colt was a pure sprinter. "I think Mr. Prospector would have stayed at least eight and a half or nine furlongs, maybe further, if he hadn't kept getting stopped by injuries," he said years later.

Walter Blum concurred. "Mr. Prospector was a jockey's dream to ride," he said in a September 2006 letter to the author. "He was a very competitive horse with an abundance of speed and stamina that one does not see in many horses ... He was not speed crazy and would rate very kindly ..."

The greatest question regarding Mr. Prospector's racing career was soundness, and at first glance he indeed seemed suspect in this regard; the hairline cannon fracture he suffered as a juvenile was without apparent excuse. But the Derby Trial was another case, as the colt may well have been injured as a result of his rough start. He also had an excuse for his career-ending injury in the heavy surface of the track over which he was being worked.

How good was Mr. Prospector as a racehorse? In a 2006 interview with the author, Croll summed up Mr. Prospector's career:

"Mr. Prospector had a lot of speed, but the timing was bad throughout his career — that rush to make the Derby compromised his entire career. He never had a fair chance to prove what he could do. He was certainly talented — if you could have matched him against Housebuster [Croll's two-time champion American sprinter] with both healthy, I think it would have been close.

"He was a really game horse."

Florida

4

O cala, Florida, is some 750 miles from Lexington and the heart of the Kentucky bluegrass country. By the standards of Kentucky horsemen in the 1970s, it was a regional backwater, drowsing under its trademark live oak trees. To be sure, a few nationally known owners and breeders were located there — Ocala Stud, Tartan Farms, and Fred Hooper had all bred and campaigned American champions and numerous stakes winners — but for the most part, the area's many horse farms were small and relatively unknown.

At the time of Mr. Prospector's retirement, Aisco Farm had a fair reputation as a rising Thoroughbred venture, having already campaigned Native Street and bred both Forward Gal and Royal and Regal. It was far from being the equal of one of the major Kentucky breeding farms, however, and had not really established itself as a top-tier breeding facility even by Florida standards.

Butch Savin meant to change that. It was for that very reason he had been willing to buy an expensive blue-blood at the Keeneland sales three years earlier. Now it was up to Mr. Prospector to fulfill his owner's dream of building Aisco Farm into a first-rate Thoroughbred nursery — if he could.

Savin set Mr. Prospector's initial stud fee at $7,500. The fee was high for a new Florida sire in those days (and quite respectable for

Florida even today), but Mr. Prospector had excellent credentials for the regional market. A very well-bred horse, he boasted excellent speed and well-balanced conformation, though his forelegs were marred by somewhat base-narrow conformation with toed-out forefeet. The colt was also rather plain about the head, a trait said by many old-timers to be reminiscent of his maternal grandsire, Nashua.

Savin was doubtless encouraged by a contact with the colt's breeder, Leslie Combs II. "I told him [Savin] that he would make a good stallion," Combs said when interviewed by Gene McLean of the Lexington *Herald-Leader* in 1987. "I knew he'd be good because he had that speed."

That fall Savin exhibited Mr. Prospector at the Parade of New Stallions at the Ocala Breeders' Sales grounds, hoping to drum up business. He was wildly successful. Breeders flocked to see the horse, and before too long the booking requests quickly flooded in —— more than could be accommodated, in fact.

With Savin able to pick and choose among the prospects for the horse's book as well as having several of his own nice mares, Mr. Prospector ended up with a solid harem of mares, better than those most Florida stallions got if not the equal of a good Kentucky stallion's book. Among the young horse's first mares were his owner's Kentucky Oaks winner, Native Street; First Nominee, a stakes-placed half sister to champion Needles; and the Northern Dancer mare Sleek Dancer, whose 1975 daughter by Native Charger would go on to win the grade I Monmouth Oaks as a three-year-old under the name Sharp Belle.

Twenty-eight named foals composed Mr. Prospector's first crop, among them a dainty bay filly out of A Wind Is Rising, by Francis S. Although she had only won her maiden race from six starts, A Wind Is Rising was a half sister to the good stakes horse Native Royalty, and her Mr. Prospector filly was promising enough to sell for $25,000 as a weanling, a fair enough price for a first-crop filly by an unproven Florida stallion.

The filly's purchaser more than got his money back. Nearly two years later Jerry Frankel would sell the A Wind Is Rising filly, by then named It's in the Air, to Louis Wolfson for $300,000. By that time the filly had run five times, had won three times and finished second twice — both times to a nice filly named Justa Reflection — and had become Mr. Prospector's first stakes winner by taking down the Mademoiselle Stakes at Arlington Park for trainer Lou Goldfine.

The purchase of It's in the Air may have involved more than a little sentiment, for Wolfson had bred and raced her "uncle," Native Royalty; had raced her paternal grandsire, Raise a Native; and had raced and stood her maternal grandsire, Francis S. In addition, It's in the Air had been bred by his sons, Gary and Stephen, in the name of their Happy Valley Farm. At any rate, the financial magnate wasted no time in getting some of his money back out of his new investment. The day after her purchase It's in the Air won the grade II Arlington-Washington Lassie Stakes, with her erstwhile conqueror Justa Reflection a well-beaten fourth.

Following the Lassie, Wolfson turned the filly over to Laz Barrera — not a surprising choice, considering that Barrera was also train-ing Wolfson's Triple Crown winner, Affirmed. Sent to Belmont Park for the important Frizette Stakes, a grade I race, It's in the Air was upset by Golferette, who had run fifth behind her in the Lassie, but finished ahead of another of the divisional leaders in the previously unbeaten Terlingua, who would later produce the great sire Storm Cat. The Mr. Prospector filly finished the season by defeating Caline (later winner of the grade I Santa Susana Stakes) in the grade II Oak Leaf Stakes at Santa Anita.

Named the co-champion juvenile filly of 1978 with the Selima

Stakes (gr. I) winner, Candy Eclair, It's in the Air earned $195,665 as a two-year-old. Her earnings helped make Mr. Prospector the leading American freshman sire of 1978, and his total progeny earnings of $309,168 ranked him sixth among all American sires of two-year-olds.

The following year It's in the Air proved she was more than just a precocious juvenile. A confirmed front runner, she could nonetheless stretch her speed if allowed to cruise unmolested on the lead. The foremost victim of this tactic was that year's three-year-old filly champion Davona Dale, who found It's in the Air just a little too much to catch in the ten-furlong Alabama Stakes (gr. I) after the daughter of Mr. Prospector was allowed to get away with an easy opening half-mile in :49 flat. It's in the Air won three other grade I races: the Delaware Oaks against her peers, and the Vanity and Ruffian handicaps against older fillies and mares. Her victims included some first-rate runners in Waya (that year's American champion older female), Jameela, Mairzy Doates, Country Queen, and Blitey, and she also placed in five other graded stakes races. It's in the Air repeated her Vanity Handicap win as a four-year-old but was unable to win a stakes at five and retired having won sixteen of her forty-three starts.

It's in the Air was much the best of Mr. Prospector's first crop, but 1979 proved that he was more than just a one-horse sire. His son out of Sleek Dancer, Northern Prospect, was hampered by a breathing problem at two but still managed to finish third in the 1978 Great American Stakes at Belmont before undergoing corrective surgery. Returning to action at Calder Race Course in Florida on December 29, the colt took down a six-furlong allowance in 1:10 4/5, a good time for the sandy Calder surface. He next won a similar event on opening day at Gulfstream Park and then won the Preview Stakes on January 27. On the same day, the filly Fine Prospect (out of First Nominee, by Rough'n Tumble) won the

Virginia Belle Stakes at Bowie in Maryland, bringing Mr. Prospector's tally up to three stakes winners.

At that point Jimmy Croll was wondering whether he might have a possible Derby prospect in Northern Prospect, an Aisco Farm homebred, but a gray streak named Spectacular Bid dashed those hopes in the Hutcheson Stakes on February 7. Although Northern Prospect bounced out of the gate first and actually opened 1 1/2 lengths on Spectacular Bid in the final turn, it was all over once the horses hit the straightaway. Spectacular Bid won easily, with a tired Northern Prospect checking in more than eleven lengths behind in third.

Although speedy and consistent, Northern Prospect turned out to be neither a stayer nor a match for top speedsters. He retired at the end of his three-year-old season having won six of fifteen starts, including two more minor sprint stakes, before becoming a useful sire of sprinters. Thirty-eight of his 598 foals became stakes winners, and his best son, 1984 San Vicente Stakes (gr. III) winner Fortunate Prospect, was a popular regional sire in Florida until he was pensioned in 2005. Fortunate Prospect is, in turn, the sire of two-time grade III winner Suave Prospect, now a sire in New Mexico, and of Suave Prospect's full sister Successful Dancer, whose son Successful Appeal (by Valid Appeal) was the leading American freshman sire of 2004.

Another Mr. Prospector filly, Patience Worth (out of Dark Duet, by Spy Song) also won a sprint stakes at three, giving the stallion four stakes winners from his first crop. In the meantime, the forty-nine named foals of Mr. Prospector's second crop were swinging into action. The best as a juvenile was Hello Gorgeous (out of Bonny Jet, by Jet Jewel), who ranked among the leading juveniles in England by winning the William Hill Futurity (Eng-I) and the Royal Lodge Stakes (Eng-II).

Hello Gorgeous trained on well enough at three to defeat Irish champion miler Master Willie by a neck in the Mecca Dante Stakes (Eng-II) over ten furlongs. He also finished second to English champion older male Ela-Mana-Mou in the Coral -Eclipse Stakes (Eng-I) at the same distance — beaten only three-quarters of a length — but did not stay well enough to finish better than sixth behind Henbit and his old rival Master Willie (second) in the Derby Stakes. He proved a poor sire in both Europe and North America and was eventually exported to Brazil. There, he found a measure of redemption by siring the group I winners Hello Costly and Itaquere Flash, both now at stud.

Gold Stage (out of Stage Princess, by Cornish Prince) spent most of the year chasing other colts while placing in five grade I events but did become his sire's third graded or group winner by capturing the grade II Breeders' Futurity over rather moderate opposition at the Keeneland fall meeting. He failed to improve on his record at three and died in 1991 after an undistinguished stud career at Spendthrift Farm.

By far the most important member of Mr. Prospector's 1977 crop turned out to be Fappiano, who like Antique Gold (out of Old Love, by Olden Times) and Stutz Blackhawk (out of Sunny Morning, by Amber Morn), was only a minor stakes winner at two. Neither Antique Gold nor Stutz Blackhawk was able to improve on his juvenile form in subsequent years, but Fappiano was better at three than at two, winning the Discovery Handicap (gr. III) and running second in the Jerome and Paterson handicaps, both grade II events. At four Fappiano won the most important race of his career, the Metropolitan Handicap (gr. I), before retiring to stud at Tartan Farms in Florida. His career as a stallion will be detailed in Chapter 9.

Mr. Prospector's five juvenile stakes winners of 1979 helped make him the leading American sire of juveniles that year. The following year the fillies Arisen, Fabulous Prospect, and Favorite Prospect and the colts

Fast Prospect, Rare Performer, and Speedy Prospect all added stakes wins to their resumes, giving the stallion an excellent eleven stakes winners from forty-nine named foals for his 1977 crop and fifteen stakes winners from seventy-seven named foals — a red-hot 19.5% percent — from his first two crops.

Butch Savin was enjoying Mr. Prospector's success, but he also was finding it overwhelming. Since the premature death of Dr. Fager in 1976, Florida's breeding market could well be described as one first-class sire — Tartan Farms' In Reality — and a fair pool of more modest successes. With the fine band of mares bred and owned by Tartan Farms, good mares owned by local breeders, and shippers from Kentucky, the state could support In Reality. But could it support two top sires, both competing for the same limited group of mares? Savin had his doubts, and he did not have the money to buy a harem worthy of the sire he had on his hands. He had syndicated the horse for $50,000 a share in 1977, but his fellow syndicate members were a motley crew, ranging from wealthy financier Peter Brant to a Connecticut baker whose shop had been a favorite of Savin's; their ability as a group to supply the horse with the kind of mares he needed was questionable.

It was Brant who proved instrumental in pushing for change. He knew that Savin was getting more offers for the stallion than he knew how to handle. He knew, too, that Savin was getting older and was concerned about estate planning. And Brant knew Seth Hancock at Claiborne Farm in Kentucky. He called Hancock and passed on two important facts: first, that Mr. Prospector was likely to be too hot a property for Savin and Florida to hang onto much longer, and second, that Savin just might be willing to sell his shares in the horse. Brant had little doubt that if Savin could be convinced, and if the price was right, the other shareholders would agree to the horse's moving to Kentucky.

Seth Hancock was interested. So was Savin, after a somewhat tougher sell from Brant. "I told him that Mr. Prospector would do much better with better mares, especially classic-type staying mares,," Brant later told David Schmitz of *The Blood-Horse*. "It took quite a long time convincing him."

Savin finally made his decision, offering Claiborne Farm the seven shares he held at a total price of $3.5 million, or $500,000 a share. Claiborne and some of its major clients snapped them up. Brant, too, sold several shares to Claiborne, though he retained two for himself.

The purchases cleared the way for Hancock to call for a vote by the syndicate on relocating and re-syndicating the stallion in the spring of 1980. When the ballots were counted, the owners of thirty-seven of the forty shares had voted yes on the proposals — the only holdouts were Gary and Steve Wolfson of Happy Valley Farm and Donald Wolfson of Regal Oak Farm — and Mr. Prospector was on his way to Claiborne Farm, where he would remain for the rest of his life.

Claiborne

5

From its inception Claiborne Farm has been the home to some of America's greatest stallions. Its name is synonymous with the finest Kentucky breeding traditions, yet its roots lie in Virginia, where its story begins with as much romance as any other in Thoroughbred history.

It was July 1863, but the calendar date probably did not matter much to Richard Hancock. Wounded in the hip, he was one of a group of injured Confederates being ferried by mule-drawn ambulance from the bloody conflict of Gettysburg to friendlier territory near Charlottesville, Virginia. He had faced the dangers of artillery fire and rifle bullets bravely, earning a battlefield promotion to captain on July 2. But now he faced a far deadlier battle: In an era lacking sulfa drugs, antibiotics, and often even basic sanitation, wound infections and dysentery killed more men in camps and medical tents than did active combat in all the battles of the Civil War combined.

Luck was with Hancock. On his arrival, the Harris family of nearby Ellerslie Farm took him in. There, the lady of the house doctored his wounds and fed him good farm fare. Hancock made an uneventful recovery and in due time rejoined his unit, Company D of the Bossier Volunteers.

Captain Hancock's remaining time in the Civil War proved adventurous. Wounded at Winchester in September 1864, he fell into Union hands but managed to escape after his chest wound healed. Apparently he remembered a more pleasant period of convalescence, however, for soon after he rejoined his unit, he requested and was given furlough to travel back to Ellerslie. There he was welcomed, and on November 22, 1864, he married Thomasia Harris, the daughter of the house.

News and people both traveled much more slowly in the mid-nineteenth century than they do today. It was not until Hancock, furlough over, was trying to find and rejoin his unit that he learned General Robert E. Lee had surrendered at Appomattox on April 9, 1865. The war was over, and so Hancock settled in with his bride to the life of a Virginia farmer.

Despite the Confederate defeat, Hancock prospered, inheriting Ellerslie after Thomasia's parents died. Many farmers turned to breeding horses to replenish the stock the war had taken away and fill the demand for practically anything that could be ridden or draw a wagon or a plow. Still, when Hancock accepted Major Thomas W. Doswell's invitation to see his colt Eolus race at Pimlico in 1871, Hancock probably thought of the trip as little more than an opportunity to enjoy a pleasant excursion with an old friend.

That changed when Hancock saw Eolus. Though Hancock had enjoyed horse racing as a youth in North Carolina, it had been primarily quarter-mile racing on an informal basis. But the young Hancock had developed an eye for a good horse, and in Eolus he saw a horse very near his personal ideal.

As it turned out, Eolus was for sale, but Hancock could not afford Doswell's asking price. For the next six years Hancock kept an ear to the ground regarding the horse's whereabouts and was finally able to acquire the animal in 1877 by trading a half brother named Scathelock for him. Hancock's faith in Eolus was proven well founded when the stallion's first Ellerslie-sired crop produced Eole, who did so well in the United States he was sent to England, where he ran second to St. Gatien in the 1885 Ascot Gold Cup.

Although Eolus was not the equal of his sire, four-time leading American sire *Leamington, he nonetheless did well at stud and established the name of Ellerslie as a source of good horses with such runners as the 1892 Futurity Stakes winner Morello, the 1884 Preakness winner Knight of Ellerslie, the 1893 Brooklyn Handicap winner Diablo, and the Suburban Handicap winners Eurus (1887) and Elkwood (1888). He was followed at Ellerslie by *Charaxus and then by *Fatherless, two stallions now little remembered but solid sires of winners in their day.

Hancock's Thoroughbred venture was not the only fruitful operation on Ellerslie, for his marriage to Thomasia was blessed with five sons (four of whom lived to adulthood) and four daughters. Hancock was a great believer in education, and he saw to it that his children were prepared for careers other than farming. Two of the sons became physicians; another became a university professor.

But if Richard Hancock had intended on discouraging his children from following in his footsteps on the farm, he failed in the case of the fourth son, Arthur Boyd. Arthur Hancock had horses in his blood from the time he could walk and talk, and by the time he was a teenager, he was helping with the family's annual consignment of sale yearlings. Sent off to Johns Hopkins University and the University of Chicago, Arthur Hancock came home with a business degree, which he proceeded to apply to managing Ellerslie.

The younger Hancock took over full management of Ellerslie in 1909, one year after marrying Nancy Tucker Clay of Paris, Kentucky. He had met the young lady while attending a 1907 yearling show as one of the judges at the Blue Grass Fair in Lexington, Kentucky, and in 1910 his bride presented him with a fine dowry indeed in the form of 1,300 acres of prime Kentucky land she had inherited in Bourbon County. The couple named their new farm "Claiborne."

(The name "Claiborne" had originally belonged to a farm owned by Mrs. Clarence LeBus, whose husband was once acknowledged as the largest landowner in Kentucky. When Mrs. LeBus elected to rename her holdings as Hinata Farm, the Hancocks decided to use the name Claiborne for their new Thoroughbred nursery. Not only was the name pleasant to the ear, but Mrs. Hancock liked it as a play on her maiden name. As for Hinata Farm, it gained a measure of fame of its own in later years when under lease to Samuel Riddle, as the great Man o' War stood his first two seasons at stud there.)

In 1910 Nancy Hancock give birth to a son, Arthur Boyd Hancock Jr., adding the duties of fatherhood to a man who was trying to juggle the management of two farms separated by hundreds of miles. Although the senior Arthur Hancock moved his base of operations to Claiborne in 1915, his balancing act between Claiborne and Ellerslie continued until 1937, when his son took over the management of Ellerslie.

The year 1912 was bittersweet for Arthur Hancock, who became the father of a daughter, Nancy Clay, but lost his own father to old age. Aside from the changes in his family, it was a most uneasy time in the Thoroughbred breeding business. Anti-gambling legislation had effectively shut down racing in New York and New Jersey, dropping the bottom out of the domestic Thoroughbred market. In 1913 the overseas market dried up as well, thanks to the infamous Jersey Act, which restricted England's *General Stud Book* to horses whose lines all traced to animals already registered in the stud book. At the stroke of a pen, the Jersey Act reduced most American Thoroughbreds to "half-breds."

Many famous Thoroughbred operations either closed or drastically reduced their holdings, but Hancock was determined to stay out dark times. He had bought out the other heirs to Ellerslie already, and in 1913 he signaled his determination to continue as a breeder with the purchase of Celt, bought from the dispersal of the late James R. Keene's Castleton Stud. Hancock had previously leased the horse for two seasons and liked the looks of the stallion's progeny, and though he had to shell out $25,000 to buy Celt, it proved money well spent. Celt died in 1919, but not before siring twenty-one stakes winners bred by Hancock and leading the American sire list posthumously in 1921.

Fortunately, Hancock had already acquired another good sire in *Wrack, a relatively minor English stakes winner purchased from Lord Rosebery in 1916 for the equivalent of $8,000 at the exchange rates then current. Although *Wrack was a modest performer who had spent part of his career racing over hurdles, he was tough and sound. He also came from a first-rate female family. His dam, Samphire, was a half sister — by the English Triple Crown winner Isinglass — to Neil Gow, winner of the 1910 Two Thousand Guineas, and his granddam Chelandry was not only a Classic winner in her own right — she had won the 1897 One Thousand Guineas — but also a half sister to Ladas, winner of the 1894 Two Thousand Guineas and Derby Stakes.

*Wrack was not a great stallion, but he proved a reliable sire of tough, hard-knocking winners and from time to time could get a really good horse. He eventually sired thirty-one stakes winners, twelve of them bred by Hancock.

Hancock was looking more and more toward European bloodlines to rejuvenate the American lines he had known in his youth, and the young Claiborne Farm reflected this. Among the farm's early sires were *Ambassador IV (Dark Ronald—Excellenza, by Haut Brion), a useful sire whose best son, St. James, was the co-champion two-year-old male of 1923 and sire, in turn, of the brilliant juvenile and good sire Jamestown; *Omar Khayyam (Marco—Lisma, by Persimmon), the 1917 Kentucky Derby winner, who did fairly well without ever siring a runner of his own merit; and *War Cloud (Polymelus—*Dreamy II, by Persimmon), winner of a division of the 1918 Preakness Stakes. *War Cloud died after only one season at Claiborne, but among the four stakes winners he left behind was the 1927 Coaching Club American Oaks winner Nimba, that year's champion three-year-old filly.

But it was *Sir Gallahad III who vaulted Claiborne from the ranks of relatively modest breeding farms to the heights of the American breeding industry. The son of *Teddy and the blue hen mare Plucky Liege had been a good but not outstanding racehorse in Europe. Speedy enough to win the 1923 Poule d'Essai des Poulains (French Two Thousand Guineas) and to defeat the excellent international runner *Epinard in a 6 1/2-furlong match race in 1924, he could not match the best of his crop over longer distances but nonetheless stayed well enough to run third, beaten two necks by Le Capucin and Niceas, in the Prix du Jockey-Club (French Derby). He was the prototype of what later came to be considered the ideal stallion for the North American market: a horse with miler speed combined with the ability to stretch that speed to ten furlongs or more.

Both American and European breeders evidenced considerable interest in *Epinard, whose brilliant victories in such races as the Grand Criterium and the Prix d'Ispahan and his game series of seconds in the three International Specials of 1924 in the United States showed him to be a first-rate horse indeed over six to ten furlongs. Hancock, however, reasoned that a horse that had shown the speed to defeat *Epinard — albeit with an eleven-pound weight concession — might make an even better stallion prospect. He did not have the money to put up an offer for *Sir Gallahad III on his own, but he had the connections to form a partnership with William Woodward of Belair Stud and two other prominent breeders, R.A. Fairbairn and Marshall Field. Together they purchased *Sir Gallahad III from Captain Jefferson Davis Cohn for $125,000 with the understanding that the horse would stand at Claiborne beginning in 1926.

*Sir Gallahad III proved an enormous success. In his first American-sired crop, he begot the Triple Crown winner Gallant Fox and went on to sire fifty-nine stakes winners while at Claiborne (he had previously sired one stakes winner in France). Four times the leader of the American general sire list, he was to have an even greater impact as a sire of broodmares, leading the American broodmare sire list no less than twelve times. (He also was indirectly responsible for another important importation to the United States. Impressed by the success of *Sir Gallahad III's first American crop, Charles B Shaffer purchased the horse's younger full brother *Bull Dog and installed him at his Coldstream Stud. The leading American sire of 1943, *Bull Dog went on to sire fifty-two stakes winners including five-time American leading sire Bull Lea and 1942 Kentucky Oaks winner Miss Dogwood, third dam of Mr. Prospector.)

Hancock's next major importation for Claiborne was *Blenheim II, already the sire of the 1936 Derby Stakes winner *Mahmoud and the brilliant Italian champion Donatello II while standing in France. Seven major Kentucky breeders, Hancock included, ponied up a total of 45,000 English pounds — about $250,000 at the exchange rate then current — to buy the stallion from the Aga Khan. Like *Sir Gallahad III, *Blenheim II also begot a Triple Crown winner in his first American crop, siring Whirlaway for Warren Wright Sr.'s famed Calumet Farm. Though not as influential in the United States as *Sir Gallahad III (other than through *Mahmoud, who was imported by C.V. "Sonny" Whitney in 1940), *Blenheim II was the champion American sire of 1941 and eventually sired thirty-seven North American-bred stakes winners in addition to the twenty-four stakes winners he had begotten during his six seasons in Europe.

Sadly, Arthur Hancock Sr. would suffer the first of a series of strokes in 1947 and never fully recovered, leaving his son Arthur Hancock Jr. (better known as "Bull") increasingly in charge until the senior Hancock's death in 1957. The younger Hancock had studied genetics at Princeton, but he had learned horsemanship from the ground up at his father's side at Claiborne, and throughout his long career at Claiborne's helm, he would prove far more comfortable with practical considerations than with esoteric theories of breeding and farm management.

The first practical consideration Bull Hancock had to make at Claiborne was how to rejuvenate the farm's bloodstock, which had fallen into a decline during the late thirties and early forties. Many of the original broodmare families that had served the farm in its early days were no longer producing well, and the farm's long partnership with Belair Stud, while resulting in many fine racehorses, had also resulted in the farm's roster being saddled with a number of stamina-laden stallions such as Gallant Fox and Johnstown, who had proven unable to maintain the standards set by *Sir Gallahad III and *Blenheim II. By 1945, when Bull Hancock returned from a stint in military service to become his father's chief assistant, *Sir Gallahad III was twenty-five, *Blenheim II was eighteen, and none of the younger stallions at the farm appeared to be worthy successors.

Bull Hancock had already made a start on bringing in new blood to the farm's stallion roster by agreeing to stand *Princequillo at Ellerslie in 1945. (Whether he initiated this or whether the colt's trainer, the colorful Horatio Luro, persuaded him, depends on which of the two men's memoirs one cares to believe.) At first glance *Princequillo seemed just another of the heavily stamina-laden type of stallion that had repeatedly proven disappointing when tried at Claiborne. Sired by the Belgian champion Prince Rose — a proven stayer and sire of stayers — out of *Cosquilla, a mare whose sire *Papyrus had proven a conduit for stamina and not much else, *Princequillo was a late-maturing sort who had developed from a cheap claimer into the Jockey Club Gold Cup (then at two miles) winner of 1943.

*Princequillo had won in allowance company at six furlongs, however, and according to the *Daily Racing Form*'s Joe Hirsch, Luro had assured Hancock that *Princequillo could run five furlongs in fifty-nine seconds any time. That was reason enough for Hancock to give the horse a chance at Ellerslie. Standing at a modest fee of $250, *Princequillo did not attract a lot of business, but both

William Woodward and Christopher Chenery of Meadow Stud sent mares to him. When Prince Simon emerged as England's best three-year-old for Woodward in 1950 while Hill Prince earned U.S. Horse of the Year honors for Chenery the same year, *Princequillo (by then at Claiborne following the sale of Ellerslie in 1946) suddenly had no more trouble filling his book. *Princequillo went on to lead the American general sire list twice and the broodmare sire list eight times.

Double Jay, a horse Bull Hancock had admired as a fleet two-year-old of 1946, joined *Princequillo on the Claiborne stallion roster in 1950. By Balladier out of the Whisk Broom II mare Broomshot, he was one of the few predominantly American-bred sires to stand at Claiborne during the mid-twentieth century, and he repaid Hancock's faith in him by siring forty-five stakes winners and leading the American broodmare sire list four times.

But it was *Nasrullah who proved the key to Claiborne's regaining and even surpassing the heights it had reached with *Sir Gallahad III and *Blenheim II. Bred by the Aga Khan, the temperamental horse had won the important Champion Stakes at Newmarket but might well have won either the Two Thousand Guineas or the Derby Stakes — or both — had he not declined to exert himself after making the lead. He had excellent conformation and regal bloodlines (by the great Italian champion Nearco out of Mumtaz Begum, a daughter of *Blenheim II out of *Mahmoud's granddam Mumtaz Mahal) and from the beginning was expected to be a stud success. By the time Bull Hancock was able to conclude a deal to buy him for $340,000 from Irish horseman Joe McGrath after the 1950 breeding season, *Nasrullah was already a proven commodity represented by runners such as *Nathoo (1948 Irish Derby), Musidora (1949 One Thousand Guineas and Oaks), and *Noor (who would end 1950 as the U.S. champion handicap male). The following year, *Nasrullah led the English general sire list.

Although *Nasrullah died in 1959 at the regrettably early age of nineteen, he led the American general sire list five times (1955, 1956, 1959, 1960, and 1962), helped in no small part by daughters of *Princequillo. *Princequillo's best sire son, Round Table, in turn enjoyed success with daughters of *Nasrullah and the latter's best son, Bold Ruler, and the *Nasrullah/*Princequillo nick would reach a peak with Secretariat (Bold Ruler—Somethingroyal, by *Princequillo), the 1973 Triple Crown winner and the first major stallion to stand at Claiborne under the management of Bull Hancock's son Seth.

Through the 1960s Claiborne continued to earn its reputation as the United States' premier stallion station. Bold Ruler and Round Table — both foaled at Claiborne on April 6, 1954 — stood at the farm throughout their careers, securing nine sire titles between them (eight for Bold Ruler, one for Round Table), and they were joined in the stallion barn by the great Argentine champion *Forli, the French champions *Ambiorix and *Herbager, and the American-bred champions Tom Rolfe, Buckpasser, Damascus, Sir Ivor, and Hoist the Flag, all successful sires.

Bull Hancock believed in continually acquiring new sire lines, and the last great champion he syndicated to stand at Claiborne was the Canadian-bred Nijinsky II, winner of the 1970 English Triple Crown and a son of the sensational young sire Northern Dancer. Unfortunately, he did not live to see Nijinsky II follow in the hoof prints of other great Claiborne sires; Hancock was diagnosed with cancer in late summer of 1972 and died on September 14, 1972.

His death marked the passing of possibly the greatest selector and maker of sires ever seen in racing history. As a measure of his influence, consider this: Stallions that Bull Hancock brought to Claiborne Farm collectively earned seventeen American sire titles, one English sire title, nineteen titles as leading American broodmare sire, and four English broodmare sire championships.

Bull Hancock's death left some question over who would succeed him at Claiborne. Although Arthur Hancock III was the elder of Bull's sons, he had developed something of a wild reputation in his youth. Ogden Phipps, William Haggin Perry, and Charles Nuckols, the advisers appointed by Bull's will, favored Seth Hancock to succeed his father. Arthur Hancock III soon went his own way with Stone Farm, which had begun as a one-hundred acre purchase by Claiborne in 1970 but was built into a two-thousand acre operation after Arthur bought it. Relations between the Hancock brothers were strained for a while but have since become amicable, with both enjoying marked success with their respective farms.

Seth Hancock was only twenty-three years old when his father died, but two early moves showed he had inherited a generous helping of both his father's horse sense and business acumen. In late 1972, at the dispersal of his father's personally owned bloodstock, Seth Hancock reached into his own pockets and paid $90,000 for a yearling son of Damascus out of Face the Facts, by *Court Martial, whom he appropriately named Judger.

And in early 1973, the young man pulled off a deal that his father would have surely appreciated: arranging the syndication of Secretariat.

Both moves paid off handsomely. Although Secretariat never became quite the replacement for his own sire, Bold Ruler, that everyone had hoped for, the publicity he generated for Seth Hancock and Claiborne was priceless; the fact that he afterward became noted as a first-rate sire of broodmares (he led the American broodmare sire list in 1992) did not hurt anything either. As for Judger, he won the 1974 Florida Derby (gr. I) and Blue Grass Stakes (gr. I) and earned $240,271 in Hancock's colors.

Judger got off to an undistinguished start at stud, however, and by 1979 Secretariat's early crops suggested that the great champion would be a good but not outstanding sire. Nijinsky II, on the other hand, was an outstanding success, as was Hoist the Flag, but Claiborne Farm could not afford to remain static. Horses are volatile commodities, and any number of events can end a horse's stud career well before the normal retirement age of the early to middle twenties. (Tragically, Hoist the Flag proved a case in point; he fractured a leg in a paddock accident and had to be euthanized in 1980 at age twelve.)

Another top-class sire younger than many of the farm's established stalwarts would be a most welcome addition, so when Peter Brant made his fateful call about Mr. Prospector's possible availability, Seth Hancock was ready to listen. Whether he knew it or not, his actions in acquiring Mr. Prospector to stand at Claiborne would have as profound of an impact on Claiborne's future as had the acquisitions of *Sir Gallahad III in his grandfather's day and *Nasrullah in his father's — an impact that continues to this day.

The Sky's The Limit

6

M r. Prospector, then ten years old, made the trip from Florida to Kentucky without incident and quickly settled into the Claiborne stallion barn, inheriting the stall and paddock that had belonged to the late Hoist the Flag. His traveling days were now behind him; for the rest of his life, his world would be bounded by his stall, his paddock, and the breeding shed.

It was a comfortable world, though not luxurious. While some of the great Kentucky stallion farms are breathtaking showplaces filled with custom architecture and expensive fittings, Claiborne's beauty is that of functional efficiency. The concrete block stallion barns are painted white with deep yellow trim; everything is spotlessly clean and the stalls are well bedded with sweet-smelling straw, but visitors will not find the walnut paneling or handsome stonework that can be seen at other farms.

For all its history, the breeding shed is equally bare of all but the necessities; except for the thick layer of shredded rubber footing on the floor and the horse gear carefully stored on wall hooks, it could almost be an empty garage for farm equipment or the hangar for a small airplane.

As Mr. Prospector settled into his new surroundings, the same intelligence and good manners that had made him easy to handle around the barn at the track carried over into his stallion career. Sometimes he would

get a bit frisky when another stallion was being sent in to breed — his paddock was right next to the breeding shed — but it was nothing that could
not be handled by putting him in his stall and keeping him there until the
mare was taken away again; he was no Northern Dancer, trying to climb
over the stall door in a bid for freedom and a chance to get to the mare.
Even in the shed, his behavior was exemplary.

"He was very easy to handle, very professional," recalled Claiborne
Farm manager Gus Koch. "He didn't have any quirks and was never a
problem."

And the winners kept rolling in. By the time Mr. Prospector started
covering his first Kentucky book, he was already the sire of another group
I winner in Miswaki, who won the 1980 Prix de la Salamandre. Produced
from the Buckpasser mare Hopespringseternal, whose dam Rose Bower
was by *Princequillo, Miswaki placed in two other European group I events
at two and went on to sire ninety-eight stakes winners in a successful stud
career that ended with his death in 2004. Miswaki's stud career reached a
pinnacle in 1991 when Black Tie Affair (Ire) was voted U.S. Horse of the
Year. Unfortunately, Black Tie Affair has been no more than useful at stud,
and his best son, 1997 Donn Handicap (gr. I) and Woodward Stakes (gr. I)
winner Formal Gold is now in California after disappointing in Kentucky.
The only other son of Black Tie Affair who seems to have any chance at
making an impact at stud is multiple graded stakes winner Sir Shackleton,
who entered stud at Castleton Lyons in Kentucky for the 2007 breeding
season.

Although Miswaki seems unlikely to have established a lasting branch
of the Mr. Prospector sire line, he has established a solid reputation as a
broodmare sire. So far, his daughters have produced 133 stakes winners,
among them champions Daylami, Galileo, Black Sam Bellamy, Hernando,

Jimwaki, and Talkin Man.

Seven other stakes winners eventually emerged from Mr. Prospector's 1978 crop including Seeker's Gold (out of I Understand, by Dr. Fager), winner of two group III races in Australia, and Sue Babe (out of Sleek Dancer, by Northern Dancer), winner of two juvenile stakes and runner-up in the 1980 Sorority Stakes (gr. I). Mr. Prospector had sired a total of twenty-three stakes winners from 118 foals in his first three crops, making him an unequivocal success. But there was a gap in his resume: He was perceived as a speed sire, not a sire likely to get a colt capable of winning an American Triple Crown race. Part of this was doubtless due to his own reputation as a non-staying speedster, but considering that It's in the Air had shown top-class form in the United States at ten furlongs and that Hello Gorgeous had won in group company over a similar distance in Europe, the belief was not entirely logical. Still, that was the perception.

That perception, however, was about to change. For Mr. Prospector's 1979 crop contained a colt who would demonstrate that with Mr. Prospector the sky was the limit.

* * *

K D Princess wasn't a great race mare, but she had enough class to place in the grade III Orchid Handicap on the turf as a five-year-old and enough durability to make sixty starts. Her pedigree was about on a par with her racing performance; by Bold Commander, sire of 1970 Kentucky Derby winner Dust Commander, she was out of Tammy's Turn, whose granddam Whirl Right was a full sister to 1941 Triple Crown winner Whirlaway. Those were sufficient credentials for her owners, Mr. and Mrs. Lewis Iandoli, to send the mare to Mr. Prospector for her first mating in 1978.

Arriving on March 20, 1979, the resulting colt was an attractive, well-balanced bay. He developed well and sold for $150,000 as a Saratoga sale yearling to Henryk de Kwiatkowski, who turned the colt over to Hall of Famer Woody Stephens for training.

Given the name Conquistador Cielo ("conqueror of the sky" in Spanish) in honor of the aviation club of which de Kwiatkowski was a member, the colt proved quick and capable in a light juvenile campaign of four starts, winning two. The more important of his victories was in the grade II Saratoga Special, in which he defeated Herschelwalker and Timely Writer in a solid 1:10 3/5 for the six furlongs. Both Herschelwalker and Timely Writer were juveniles of some ability; the former was also runner-up in the Futurity Stakes (gr. I) at Belmont, while the latter went on to win the Hopeful Stakes (gr. I) at Saratoga and the Champagne Stakes (gr. I) at Belmont.

Conquistador Cielo followed up his Saratoga Special win with a fourth-place finish in a roughly run Sanford Stakes (gr. II) on August 12. Following the race, a saucer fracture was found in the colt's left foreleg. The injury kept him away from the races until February 16, 1982, when he ran fourth in a seven-furlong allowance at Hialeah. Ten days later the colt won a similar event in a brisk 1:22 1/5 for the distance.

But the next day Conquistador Cielo turned up lame. X-rays showed that the saucer fracture had recurred. This time, on the advice of a New York veterinarian, Stephens had the leg treated with a machine advertised as using electrical stimulation to speed bone formation. Apparently, the treatment worked, as Conquistador Cielo was breezing again in April.

The colt reappeared in the Preakness Prep, a 1 1/16-mile allowance race, on May 8 at Pimlico. He duly won by three lengths under a strong hand ride from Eddie Maple, but Stephens had no illusions that Conquistador Cielo was quite ready for the Preakness itself. Instead, he shipped the colt to Belmont Park.

Conquistador Cielo's injuries had been frustrating to his owner and trainer, but they may have been a blessing in disguise. Instead of being rushed as his sire had been to try to make the Derby, Conquistador Cielo was allowed to come along at a slower pace and came roaring into the Belmont spring meeting as a fresh, fit, and eager horse.

The railbirds apparently noticed the colt's condition, for Conquistador Cielo went into a May 19 allowance race against older males as an odds-on favorite. Living up to those odds, the colt won laughing, beating four-year-old Swinging Light by eleven lengths in a sharp 1:34 1/5 for the mile. Then Stephens made a more audacious move: He entered the colt in the one-mile Metropolitan Handicap (gr. I) against older males on May 31.

Conquistador Cielo was one of only two three-year-olds in the field of fourteen, and he was assigned 111 pounds, equal to 125 pounds on an older horse by the scale of weights. He had not won a stakes since his victory in the Saratoga Special the year before, but so impressive had his allowance victory been that he was made the 2-1 favorite. He did not disappoint the fans, winning by 7 1/4 lengths over four-year-old Silver Buck (who also carried 111 pounds) in track-record time of 1:33 flat. In his next start Silver Buck would win the Suburban Handicap (gr. I).

Unconventional as his decision to put Conquistador Cielo in the Met was, Stephens' next move raised even more eyebrows. He entered Conquistador Cielo in the Belmont Stakes.

"Impossible," the pundits said. Only five days separated the two races, and anyway, the conventional wisdom was that Conquistador Cielo was a brilliant miler, nothing more. A Mr. Prospector colt couldn't be expected to stay 1 1/2 miles. Even Seth Hancock, impressed though he was with Mr. Prospector as a stallion, had his doubts and said as much to author Ed Bowen in the paddock immediately prior to the running of the Belmont.

As if the pedigree question were not enough, Eddie Maple, who had ridden the colt throughout the season, went down in a nasty racing spill the day before the Belmont and suffered fractured ribs and a bruised kidney. Stephens made a hasty call to Laffit Pincay Jr., who flew from California to pick up the mount.

On June 5, 1982, with his new jockey in the saddle, Conquistador Cielo pranced to the post over a sloppy track. Ten other horses were in the field, including the Derby winner, Gato Del Sol, and the Preakness winner, Aloma's Ruler.

Two minutes, twenty-eight and one-fifth seconds later, Conquistador Cielo cruised home all alone, fourteen lengths in front of Gato Del Sol; Aloma's Ruler, who clearly wanted neither the distance nor the footing, was some forty lengths behind the Derby winner in ninth place. In six days and just over four minutes' total racing time, Conquistador Cielo had locked down honors as U.S. champion three-year-old male and, as it turned out, Horse of the Year.

For those who thought Conquistador Cielo's stunning victories were flukes, the colt next tacked on the Dwyer Stakes (gr. II) on July 5, running nine furlongs in 1:46 4/5 after spinning the opening six furlongs in a blistering 1:08 3/5 — time that would win many a graded sprint. A one-length win over Lejoli in the Jim Dandy Stakes (gr. III) at Saratoga followed on August 8, setting the colt up for a rematch with a freshened Aloma's Ruler in the Travers Stakes.

To no one's surprise, a North American classic winner took the Travers. The shocker was which one. Running the race of his life, Runaway Groom — previously winner of the second leg of the Canadian Triple Crown, the Prince of Wales Stakes — charged up from off the pace to defeat Aloma's Ruler by a half-length with Conquistador Cielo another three-quarters of a length back in third. (The following month, Runaway Groom went on to win the last race of the Canadian Triple Crown series, the Breeders' Stakes.)

It was a rude awakening for those who were starting to hail Conquistador Cielo as the next Secretariat, but the colt did have excuses. Although rumors had been flying among horsemen at the Saratoga meeting that all was not well with Conquistador Cielo, most fans were unaware he had injured his left front ankle shortly after the Jim Dandy. Then, the Thursday before the Travers, the colt blew through his final pipe-opener in :34 flat for the three furlongs — too fast. Though the troublesome ankle held up, the colt was now too tightly wound. In the Travers itself, he was rank and could not be hauled back from a speed duel with Aloma's Ruler, setting the race up for Runaway Groom. And after the race, he was once again lame.

Conquistador Cielo never started again, retiring with nine wins from thirteen starts and earnings of $474,328. Syndicated for a record $36 million, the colt entered stud alongside his sire at Claiborne Farm in 1983, inheriting the paddock that had once belonged to Buckpasser. While he never reached the heights attained by the great Claiborne stallions — his only champion, Montauciel, earned his honors in Hungary and Slovakia — he had a long and honorable stud career, with seventy stakes winners and international earnings of nearly $64 million for his progeny credited to him as of July 2007. Conquistador Cielo died on December 17, 2002.

Marquetry proved the best of Conquistador Cielo's progeny on the racetrack, capturing three grade I wins among his ten victories from thirty-six starts and earning $2,857,886. He also has been Conquistador Cielo's most important son at stud. Although the overall quality of his stock has been fairly modest, Marquetry has sired two brilliant runners in American champion sprinters Artax (1999) and Squirtle Squirt (2001). Both won the Breeders' Cup Sprint (gr. I) to cap off their championship seasons, and Artax still holds the stakes record of 1:07.89 — a time that also made him the co-holder with Mr. Prospector himself of the Gulfstream Park six-furlong track record. Marquetry is still active at Stonewall Farm in Kentucky as of this writing, while Artax is at stud in New York; Squirtle Squirt is in Japan.

As a broodmare sire, Conquistador Cielo also has done well. Ninety-nine stakes winners were credited to his daughters as of July 2007, among them 1999 Canadian Horse of the Year Thornfield, 1993 Canadian champion sprinter Apelia, and 2006 Canadian champion turf male Sky Conqueror, winner of the inaugural Northern Dancer Breeders' Cup Stakes (Can-II). Still in training in 2007, Sky Conqueror served notice that he might be a factor in the U.S. turf male division by winning the Early Times Turf Classic (gr. IT) on the Kentucky Derby undercard.

***

Conquistador Cielo may have put to rest the notion that Mr. Prospector could not get a horse capable of going classic distances, but there were plenty of speedsters among the stallion's 1979 crop as well. Chief among them was Gold Beauty (out of Stick to Beauty, by Illustrious), who made her sire only the tenth North American stallion to sire two or more divisional champions in one year by earning an Eclipse Award in 1982 as champion sprinter.

Only the seventh filly or mare to win honors as champion sprinter — and only the second to do it as a three-year-old, following the phenomenal Ta Wee in 1969 — Gold Beauty was still an unraced maiden at the beginning of 1982. After breaking her maiden by twelve lengths in February, she did not resurface until June, when she ran away from an allowance field by the same twelve-length margin.

By this time it was pretty obvious that Gold Beauty was stakes material. Sent to Keystone Park in Pennsylvania for the six-furlong Rushland Stakes, Gold Beauty was just as devastating against stakes company, romping by ten lengths.

A second stakes win at Keystone followed, this in the Spring Valley Handicap. Then it was off to Saratoga for the Test Stakes (gr. II), a race that normally draws the best among the sprinting three-year-old fillies. Getting five pounds (116 to 121) from Ambassador of Luck, who would reign as American champion older female the following year, Gold Beauty won in a solid 1:22 4/5 for the seven furlongs.

Having demonstrated her superiority over sprinters of her own age and sex, Gold Beauty next tackled open competition in the Fall Highweight Handicap (gr. II) and turned in the most impressive performance of her career. Carrying 126 pounds against 131 on the stakes-winning four-year-old colt Engine One — a four-pound concession by the filly when allowances for her age and sex are taken into account — Gold Beauty sped home first in 1:09 1/5.

The fleet filly finally met defeat in her next race when Engine One beat her by a length for the Vosburgh Stakes (gr. I). She had actually finished third but was moved up a place on the disqualification of Duke Mitchell, who had interfered with fourth-place Maudlin. As it turned out, Gold Beauty had an excuse for her defeat; a saucer fracture was found in her left foreleg after the race, and the filly ran no more that year. She returned to racing as a four-year-old and added the True North Handicap (gr. III) to her trophy case before retiring with eight wins from twelve starts and earnings of $251,901.

Three other runners from Mr. Prospector's 1979 crop added graded stakes wins to their sire's resume. The best of them, Fast Gold (out of Flack Attack, by Ack Ack), won the 1982 Paterson Handicap (gr. II) and the 1983 Excelsior Handicap (gr. II) before a modest stud career in Kentucky. Eventually exported to Brazil, Fast Gold is the sire of the Brazilian group I winners Be Fair, El Paso, Guacho, Lingote de Ouro, Nugget do Faxina, Puerto-Madero, Setembro Chove, Soft Gold, and Ze de Ouro, as well as of India Brava, a champion in Peru. Fast Gold was fourth on the Brazilian general sire list in 2005/06.

The filly Vain Gold (out of Chancy Dance, by Bold Reason) proved a more precocious type than Fast Gold, winning the 1981 Gardenia Stakes (gr. III) and running third in the Demoiselle Stakes (gr. I) as a juvenile. Between these two was the Aisco Stable homebred Distinctive Pro (out of Well Done, by Distinctive), who tallied his biggest score in the 1982 Hutcheson Stakes (gr. III). A useful regional sire in New York, Distinctive Pro very appropriately sired his best runner for Jimmy Croll, who bred Quick Mischief from his mare Mischief Pronto. Racing in the colors of Charles Carlesimo and Greg Mordas, Quick Mischief won the 1990 Ruffian Handicap (gr. I) and the 1992 John A. Morris Handicap (gr. I).

All told, Mr. Prospector sired ten stakes winners from the forty-three named foals of his 1979 crop, and he nearly had an eleventh when Crafty Prospector missed by a neck against the top filly Christmas Past in the 1983 Gulfstream Park Handicap (gr. I). A smallish, low-slung chestnut with a strong resemblance to his maternal grandsire, In Reality, Crafty Prospector entered stud with very modest expectations but became a consistent stallion with one of the best reputations for throwing soundness among Mr. Prospector's foals. Few of his progeny cared for much more than a mile or were of the highest class — not that surprising when one considers that Crafty Prospector spent his stud career covering mares of more modest class than most of Mr. Prospector's top sire sons — but Crafty Prospector did manage to sire 2001 Japanese champion older male Agnes Digital and 1997 Cigar Mile Handicap (gr. I) winner Devious Course among his eighty-nine stakes winners before being pensioned following the 2006 breeding season.

Nine more stakes winners came from Mr. Prospector's 1980 crop, headed by 1984 champion sprinter Eillo (out of Barbs Dancer, by Northern Dancer). Eillo waited until he was four to hit the big time, and he did so with a flourish by winning the inaugural Breeders' Cup Sprint (gr. I) to go with four wins in minor sprint stakes. Unfortunately, he did not live to go to stud as he died following colic surgery, but his year-younger full brother Sam M., though only stakes-placed on the racecourse, was a leading sire in Chile until his death in December 2002 and sired two Chilean champions in Sahumerio and Satanico.

Widaad (out of Attache Case, by Diplomat Way) was probably the best of Mr. Prospector's other 1980 foals, winning the 1982 Queen Mary Stakes (Eng-II) and running third in the all-aged Flying Childers Stakes (Eng-II) as a juvenile. She did not run at three or afterward, but Proclaim (out of Maybellene, by Fleet Nasrullah) and Strike Gold (out of Newchance Lady, by *Roi Dagobert) both captured group/grade III events as sophomores in 1983. Strike Gold, a top California sire by number of winners, sired two well-regarded fillies in Arches of Gold (1992 La Brea Stakes, gr. III) and Traces of Gold (1996 California Jockey Club Handicap, gr. III, and 1998 Brown Bess Handicap, gr. III).

Mr. Prospector's sixth and final Florida-bred crop, foals of 1981, produced "only" eight stakes winners among its forty-nine named foals, but among them was the stallion's first European champion, the filly Proskona (out of Konafa, by Damascus), who earned a divisional highweight in Italy with a victory in the 1984 Premio Umbria (Ity-II). Another notable from the 1981 foal crop was Procida (out of With Distinction, by Distinctive), who won the 1984 Prix de la Foret (Fr-I) and then crossed the Atlantic to win the Hollywood Derby (gr. IT). Procida proved a disappointing sire other than for Shanghai, the upset winner of the 1992 Poule d'Essai des Poulains (Fr-I).

The Florida chapter off Mr. Prospector's stud career ended with the stallion having proved himself a sire of rare versatility and brilliance. He had begotten five champions, ranging from a colt and filly capable of winning impressively at Classic distances to first-rate sprinters. Fifty of his 257 Florida-sired foals eventually won stakes — a strike rate of 19.5 percent — and nineteen, or 7.4 percent, became graded/group stakes winners, a status normally achieved by less than 1 percent of all Thoroughbreds.

And the best was yet to come.

Blue Blood

7

Mr. Prospector's first Kentucky-sired crop arrived in 1982. Among the forty-six foals struggling to their feet that spring was a rather coarse but powerful bay youngster who hearkened back to Mr. Prospector's Florida connections; his dam, Midnight Pumpkin, was a stakes-winning daughter of Me Next, a full sister to In Reality's dam My Dear Girl.

Although Seth Hancock was doubtless pleased by what he saw in Claiborne's pastures that spring — the same well-muscled, close-coupled, powerfully quartered types that Mr. Prospector had been getting in Florida — he could hardly have been blamed if he had his worries. After all, as he had told Peter Brant when the possibility of Mr. Prospector's coming to Claiborne was first being discussed, he had seen a number of stallions who had done well as regional sires but had disappointed on coming to Kentucky.

He needn't have worried. The bay colt out of Midnight Pumpkin, who went to Eugene Klein for $625,000 at the 1983 Keeneland July sale, came out running well enough to be second to eventual champion juvenile Chief's Crown in the inaugural Breeders' Cup Juvenile (gr. I). (The field was first-rate indeed, for the third-place horse was Spend a Buck, who went on to become champion three-year-old male and Horse of the Year in 1985.) The young Tank's Prospect went on to win the Arkansas Derby (gr. I) and Preakness Stakes (gr. I) before bowing a tendon at the top of the stretch in the Belmont (gr. I) to end his career with five wins from fourteen starts. He died in 1995 after a disappointing stud career.

The career of Tank's Prospect signaled a turning point for his sire. With Mr. Prospector's reputation as a classic sire now thoroughly established, blue-blooded mares lined up for his book by tens and dozens. Somewhat surprisingly, they would not improve on the numbers of stakes winners he had racked up with his Florida mates; of the 931 foals he sired during his nineteen years at Claiborne, 131, or 14.1%, would become stakes winners. But they would do two things: They would produce an ever-lengthening stream of champions, and they would lay the foundation for the majority of the sons and daughters that would gain Mr. Prospector a reputation as one of the greatest all-around sires of the twentieth century.

The year 1982 also saw the birth of two sons of Mr. Prospector who, while not stakes winners, gained some note as sires. Allen's Prospect, a half brother to 1994 Broodmare of the Year Fall Aspen, showed marked promise in winning three of his seven starts but did not stay sound long enough to win in stakes company. Although not nearly the racehorse that Tank's Prospect was, Allen's Prospect outdid him as a sire, becoming one of the most sought-after stallions in Maryland. Allen's Prospect, who died in September 2003, has sired sixty-eight stakes winners headed by 1996 Malibu Stakes (gr. I) winner King of the Heap, now at stud in Texas.

Silver Ghost, a gray colt out of the good race mare Misty Gallore, also showed some ability in a brief racing career, finishing out of the money only once in six starts. Given a chance at stud in Kentucky despite his lack of marquee wins and a nasty temperament that did not improve with age, he did quite well given the modest quality of his mates. Pensioned in October 2006, he has fifty stakes winners to his credit, including the grade I-winning fillies Dreams Gallore, Love Lock, and Lunar Spook.

Woodman, a foal of 1983, was the first of Mr. Prospector's Claiborne-sired champions. Produced from Playmate, a daughter of Buckpasser and Intriguing and so a full sister to 1971 U.S. champion juvenile filly Numbered Account, the husky chestnut fetched $3 million at the 1984 Keeneland July sale.

Sent to Europe, Woodman proved the best Irish-based juvenile of 1985 but was no match for the better English youngsters, running unplaced in the Dewhurst Stakes (Eng-I). He raced only once at three before being retired due to injury.

Syndicated and sent to stud at Ashford Stud in Kentucky, Woodman got off to a tremendous start at stud by siring three champions — two of them also classic winners — in his first crop. After earning honors as France's champion juvenile in 1990, Hector Protector won the 1991 Poule d' Essai des Poulains (Fr-I) before failing to stay on in the Derby Stakes (Eng-I). Meanwhile, the handsome Hansel rated among the better American juveniles by winning the Arlington-Washington Futurity (gr. II). Injury kept him from making a run at the juvenile championship, but Hansel returned at age three to win the Preakness and the Belmont, earning honors as U.S. champion three-year-old male. Woodman's third champion of the 1988 crop was Mujtahid, rated the best English juvenile of 1990 with wins in the Scottish Equitable Gimcrack Stakes (Eng-II) and Anglia Television July Stakes (Eng-III).

None of the trio became overwhelming successes at stud, and Woodman himself has had an uneven stud career. A forerunner of the modern trend to huge books, Woodman has sired 1,957 foals as of July 2007, of which 109 have become stakes winners. His best have been very good indeed. Although he did not sire another champion until 1992, he struck gold with two that year — Hishi Akebono, champion sprinter and miler in Japan, and Timber Country, winner of the 1995 Preakness and U.S. champion two-year-old male in 1994. The following year Woodman sired Bosra Sham, a full sister to Hector Protector whom many considered to be one of the best English-based fillies seen in years. The winner of the 1996 One Thousand Guineas, Bosra Sham earned back-to-back titles as English champion three-year-old filly and English champion older female.

Dr. Johnson (highweighted three-year-old stayer in Ireland in 1997), Way of Light (1998 French champion juvenile mile), and Woodcarver (1999 Queen's Plate and Canadian champion three-year-old male) followed Bosra Sham, along with 1999 Irish One Thousand Guineas (Ire-I) winner Hula Angel. The best horse that Woodman has sired since Bosra Sham, however, is unquestionably Hawk Wing, champion three-year-old male in both England and Ireland in 2002 and the highweight on the 2003 International Classifications with a rating of 133 pounds. Hawk Wing, whose career was cut short by a knee injury in the 2003 Queen Anne Stakes (Eng-I) after a breathtaking eleven-length win in the Juddmonte Lockinge Stakes (Eng-I), is now at stud in Ireland.

Sired from 1980 U.S. champion filly Heavenly Cause, Two Punch did not manage to match Woodman's record as a racer; though he won half his eight starts, his only stakes win was in the listed Bachelor Stakes as a three-year-old in 1986. He added to Mr. Prospector's reputation as a sire of sires, however. Sent to stud in Maryland, Two Punch not only forged a career as a good regional sire but got himself a successor in Smoke Glacken, the U.S. champion sprinter of 1997. As of July 2, 2007, Smoke Glacken has sired twenty-nine stakes winners from 471 foals of racing age, headed by multiple grade II winners Smok'n Frolic and Read the Footnotes. The latter, after standing the 2005 breeding season at Sequel Stallions in Florida, is now at stud in New York.

Mr. Prospector sired two more champions in 1984 that were part of a crop that many experts consider to have been the best in the last quarter of the twentieth century in North America. Gulch, bred by Peter Brant from his multiple grade I-winning mare Jameela, showed his merit first, though the later to earn his championship. One of the best juveniles of 1986, Gulch won four graded stakes including the Hopeful Stakes (gr. I) at Saratoga and the Futurity Stakes (gr. I) at Belmont but could not contest the Breeders' Cup Juvenile due to injury. In his absence, the race was won by Capote, previously an impressive winner of the Norfolk Stakes (gr. I), who thereby assured himself the crown as 1986 U.S. champion juvenile male.

Returning at age three, Gulch won the nine-furlong Wood Memorial Invitational Stakes (gr. I) and ran third in the Belmont but showed his best form in the Metropolitan Handicap, which he won over the classy older horses King's Swan and Broad Brush. His earnings helped lift Mr. Prospector to his first title as leading American sire.

At four, Gulch finally earned his crown by winning the Breeders' Cup Sprint (gr. I) and with it the championship of the American sprint division over a field that included the brilliant Mining, another 1984 son of Mr. Prospector who was none too sound but was previously unbeaten in six starts including the Vosburgh Stakes (gr. I). Gulch, one of the soundest and most durable of Mr. Prospector's top sons, retired with thirteen wins from thirty-two starts for earnings of $3,095,521, making him Mr. Prospector's leading earner.

At stud, Gulch has had an honorable career just below the top rank. As of July 2, 2007, he has sired sixty-four stakes winners from 943 foals of racing age. His best year was in 1995, when his daughter Harayir won the One Thousand Guineas while his son Thunder Gulch won the Kentucky Derby, Belmont, and Travers Stakes en route to honors as U.S. champion three-year-old male.

A compact chestnut that trainer D. Wayne Lukas nicknamed "Mighty Mouse," Thunder Gulch went to stud in 1996 at Ashford Stud alongside his elder kinsman, Woodman. Like Woodman, he has had trouble with consistency among his foals, a problem perhaps not helped by the huge books he has served (he has averaged over 140 foals per year through his first ten years at stud). He numbers more fillies than colts among his best runners, most notably the 2000 Breeders' Cup Distaff (gr. I) winner, Spain, but his one North American champion is Point Given, U.S. champion three-year-old male and Horse of the Year in 2001.

Point Given narrowly missed another title at two, when he just failed to run down eventual champion juvenile Macho Uno in the Breeders' Cup Juvenile. At three he ran fifth behind Monarchos in the Kentucky Derby but took his revenge in the Preakness and Belmont. A huge, rambunctious chestnut that trainer Bob Baffert sometimes called "The Big Red Train" and "The T-Rex," Point Given has so far sired eight stakes winners including 2006 Del Mar Debutante Stakes (gr. I) winner Point Ashley.

Afleet, Mr. Prospector's second champion in the 1984 crop, was a little slower to get going than Gulch and did not race at two. He made up nicely for lost time at three, however. After winning three Canadian stakes races and finishing second behind Market Control in the Queen's Plate, Afleet invaded the United States to capture the Pennsylvania Derby (gr. II) and Jerome Handicap (gr. I). He then ran second to 1985 Belmont Stakes winner Creme Fraiche in the Meadowlands Cup Handicap (gr. I). Although he could do no better than tenth behind Ferdinand in the Breeders' Cup Classic, his record earned him Sovereign Awards as Canadian champion three-year-old male and Horse of the Year.

At four Afleet won the Toboggan Handicap (gr. III) and earned placings in the Breeders' Cup Sprint and three other graded stakes before retiring to stud at Gainesway Farm with a record of seven wins from fifteen starts and earnings of $995,235. He stood six seasons in Kentucky before being exported to Japan in 1994. To date, Afleet has been credited with fifty-eight stakes winners including the 1999 Oka Sho (Japanese One Thousand Guineas, Jpn-I) winner Primo Ordine and the 2003 Japan Dirt Derby (Jpn-I) winner Big Wolf.

While at Gainesway, Afleet sired 2001 Canadian champion older male A

Fleets Dancer and 1994 Italian champion juvenile Blu Tusmani, but his best sire son so far was a runner of somewhat lesser stature. Produced from the great Canadian family of Square Angel (his third dam), Northern Afleet showed speed over sprint distances at two and three but did not become a stakes winner until age four, when he won the San Carlos Handicap (gr. II), the San Fernando Breeders' Cup Stakes (gr. II) and the San Diego Handicap (gr. III).

Retired to Double Diamond Farm near Ocala, Florida, at an initial fee of $5,000, Northern Afleet stood his first season in 1999 and has sired fourteen stakes winners so far from his first six crops of racing age. By far the best has been Afleet Alex, who won the 2005 Preakness after a heart-stopping stumble caused by interference from Scrappy T at the top of the lane. Afleet Alex went on to win the Belmont by seven lengths, easily defeating Kentucky Derby winner Giacomo (who finished seventh after having been third in the Preakness). Though Afleet Alex was forced to the sidelines thereafter by injury and eventually retired without ever having raced again, he won an Eclipse Award as the U.S. champion three-year-old male of 2005 and is now at stud at Gainesway. As for Northern Afleet, he moved from Florida to Taylor Made Farm in 2005. He is slated to shuttle to Stud TNT in Brazil for the 2007 Southern Hemisphere breeding season.

Gone West never won a championship, but the 1987 Dwyer Stakes (gr. I) winner is arguably the best sire produced from Mr. Prospector's 1984 crop. Standing at Mill Ridge Farm near Lexington throughout his career, he has sired eighty-seven stakes winners as of July 2007. His accomplishments will be profiled in greater detail in a later chapter.

Among the fifty-one named foals of Mr. Prospector's 1985 crop were two whose destinies would be closely linked. Both foaled at Claiborne from backgrounds filled with Claiborne-linked bloodlines, the pair would be rivals on the racetrack as well as contributors to Claiborne's great heritage of fine sires.

Bred and owned by Claiborne itself, Forty Niner traced his descent from one of the fine broodmares brought in by Bull Hancock to rejuvenate the Claiborne broodmare band during the late 1940s and the 1950s. This was *Highway Code, a daughter by the great English sire Hyperion out of Book Law, winner of the 1927 St. Leger Stakes. Although not a great producer herself, *Highway Code founded a first-rate American family through her stakes-placed 1952 daughter by *Nasrullah, Courtesy.

Courtesy produced three good stakes winners by Round Table for Claiborne — Knightly Manner, Respected, and Dignitas — as well as the appropriately named Continue. A 1958 daughter of Double Jay, Continue won five of her seven starts but never earned black type. Her legacy was to be in the paddocks, where she produced five stakes winners. The best on the track was Yamanin, a son of *Herbager who scored his biggest win in the 1977 Widener Handicap (gr. I), but the most important to the future were Tuerta, a 1970 daughter of *Forli, and File, a 1976 daughter of Tom Rolfe.

Bull Hancock was reportedly none too pleased when Tuerta was born. Not only had he been hoping for a colt, but the filly turned out to be one-eyed (the source of her name, which means "one-eyed" in Spanish) and with a deformed ear. But had Hancock been able to see the future, he doubtless would have been delighted. Not only did Tuerta become a two-time grade III winner in her own right, but in 1981 she produced a near-black colt by Seattle Slew who took Claiborne to both the heights of ecstasy and the depths of agony. Named Swale, the colt became the first horse bred and owned by Claiborne to win the Kentucky Derby. On June 9, 1984, the colt added the Belmont Stakes in stylish fashion ... and eight days later he was dead, the victim of an apparent heart attack. He was posthumously named the U.S. champion three-year-old male of 1984.

File was not quite as talented as Tuerta but did become a stakes winner, taking the 1979 Cinderella Stakes as a three-year-old. Her first foal, Stack (by Nijinsky II), was only an allowance winner but became a three-time champion sire in Peru before returning to the United States in 1997. Two Mr. Prospector fillies of no great importance followed before File hit the jackpot with her wiry chestnut son in 1985.

Sent to Woody Stephens for training, Forty Niner was named U.S. champion two-year-old male of 1987 off victories in the Sanford Stakes (gr. II), Futurity Stakes (gr. I), Champagne Stakes (gr. I), and Breeders' Futurity (gr. II). His spring campaign began with high hopes that he might bring another Kentucky Derby trophy home to Claiborne, but the colt ran into one frustration after another, losing the Hutcheson Stakes (gr. III) to an upstart named Perfect Spy, the Florida Derby (gr. I) to Brian's Time, and the Lexington Stakes (gr. II) to a rapidly-developing son of Secretariat named Risen Star. A victory in the major prep race for the Florida Derby, the Fountain of Youth Stakes (gr. II), probably seemed like a mere consolation prize to the colt's connections, and the final stroke was the colt's game but futile charge in the Kentucky Derby, which saw him come up short by a neck to front-running Winning Colors.

Woody Stephens changed tactics in the Preakness Stakes, ordering jockey Pat Day to go head to head with Winning Colors from his post position just inside the filly. But the decision proved suicidal; while Forty Niner may have cost Winning Colors any chance of winning the race — between the speed duel and carrying her wide on the final turn (she finished third) — the effort exhausted the game colt, who finished well up the track behind eventual winner Risen Star. That gave Risen Star a two-to-one advantage in head-to-head confrontations with Forty Niner (he had been third in the Derby after encountering traffic problems) and, coupled with the Secretariat colt's runaway victory in the Belmont, may well have helped swing voter sentiments to Risen Star in year-end championship voting, despite the brilliance of Forty Niner's summer and fall campaign.

Rested for nearly three months following the Preakness, Forty Niner came back in August ready to make his bid for his second straight championship. Risen Star was gone from the scene, having been forced into retirement by injury after the Belmont, but a new contender was waiting: Seeking the Gold.

The association of the Phipps family with Claiborne has been so long and close that horses bred by the former might almost be considered adopted sons and daughters of the latter. The association began with Mrs. Henry Carnegie Phipps, who often consulted Bull Hancock on the selection of breeding stock and matings for her Wheatley Stable. Mrs. Phipps' professional relationship with Hancock eventually resulted in the best horse she was ever to breed after Hancock offered to sell her a stakes-winning Discovery mare, Miss Disco, in place of a mare he had unsuccessfully tried to buy as agent for Mrs. Phipps. The lady, no dolt, took him up on the offer. Bull Hancock must have sometimes regretted his sale of Miss Disco later, for following a 1953 mating to *Nasrullah, the mare produced Bold Ruler, the 1957 Horse of the Year and a great sire. As Bold Ruler stood his entire career at Claiborne, however, Hancock was at least partially compensated for losing the glory of being the horse's breeder and owner.

Mrs. Phipps' son, Ogden Phipps, had a long association with Claiborne in his own right, for he had bred his first stakes winner, the 1935 Youthful Stakes winner White Cockade, from a mare bred by Arthur B. Hancock, Sr. He also boarded his horses at Claiborne during most of his Turf career. Among the Phipps mares whose foals took their first steps at Claiborne was Con Game, a daughter of Phipps' homebred stallion Buckpasser.

Both Con Game and Buckpasser belonged to families acquired from the dispersal of Colonel E. R. Bradley's stock in 1946. Buckpasser, of course, descended from *La Troienne through her Blue Larkspur filly Businesslike, who was carrying a War Admiral foal at the time of her acquisition by Phipps. The foal turned out to be Busanda, a moody but high-class mare who won the 1950 Alabama Stakes, the 1951 Suburban Handicap and Saratoga Cup, and the 1952 Saratoga Cup in Phipps' colors before retiring to produce three stakes winners, Buckpasser included.

Flitabout, who became Phipps' property as a yearling, was a granddaughter of the Son-in-Law mare *La Mome, another of Bradley's importations. A staying filly whose best race was a second to Scattered in the 1948 Coaching Club American Oaks, Flitabout produced three stakes-winning fillies for Phipps, among them Broadway. A daughter of the 1954 Preakness winner, Hasty Road, Broadway won the 1961 Polly Drummond Stakes and finished second in the important Selima Stakes the same year before retiring to the Phipps broodmare band. In addition to Con Game — a minor winner — Broadway produced four stakes winners, the best of which were 1967 U.S. champion two-year-old filly Queen of the Stage and the very fast Reviewer, both by Bold Ruler. Reviewer, in turn, took up stud duties as a Claiborne stallion until his untimely death in 1977, two years after the tragic death of his great daughter, Ruffian.

Seeking the Gold started only once at two, winning a maiden race, and was allowed to take his time as he developed at three. Although he came to hand rapidly enough to win the Swale Stakes at Gulfstream Park in the spring, seconds to then-unbeaten Private Terms in the Gotham Stakes (gr. II) and Wood Memorial Stakes (gr. I) at Aqueduct and a seventh in the Kentucky Derby indicated that Seeking the Gold was not quite ready to contend with the very best of the division. Instead of continuing on the Triple Crown trail, the colt scored his first graded stakes win in the Peter Pan Stakes (gr. II) at the Belmont spring/summer meeting, followed by a win in the Dwyer Stakes (gr. I).

Seeking the Gold was sent in search of a second grade I win in the Haskell Invitational Handicap (gr. I) at Monmouth, a race also targeted by the freshened

Forty Niner. The two were weighted one pound apart, with Forty Niner carrying 126 pounds against 125 on Seeking the Gold, and they finished locked together, with Forty Niner winning the head bob in a lively 1:47 3/5 after a prolonged stretch duel. (Many handicappers equate a two-pound weight difference with a length in margin, so the weights for the Haskell suggest that the official handicapper felt that Forty Niner was about a half-length superior to Seeking the Gold at the time the weights were declared. Forty Niner's actual margin was a nose, so the handicapper came very close to achieving the theoretical handicapping goal of creating a dead heat.)

Ordinarily, such an effort would have drained one or both rivals. But when the action moved to the Travers Stakes (gr. I) at Saratoga, the pair turned in an equally spine-tingling repeat performance, with Forty Niner once again the winner by a nose. This time the weights were even, as both colts carried 126 pounds.

Sent to tackle somewhat softer competition in the Super Derby (gr. I) at Louisiana Downs, Seeking the Gold romped home at the expense of local hope Happyasalark Tomas. The Phipps colt closed out his sophomore season with a game second to eventual champion older male and Horse of the Year Alysheba in the Breeders' Cup Classic (gr. I) while Forty Niner, who got a less than ideal trip, finished fourth in the same race. The purses from their placings, along with Gulch's win in the Breeders' Cup Sprint, helped ensure Mr. Prospector a second consecutive title as leading American sire.

That was all for Forty Niner, who became the second of Mr. Prospector's sons to join his sire at Claiborne with a record of eleven wins and five seconds from nineteen starts. As for Seeking the Gold, he was to make only two more starts, winning a prep race for the Metropolitan Handicap (gr. I) but losing the big event to Proper Reality, who was carrying 117 pounds to 126 on Seeking the Gold. More than weight may have been behind Seeking the Gold's defeat, for he came out of the race with an injury and was retired, joining Forty Niner at Claiborne. With earnings of $2,307,000, he and Forty Niner ($2,726,000) made their sire the first North American stallion to sire three earners of more than $2 million. Both would play further roles in the Claiborne saga.

Forty Niner's contributions will be outlined later, but Seeking the Gold has been a fine sire and as of this writing is still active at Claiborne with eighty stakes winners to his credit. Although best known as a sire of top fillies, including four champion females, his leading runner is Dubai Millennium, a multiple champion in England and the United Arab Emirates. Sadly, Dubai Millennium sired only one partial crop before dying of grass sickness in April 2001, midway through his first season at stud, but that crop included the 2005 Irish Two Thousand Guineas (Ire-I) winner Dubawi, now at stud in England.

Mutakddim, a minor stakes winner in England, has been Seeking the Gold's best son at stud to date. A good sire in Argentina, he has at least eleven Group I winners to his credit in that country. His best runner in North America has been the popular Lady Tak, a grade I winner at three and four. As of July 2, 2007, Mutakddim has sired fifty-nine stakes winners — thirty-two of them winners in group or graded races — from 785 foals of racing age.

Given both his own excellent pedigree and the quality of the mares to which he has been bred, it should not be surprising that Seeking the Gold has also proven to be a solid broodmare sire. Twenty-fourth on the U.S. broodmare sire list in 2006, Seeking the Gold has so far been credited with fifty stakes winners from 909 foals of racing age produced by his daughters, headed by 2000 U.S. champion three-year-old filly Surfside and grade I winners Riskaverse, Pomeroy, Pine Island, and Good Reward.

The year 1985 was also notable for the birth of Ravinella, arguably the best daughter of Mr. Prospector since It's in the Air nine years earlier. Produced from the stakes-winning Northern Dancer mare Really Lucky, Ravinella was named champion juvenile filly in both England and France in 1987 on the strength of victories in the Prix d'Arenberg (Fr-III) and the Tattersalls Cheveley Park Stakes (Eng-I). The following year Ravinella won a classic double in the One Thousand Guineas (Eng-I) and the Poule d'Essai des Pouliches (Fr-I) for owner Alec Head and was the European highweight for three-year-old fillies at 1,400 to 1,900 meters.

All told, Mr. Prospector sired five grade or group I winners from the ten stakes winners of his 1985 crop, more than many stallions sire in a lifetime. (The remaining two were Over All, a filly from the same family as Conquistador Cielo, and Classic Crown, a half sister to 1984 champion two-year-old male Chief's Crown.) He had also established two crosses that would be important to the future: with the daughters of Buckpasser, and with the daughters and granddaughters of Northern Dancer. Both would prove golden many times over, and the latter would prove important in reverse as well, with Mr. Prospector daughters matched to Northern Dancer-line sires.

Parade Of Champions

8

By the time the 1986 crop reached the races, siring champions was almost routine for Mr. Prospector, whose reputation in that department was rapidly becoming second only to that of Northern Dancer. Two more champions would come out of the stallion's 1986 foals, and their contrasting aptitudes helped emphasize Mr. Prospector's versatility as a sire.

Tersa struck first. A half sister to Gato Del Sol, she could not have been less like her half brother in anything but talent. Whereas he had been a late-running stayer who won the Kentucky Derby on superior stamina, she was a precocious two-year-old who was named champion juvenile filly in France after winning the Prix du Bois (Fr-III) and the Prix Morny (Fr-I). She was unable to sustain her form at three, however.

In contrast to Tersa, Queena (out of Too Chic, by Blushing Groom) never even made it to the races until age four, winning five of nine starts. At five, however, she lived up to her name by ruling over the American older female division with wins in the Maskette Stakes, Ruffian Handicap, and Ballerina Stakes, all grade I events.

Ten stakes winners came out of Mr. Prospector's 1986 crop, and he matched that total in 1987 with two more champions and a national high-weight included in the group. In North America, the stallion was represented by Rhythm, who followed up a good second-place finish in the Champagne

Stakes (gr. I) with an impressive victory in the Breeders' Cup Juvenile to earn an Eclipse Award as 1989 U.S. champion juvenile male.

But Rhythm's three-year-old season was a study in frustration. After undergoing surgery for a displaced palate in the spring, the colt came back for the grade II Dwyer Stakes in June but was beaten a length by Profit Key after ducking out in the stretch, and he never really fired while finishing third in the grade I Haskell Invitational Handicap in late July. The colt turned around with a powerful victory in the Travers Stakes (gr. I), raising hopes for a strong fall season. Autumn started promisingly enough with a respectable third to the older Dispersal and Quiet American in the Woodward Handicap (gr. I), but in a wide-open field for the Breeders' Cup Classic, in which he was made a slight favorite, he was done after a mile and finished eighth, some thirteen lengths behind that year's Kentucky Derby winner, Unbridled.

Although he continued racing at age four, Rhythm never recovered his best form and retired having won six of twenty starts and earning $1,592,532. High expectations awaited him at stud, given that his dam, the Northern Dancer mare Dance Number, was a grade I-winning half sister to the fine stallion Private Account. But Rhythm had been a willful and temperamental sort who had taxed Hall of Fame trainer Shug McGaughey's patience while in training, and he passed on his disposition all too often. Over time, Rhythm's progeny gained a reputation as being late-maturing animals with a proclivity for mental issues.

Rhythm must generally be reckoned as a disappointment while standing in Japan, Australia, and later California, but he did get a few high class animals among his progeny. The best was the multiple Australian group I winner and champion stayer Ethereal, one of the best Australian race mares of the late twentieth century. He is also the sire of 2001 New Zealand Oaks (NZ-I) winner Tapildo, 2005 Wellington Cup (NZ-I) winner Zabeat, 2004

Auckland Cup (NZ-I) winner Upsetthym, and 2004 Thorndon Mile (NZ-I) winner Sir Kinloch.

Rhythm's younger full brother Not For Love (foaled in 1990), although only stakes-placed on the track, has been a much more consistent sire, getting thirty-five stakes winners from 556 foals of racing age so far while standing in Maryland. His best runners to date have been the grade II winners Duckhorn (now at stud in Pennsylvania), Love of Money, and Touch Love.

Mr. Prospector's second champion from the 1987 crop, Machiavellian (out of Coup de Folie, by Halo) was more consistent in his briefer racing career. Rated the best two-year-old in Europe in 1989 off wins in the Prix Morny (Fr-I) and Prix de la Salamandre (Fr-I), the colt was second to Tirol in the Two Thousand Guineas the following year and fourth to that rival in the Irish Two Thousand Guineas, a race in which he did not get clear until the final furlong and still was beaten less than a length for it all. His only bad race was in his final start, the Prix Maurice de Gheest (Fr-II), where he failed to show his previous form and ran fifth and last, beaten nearly seven lengths by winner Dead Certain. Machiavellian won four of his seven starts, with all his wins coming in stakes.

At stud Machiavellian proved Mr. Prospector's best son in Europe and one of his best sons overall. Standing at Sheikh Mohammed bin Rashid al Maktoum's Dalham Hall Stud in Newmarket, England, Machiavellian died at age seventeen from laminitis in June 2004; as of July 2007, his tally of stakes winners stood at sixty-nine. Eight of his progeny have been named champions or highweights in various countries, headed by the Dubai World Cup (UAE-I) winners Almutawakel (GB) (1999) and Street Cry (Ire) (2002).

A descendant of Natalma (his third dam), Machiavellian proved particularly effective with mares carrying Northern Dancer (Nearctic—Natalma) blood. An example of the cross is 2007 Prix de Diane (French Oaks, Fr-I) winner West Wind, a member of Machiavellian's penultimate crop, who was produced from the Nureyev mare Red Slippers.

Although it is probably too early to declare him to be Machiavellian's heir at stud, Street Cry is off to an excellent start with eleven stakes winners (seven of them graded or group winners) having emerged so far from the eighty-eight foals of his first crop. The star of the group is Street Sense, whose record-breaking ten-length victory in the 2006 Breeders' Cup Juvenile propelled him to an Eclipse Award as U.S. champion juvenile male. In May 2007 Street Sense became the first colt to complete the Breeders' Cup Juvenile–Kentucky Derby double before losing the Preakness by a short head to Curlin.

Another of Mr. Prospector's sons, Maximilian (out of Mystery Mood, by Night Invader) was weighted atop German three-year-old males in the 1,400 to 1,900 meter range after winning the 1990 Ostermann Pokal (Ger-III). However, as German racing places little emphasis on sprinters or milers, this was something of a hollow honor, and Maximilian has been less distinguished as a sire than as a racer.

Two-time grade II winner Carson City (out of Blushing Promise, by Blushing Groom) was not quite up to the racing standards set by Rhythm and Machiavellian, but he surprised many pundits by becoming a very good stallion. Like Machiavellian, he died in 2004, but so far he has sired eighty-seven stakes winners including 2002 Canadian champion older female Small Promises and 2003 UAE champion older male State City. Carson City has several young sons at stud, among them 2000 Hopeful Stakes (gr. I) winner City Zip, whose seven stakes winners to date are headed by 2006 Lane's End Stakes (gr. II) winner With a City.

Although the 1988 crop also contained ten stakes winners, none were quite up to championship stature. The best runners from this group were the 1990 Hollywood Starlet Stakes (gr. I) winner Cuddles (out of Stellarette, by Tentam); two-time grade I winner Scan (out of Video, by Nijinsky II), who was exported to Japan for stud duty; and Lycius, who became Mr. Prospector's one hundredth stakes winner when he captured the Prix du Haras de la Huderie on August 20, 1990. Out of the Lyphard mare Lypatia, Lycius followed up by winning the Middle Park Stakes (Eng-I) and placed in both the Two Thousand Guineas and the Irish Two Thousand Guineas at three. He is the sire of Italian champions Hello and Slap Shot and of 2005 Canadian champion three-year-old male Palladio and is still active in New York as of this writing.

Also worthy of note is 1992 Fayette Stakes (gr. II) winner Barkerville (out of Euryanthe, by Nijinsky II), who is the sire of Chilean Horse of the Year Ballistic and two-time Chilean group I winner Big Ten. The latter horse also won the 2000 Californian Stakes (gr. II) and is now at stud in his native country. Thanks to his successes in Chile as a shuttle stallion, Barkerville was brought back to stud in Kentucky in 1998 but has not achieved much success while there.

The seven stakes winners of Mr. Prospector's 1989 crop were headed by two high-class fillies: Preach, winner of the 1991 Frizette Stakes (gr. I), and Prospectors Delite, winner of the 1992 Ashland (gr. I) and Acorn (gr. I) stakes. Both were later successful broodmares (see Chapter 11). The crop also included Lion Cavern, a full brother to Gone West who became a group III winner in England and France and took down the 1993 True North Handicap (gr. II) in the United States. A less consistent sire than Gone West, Lion Cavern nonetheless had his moments, his best progeny including 2000 Irish One Thousand Guineas winner and English, Irish, and German champion three-year-old filly Crimplene, 1997 Italian champion juvenile Silent Tribute, and two-time Yugoslavian highweight Catarinadimedici. Lion

Cavern was sold for export to Greece in 2004 but died of colic shortly after arriving in his new country.

* * *

Mr. Prospector sired nine stakes winners among his 1990 crop, but had he begotten only Kingmambo that year, his efforts in the breeding shed would have been well spent. A handsome, regally bred colt out of multiple European and American champion Miesque (by the excellent Northern Dancer stallion Nureyev), Kingmambo showed himself to be a worthy son of his dam by winning three group I events as a three-year-old, among them the classic Poule d'Essai des Poulains.

Retired to stud at Lane's End in Kentucky, Kingmambo has joined the ranks of the world's elite commercial sires. As of July 2, 2007, he has sired seventy stakes winners and has eight champions to his credit so far, headed by 1999 Japanese Horse of the Year El Condor Pasa. As a rule, his progeny seem best suited to European turf, but Lemon Drop Kid, winner of the 1999 Belmont Stakes and U.S. champion older male in 2000, has demonstrated Kingmambo's ability to get a top dirt runner as well. The stallion's most recent star is Light Shift, winner of the 2007 Oaks (Eng-I).

How much longer Kingmambo will be able to remain at stud is somewhat in doubt. Although demand for the stallion's services or for his progeny has not diminished — a yearling son of his out of the stakes-winning Seattle Slew mare Crown of Crimson sold for $11.7 million at the 2006 Keeneland September sale, becoming the second most expensive auction yearling in history — Kingmambo was forced to miss nearly six weeks of the 2005 breeding season due to an arthritic neck, a protozoal infection, and a minor leg injury. He covered only thirty-six mares that year. While the infection and the leg injury have healed, the arthritis in the stallion's neck may eventually force his retirement if it progresses. As a result of Kingmambo's physical issues, William S. Farish of Lane's End announced the stallion's book would be limited to no more than sixty or seventy mares for 2007, in line with the sixty-five mares that Kingmambo covered in 2006.

As Kingmambo's eldest sons are still relatively young, the jury is out as to how he will fare as a sire of sires. Unfortunately, El Condor Pasa died of colic after only three seasons at stud in Japan. Lemon Drop Kid, on the other hand, may be on the rise; after a slow start at stud, he is now the sire of eighteen stakes winners including 2006 Kentucky Oaks (gr. I) victress Lemons Forever, 2007 Gamely Stakes (gr. IT) winner Citronnade, and 2007 Ashland Stakes (gr. I) winner Christmas Kid.

Another son of Kingmambo, 2004 Japanese champion three-year-old male King Kamehameha, apparently has been very well received by Japanese breeders and buyers; a weanling filly from his first crop sold for a world-record 600 million yen ($5,217,391 at the exchange rate) at the Japan Racing Horse Association select sale in July 2006, eclipsing the previous record price for a weanling sold at auction by more than $680,000.

Faltaat (out of U.S. champion juvenile filly Epitome, by Summing) spent most of his racing career in Dubai. In 1995 he added to Mr. Prospector's list of champions and highweights by becoming the highweighted older male in the United Arab Emirates over 1,000 to 1,400 meters. In New Zealand, he has sired 2002/03 Horse of the Year Tit for Taat and group I winners Jury's Out, Sedecrem, and Taatletail.

Two other outstanding members of Mr. Prospector's 1990 crop are Educated Risk and Miner's Mark, both bred and owned by the Phipps family. A daughter of the Key to the Mint mare Pure Profit, Educated Risk won the 1992 Frizette Stakes (gr. I) and the 1994 Top Flight Handicap (gr. I) as well as placing in six other grade I races during her career. Miner's Mark, a son of the great race mare Personal Ensign, ranked among the best sophomore males of 1993 with a win in the grade I Jockey Club Gold Cup. A horse who clearly relished the American classic distance of ten furlongs, Miner's Mark retired to Lane's End in 1995 but disappointed as a sire and was moved to Pennsylvania before being pensioned from stud duty in 2004.

* * *

Mr. Prospector's 1991 crop contained only five stakes winners — the smallest number to come from any of his crops since his first — but among them was the first champion he had sired in three years, as well as two highweights. The champion was Coup de Genie, a full sister to Machiavellian who was named French champion juvenile filly on the strength of wins in the Prix de Cabourg (Fr-III), Prix Morny (Fr-I), and Prix de la Salamandre (Fr-I). Like her brother, she went on to be classic-placed at three, running third in the One Thousand Guineas.

Mr. Prospector's best son from the 1991 crop was Distant View (out of Seven Springs, by Irish River), a hard-trying colt who won the 1994 Sussex Stakes (Eng-I) and was given the 128-pound topweight among three-year-old males in the miler category on the International Classifications. Now pensioned, Distant View had a fairly useful stud career at Juddmonte Farms' Kentucky division, his best runners being 2000 English champion three-year-old male Observatory and multiple grade I winner Sightseek. Observatory is now at stud at Banstead Manor Stud in England and as of 2007 has been represented by three crops of racing age. Another Mr. Prospector son of 1991, Desert Symphony (out of Ma Biche, by Key to the Kingdom) was weighted atop older males in Scandinavia in 1996 but as a gelding had no opportunity to earn further honors as a sire.

One other member of the 1991 crop worthy of brief mention is Manshood, a son of Storm Bird's champion daughter Indian Skimmer. Sent to Zimbabwe as a stallion (he is now in South Africa), Manshood sired South

African Horse of the Year Ipi Tombe, whose successes outside South Africa include the 2003 Dubai Duty Free (UAE-I) and the 2003 Locust Grove Handicap (gr. III).

The 1992 crop doubled the production of stakes winners to ten. Its most important member is doubtless Smart Strike, a son of 1984 Canadian champion three-year-old filly Classy 'n Smart and a half brother to 1991 Canadian Horse of the Year Dance Smartly. The colt nearly did not get a chance to show his true ability; unraced at two, he won three of his first four starts at three and was being considered a candidate for the Canadian classics when he took a freakish step and managed to damage the tendons in both hind legs. It took thirteen months for Smart Strike to get back to the races, but the colt rewarded trainer Mark Frostad's patience by winning the 1996 Philip H. Iselin (gr. I) and Salvator Mile (gr. III) handicaps.

Frostad intended to point the colt toward the Breeders' Cup Classic, which was at Woodbine that year. But during a routine workout on September 30, the hard-luck colt fractured a bone in his left foreleg, ending his career with six wins and a second from eight starts. Lane's End won the bidding war for the future stallion, aided by the fact that Smart Strike's breeder and owner, Ernie Samuel of Sam-Son Farm, did not want the colt to leave North America for either Japan or shuttle duty.

While Smart Strike has not gotten the commercial respect accorded to some other sons of Mr. Prospector, he has done very well as a sire. Getting some 9 percent stakes winners from foals, he has sired forty-eight stakes winners as of July 2007, including 2006 and 2007 United Nations Stakes (gr. IT) winner English Channel and Canadian champions Soaring Free, Eye of the Sphynx, Portcullis, and Added Edge. His most recent star is Curlin, winner of the 2007 Preakness Stakes and close runner-up in the Belmont after a troubled third in the Kentucky Derby.

The year 1992 also saw the births of Macoumba (out of Maximova, by Green Dancer), winner of the 1994 Prix Marcel Boussac (Fr-I), and of Miesque's Son, a full brother to Kingmambo. Winner of the 1996 Prix de Ris-Orangis (Fr-III) and runner-up in two group I events, Miesque's Son was not quite so talented as Kingmambo on the racecourse and has not been as consistent a sire either. Nonetheless, he has gotten two good runners in multiple group I winner Whipper, now at stud in Ireland, and 2006 U.S. champion turf male Miesque's Approval, upset winner of the 2006 Breeders' Cup Mile.

Golden Attraction, a member of the 1993 crop, became Mr. Prospector's nineteenth champion or highweight by winning an Eclipse Award as champion juvenile filly in 1995. A daughter of 1990 Kentucky Oaks victress Seaside Attraction (by Seattle Slew), Golden Attraction sealed her title with consecutive wins in the Spinaway Stakes at Saratoga and the Matron and Frizette stakes at Belmont, all grade I events. She did not perform as well at three but did pick up a win in the grade II Turfway Breeders' Cup Stakes before retiring with eight wins and two placings from eleven starts. The best of the other eight stakes winners from the 1993 crop was Sheikh Hamdan bin Rashid al Maktoum's homebred Ta Rib, who won the 1996 Poule d'Essai des Pouliches to become her sire's fifth classic winner.

Pioneering was not among Mr. Prospector's stakes winners from the 1993 crop, winning two of six starts against more modest competition. At stud, however, the half brother to champion sire Storm Cat appears to be on the rise. Standing alongside Storm Cat at Overbrook Farm, Pioneering has so far sired twenty-eight stakes winners from 370 foals of racing age. His best runners include Behaving Badly, winner of the 2006 Santa Monica Handicap (gr. I), and Venezuelan group I winner Canoa. Represented by thirteen stakes winners in 2006, Pioneering finished forty-third on the 2006 North

American general sire list, ahead of more vaunted sons of Mr. Prospector such as Fusaichi Pegasus and Kingmambo.

* * *

Although Mr. Prospector sired six stakes winners from his thirty-seven foals in 1994, his crop's quality didn't match that of previous years. Only Sahm (out of Salsabil, by Sadler's Wells), who won the 1998 Knickerbocker Handicap (gr. IIT), became a graded stakes winner, ending a run of eighteen years during which Mr. Prospector had sired at least one grade/group I winner per crop. The stallion was back on track in 1995, however, getting Chester House and two other graded/group stakes winners among the five stakes winners from that crop. Chester House, whose dam Toussaud was a future Broodmare of the Year, won the 2000 Arlington Million (gr. IT) but died after only three seasons at stud. His best runners so far have been Warning Zone, winner of the 2006 Generous Stakes (gr. IIIT), and Divine Park, winner of the 2007 Withers Stakes (gr. III).

In terms of racing quality, 1996 was arguably Mr. Prospector's worst crop. Only two stakes winners emerged from thirty-three foals, with the better being 1999 San Miguel Stakes (gr. III) winner Cape Canaveral, a full brother to Golden Attraction. Then, in another turnaround, Mr. Prospector got one of the most talented colts of his entire career in the 1997 crop: Fusaichi Pegasus, whose career both tantalized and frustrated racing fans across North America.

Produced from the Danzig mare Angel Fever, a stakes-placed full sister to 1992 Preakness Stakes winner Pine Bluff, the colt was exceptionally handsome from birth, earning the nickname "Superman" from co-breeder Arthur Hancock III. The striking youngster garnered his first headlines by topping the 1998 Keeneland July yearling sale on a bid of $4 million from Japanese entrepreneur Fusao Sekiguchi.

Had Mr. Sekiguchi watched the colt as he was led away to John T. Ward Jr.'s training barn, he might have wondered about the wisdom of his purchase. The colt was quite a handful, repeatedly trying to rear and strike as he was walked over. He might have further questioned himself if he had watched the colt's early training in Florida. Intelligent, self-willed, and physically powerful, Fusaichi Pegasus quickly became bored with the routine of training and decided he would use his size and athleticism to intimidate his riders. It took all the strength and skill of Ward's assistant Blaine Holloway, a husky man who had been a top show-jumping rider in his younger days, to teach the rebellious colt some basic respect for human commands without turning the situation into all-out war.

Once the colt had decided to accept human direction, he was sent on to Neil Drysdale's barn. In his only start at two, he ran second to future grade III winner David Copperfield. At three Fusaichi Pegasus exploded into the Kentucky Derby picture with wins in the San Felipe Stakes at Santa Anita and the Wood Memorial Stakes at Aqueduct, both grade II races. But his unruly behavior re-emerged just before the Wood, when he balked at the starting gate. Further speculation about his ability to handle the barely controlled chaos of a typical Derby ran rampant after he managed to dump his exercise rider in an April 27 workout, just nine days before the big race.

Still, the tremendous burst of acceleration the colt had displayed in winning the Wood was enough to make him the Derby favorite in a year that otherwise lacked a clear standout, as evidenced by the field of nineteen that eventually went to the post. And the colt delivered on his favorite's status. Although Fusaichi Pegasus lathered up while in the paddock, Drysdale's careful schooling held, aided by his keeping the colt in his saddling stall and away from the crowd until the last possible moment. The race itself was deceptively simple. Sent up the inside in a ground-saving ride by Kent

Desormeaux, Fusaichi Pegasus angled out to gain a clear path with about five-sixteenths of a mile to go, took command with an eighth of a mile left, and won by 1 1/2 lengths under a hand ride.

So dominant had Fusaichi Pegasus' victory appeared that he immediately was declared the strongest hope to win the Triple Crown since Affirmed had turned the trick twenty-two years earlier. But two weeks later rainy weather and another horse of Mr. Prospector's blood brought that dream crashing back to earth. Over a drying-out track labeled "good," Fappiano's grandson Red Bullet, who had been a well-beaten second in the Wood Memorial — the first defeat of his career — turned the tables on Fusaichi Pegasus, winning by 3 3/4 lengths. Never seeming truly comfortable on the track, favored Fusaichi Pegasus barely saved second by a head over the late-running Impeachment.

Although originally targeted toward the Belmont Stakes, Fusaichi Pegasus was declared out a week before the race due to a minor foot injury suffered in his stall. He did not reappear until the fall meeting at Belmont, and his fall campaign was both enigmatic and brief. He won the mile Jerome Handicap (gr. II) with apparent ease but never got untracked during the running of the Breeders' Cup Classic, finishing in sixth about eight lengths behind the late-blooming three-year-old Tiznow. Tiznow's victory over European champion Giant's Causeway crushed any chance Fusaichi Pegasus had of claiming an Eclipse Award, and the Mr. Prospector colt retired with a somewhat tarnished reputation to Coolmore's Ashford Stud, which had acquired his breeding rights for a reported $60 million to $70 million.

Thanks to large books and the fact that he has been shuttling to Australia in addition to standing the Northern Hemisphere season, Fusaichi Pegasus has to date been credited with siring 890 foals in his first five crops. To put this into some kind of perspective, that is more foals than Northern Dancer sired during his entire twenty-three-year stud career and equal to the number of foals that Mr. Prospector sired in his first eighteen crops. Whether the results have justified this kind of intensive use is debatable, at least so far as racing results go. Of Fusaichi Pegasus' 676 foals of racing age, twenty-eight have won stakes races through July 2007. Twelve have won graded/group stakes, headed by 2005 Blue Grass Stakes (gr. I) winner Bandini and 2005 Haskell Invitational Handicap (gr. I) winner Roman Ruler; both are now at stud after racing careers marked by talent but marred by physical issues.

* * *

For Mr. Prospector, the Kentucky Derby victory of Fusaichi Pegasus was a posthumous achievement, for the great sire had died on June 1, 1999, at the age of twenty-nine. But the stallion bowed out with a flourish. Less than two months after Fusaichi Pegasus' Derby win, Mr. Prospector's son Scatter the Gold followed in the hoof prints of his dam, Canadian Horse of the Year Dance Smartly, by winning the Queen's Plate. A month later the colt won the second leg of the Canadian Triple Crown, the Prince of Wales Stakes, before bowing to Lodge Hill and Master Stuart in the final leg, the Breeders' Stakes. He did not run again and is now at stud in Japan, but the following year, his full sister Dancethruthedawn won the Woodbine Oaks and the Queen's Plate on her way to honors as Canada's champion three-year-old filly. And in 2003, Aldebaran (out of Chimes of Freedom, by Private Account) was voted U.S. champion sprinter off grade I wins in the San Carlos Handicap, Metropolitan Handicap, and Forego Handicap, and grade II wins in the Churchill Downs, and Tom Fool handicaps, becoming the twenty-second and last of Mr. Prospector's champions or highweights.

Mr. Prospector's stud career closed with his having sired 1,195 foals in twenty-five crops. He retained exceptional libido and fertility right up to the end of his long stud career, covering forty-seven mares in his final season;

thirty-nine of those mares produced live foals the following spring.

On April 24, 2005, a gelding named Subsidy rolled home first in the Owners Association Trophy, a Korean group III race, becoming the last of Mr. Prospector's 181 stakes winners. On December 18 of the same year, Subsidy captured the Grand Prix (Kor I), adding one final embellishment to the legacy of his sire.

Today, Mr. Prospector rests quietly in his grave in the famous Claiborne horse cemetery, where he lies between Nijinsky II and Secretariat. But on racetracks around the world, his blood runs on.

Branches From The Tree: Fappiano

9

By the time of his death, Mr. Prospector had already earned a reputa-tion as a sire of sires second only to Northern Dancer among modern stallions. Among his sons to have done well at stud are Afleet, Carson City, Conquistador Cielo, Fast Gold, Gulch, Kingmambo, Machiavellian, Miswaki, Seeking the Gold, and Woodman, who have all been briefly profiled in con-nection with their racing careers.

Even sons of Mr. Prospector without good race records have compiled some enviable sire records. Hussonet, for instance, was only stakes-placed at two and three despite being a son of 1987 U.S. champion three-year-old filly Sacahuista; yet on export to Chile, he rapidly made a great name for himself and was leading sire from 2000 through 2006 and at press time was leading the 2007 Chilean general sire list. His best-known runners in North America are Wild Spirit, 2003 Chilean Horse of the Year and a three-time graded winner in the United States, and Host, 2003 Chilean champion juvenile male and winner of the 2005 Shadwell Turf Mile Stakes (gr. IT).

One of Mr. Prospector's most successful sire sons, Hussonet has sired 105 stakes winners. His other top runners include Argentine group I winner Husson and the Chilean group I winners Printemps (also a grade II winner in the United States), Penamacor, Desert Fight, National Park, Lhiz, El Cumbres, Mar De Kara, Hush Money, Franbulo, River Café, Marzuk, Mail Coach, Byblos,

Shapira, Personnet, Spontaneous, Trotamondo, and Athenea. Hussonet stood the 2004 and 2005 Northern Hemisphere seasons at Vinery in Kentucky and is now standing at Arrowfield Stud in Australia. His first Australian-bred crop, juveniles of 2006/07, has so far produced 2006 Maribyrnong Stakes (Aus-III) winner Husson Lightning.

In acquiring Hussonet for its roster, Arrowfield may have been remembering the stud career of another Mr. Prospector son with a modest racing record. Straight Strike, out of the Never Bend mare Bend Not, earned only four wins and two minor stakes placings from twenty starts but got some notable runners in New Zealand, among them the 1992 New Zealand Two Thousand Guineas (NZ-I) winner Hulastrike, 1996/97 New Zealand champion juvenile filly Good Faith, 1988 New Zealand One Thousand Guineas (NZ-I) winner Olga's Pal, and group I winners Bawalaksana, Shindig, and Straight Order.

A third stakes-placed Mr. Prospector son to have done well in the Southern Hemisphere is Lode (out of Grand Luxe, by Sir Ivor), who has sired twenty-four group I winners while standing in Argentina Among his best are Argentine champion juveniles Lord Jim and Safari Queen and Argentine classic winners Kesplendida and Kiss Me Sweet. Lode was champion sire in Argentina in 2005 after having ranked among the top ten Argentine sires seven times from 1997 through 2004.

As with most stallions, however, Mr. Prospector's most successful racing sons have generally become his most successful sire sons as well. Three in particular appear to have established distinct branches of the Mr. Prospector male line. They are Fappiano, Forty Niner, and Gone West.

* * *

Ironically, the best stallion Mr. Prospector ever sired was from one of his Florida crops, which by and large were produced from mares with weaker female families than those from his Kentucky crops. Fappiano, however, was an exception to the rule. His dam, Killaloe, was a good allowance-class filly in her own right and a daughter of the great Dr. Fager from the stakes-winning mare Grand Splendor, a half sister to three other stakes winners and the dam of the stakes-winning Tom Rolfe colt Paddock Park. The female line traces back to *Marguerite de Valois, a full sister to *Sir Gallahad III and *Bull Dog. Killaloe lived up to this royal heritage by producing five stakes winners as well as the dam of 2000 Belmont Stakes winner Commendable.

Retired to Tartan Farms in 1982, Fappiano started his career with a flourish, getting Tasso in his first crop. After winning the 1985 Del Mar Futurity (gr. I) and Breeders' Futurity (gr. II), the colt just managed to run down Storm Cat in the Breeders' Cup Juvenile (gr. I), securing both the race and U.S. champion juvenile male honors by a mere nose.

Tasso did not live up to expectations at either three or four and was equally disappointing as a stallion, eventually being exported to Saudi Arabia. But another member of Fappiano's first crop more than made up for Tasso's shortcomings as a sire. Roy, whose best effort on the racetrack was a second in the 1985 Sanford Stakes (gr. II), quickly made a name for himself after export to Chile in 1988, getting four group I winners in his first crop including champion juvenile colt Campo Marzio and champion juvenile filly Porta Pia. He continued to excel in Chile, becoming a champion sire there, and was purchased in late 1995 by a group headed by John Phillips of Darby Dan Farm.

Roy was never as successful in Kentucky as he had been in South America, his North American-bred stakes winners being headed by 2003 Desert Stormer Handicap (gr. III) Madame Pietra. He shuttled to Brazil in 1996 and to Argentina in 1997–1999, however, and his South American-bred runners continued to promote him at the same high level he had enjoyed as a stallion in Chile. This success resulted in the stallion's permanent return to South America following the 2000 Northern Hemisphere breeding season.

Roy was credited with siring his one hundredth stakes winner on May 8, 2004, when his Argentine-bred son Candidato Roy won the Bloodstock South African Nursery (SAf-I). Although Roy died of a respiratory ailment on January 7, 2005, his legacy continues to grow. To date, he has been credited with siring at least 123 stakes winners and fifteen champions headed by 2002/03 Argentine Horse of the Year Freddy (Arg). Nine times champion sire in Chile (1991–1999) and champion sire in Argentina in 2002, Roy led the 2007 Argentine general sire list as of July 2007.

Fappiano's first crop also contained the graded stakes winners Funistrada, Mustin Lake, and With a Twist, and his second crop was headed by Cryptoclearance, whose twelve victories from forty-four starts included grade I wins in the 1987 Florida Derby and Pegasus Handicap and the 1989 Donn and Widener handicaps. A useful sire, Cryptoclearance has so far been credited with forty-one stakes winners headed by 1999 U.S. champion older male Victory Gallop and 2002 Breeders' Cup Classic winner Volponi. Victory Gallop, in turn, has become a useful breed-to-race sire and has sired eighteen stakes winners so far, headed by 2004 Stonerside Beaumont Stakes (gr. II) winner Victory U. S. A and 2007 Keio Hai Spring Cup (Jpn-II) winner Eishin Dover.

Tappiano was another standout from Fappiano's second crop. One of the leading juvenile fillies of 1986, she won the Spinaway (gr. I) and Matron (gr. I) stakes before losing the Breeders' Cup Juvenile Fillies to Brave Raj, deciding the juvenile filly championship in the latter's favor. Tappiano added a victory in the Demoiselle Stakes (gr. I) to close out her juvenile season and won eleven more stakes before ending her career as a five-year-old with seventeen wins from thirty-four starts for earnings of $1,305,522.

Fappiano's 1985 crop contained another grade I victor in Aptostar, winner of the 1988 Acorn Stakes, but his next important son did not emerge until 1986, when Quiet American first saw the light of day. A good-sized, masculine bay who many observers feel resembles both his own sire and his broodmare sire Dr. Fager (who, of course, is also the broodmare sire of Fappiano), Quiet American won the 1990 NYRA Mile Handicap (gr. I) and placed in two other grade I races.

Quiet American started his stud career in handsome style by getting 1997 U.S. champion older female Hidden Lake and 1995 Hollywood Starlet Stakes (gr. I) heroine Cara Rafaela in his first crop. Cara Rafaela has since gone on to further honors as the dam of Bernardini, champion three-year-old colt and winner of the 2006 Preakness Stakes (gr. I), Travers Stakes (gr. I), and Jockey Club Gold Cup (gr. I). Although Bernardini is Cara Rafaela's only stakes winner to date, he was enough for her to be voted U.S. Broodmare of the Year honors for 2006.

Since then, Quiet American has had a somewhat uneven stud career but has overall done fairly well, getting forty-four stakes winners from 645 foals of racing age as of July 2007. He became the second of Fappiano's sons (following Unbridled, about whom more will be said later) to sire the winner of an American Triple Crown race when his son Real Quiet won the 1998 Kentucky Derby and Preakness before being run down by Victory Gallop in the Belmont. (As already mentioned, Victory Gallop is by Cryptoclearance, so his nose victory made it a Triple Crown sweep for sire sons of Fappiano.)

A narrowly built colt who gained the nickname "The Fish" from trainer Bob Baffert, Real Quiet was retired after his four-year-old season and entered stud at Vinery in Kentucky but was viewed with some suspicion by breeders despite his having been a grade I winner every year he raced. He had suffered from frequent physical problems during his career; further, it was common knowledge that he had undergone surgery to correct crooked forelegs as a foal. As a result, he did not get the quality of mares one might normally expect for a well-bred horse with five grade I wins under his belt — two of them in classics

— and was moved to Pennsylvania in 2006. Perhaps the move from Kentucky was a catalyst, for the stallion was represented by eight stakes winners in 2006, headed by Coaching Club American Oaks (gr. I) winner Wonder Lady Anne L and Humana Distaff Handicap (gr. I) winner Pussycat Doll. Overall, Real Quiet has sired thirteen stakes winners from 433 foals of racing age.

Quiet American has been considered a somewhat better sire of fillies than colts, and this appears to be reflected in his rising status as a broodmare sire. In addition to the already-mentioned Bernardini, Quiet American is the broodmare sire of 2005 U.S. Horse of the Year Saint Liam, 2005 Gran Premio del Jockey Club (Ity-I) winner Cherry Mix, and 2002 Futurity Stakes (gr. I) winner Whywhywhy. As of this writing, Quiet American's daughters have produced 25 stakes winners from 387 foals of racing age; ninth among American broodmare sires in 2005, Quiet American finished fifteenth on the 2006 list.

Some Romance was another standout of Fappiano's 1986 crop. One of five stakes winners produced from the excellent broodmare Zippy Do, Some Romance won the 1988 Frizette Stakes (gr. I) and Matron Stakes (gr. I) to rank among the year's leading juvenile fillies. She added the grade III Post-Deb Stakes to her trophy case and placed in four grade I events as a sophomore, but she has been a rather disappointing broodmare with the minor stakes winner Polish Love (by Danzig) as her only black-type runner.

The 1987 foal crop was the next to last that Fappiano sired in Florida before moving to Lane's End in Kentucky (the last crop, conceived in 1987, was born after the stallion's transfer in June 1987), and it was the best of his entire career. No less than four grade I winners emerged from this crop, including two champions.

Perhaps a third champion might have come from this crop if not for ill fate. Grand Canyon, an $825,000 purchase at the 1988 Keeneland July yearling sale, won the 1989 Norfolk Stakes (gr. I) at Santa Anita, ran second in the Breeders'

Cup Juvenile, then ran a dazzling mile in 1:33 flat to win the Hollywood Futurity (gr. I). But the brilliant colt contracted laminitis the following spring and all efforts to save his life proved futile.

Defensive Play was a runner of a different sort from Grand Canyon. A later-maturing colt who proved capable on both turf and dirt, he took his biggest victories in the 1990 Man o' War Stakes (gr. IT) and the 1991 Charles H. Strub Stakes (gr. I). He did not meet with great success when tried at stud in Kentucky, however, and is now a regional sire in Washington.

Rubiano, a striking gray horse who had bleached to nearly white by the time he really hit his stride, won the 1991 NYRA Mile Handicap (gr. I) at four but was better at five in 1992, when he earned honors as U.S. champion sprinter. His come-from-behind style was not really suited to the six furlongs of the Breeders' Cup Sprint, in which he ran third, but he earned his title based on wins in five graded races including the Carter Handicap (gr. I) and Vosburgh Stakes (gr. I), both over seven furlongs.

Although he was from the immediate family of the excellent sire Relaunch, Rubiano did not quite live up to expectations as a stallion. Nonetheless, he had a useful career before dying from laminitis in 2002. He sired thirty-one stakes winners, the best of whom were the Argentine group I winner Impression and Burning Roma, winner of the 2000 Futurity Stakes (gr. I). A stakes winner every year he raced and a graded stakes winner on both dirt and turf, Burning Roma is now at stud at Hidden Point Farm in Florida and will be represented by his first crop to race in 2008. Another good son of Rubiano, multiple grade II-winning sprinter, Too Much Bling, entered stud in 2007 at Sequel Stallions in Florida.

* * *

By far the most important member of Fappiano's 1987 crop, however, was a massive, good-natured bay with knock knees and toed-out forefeet. This was Unbridled, who sold to Frances A. Genter for $70,000 as a weanling out of the Tartan Farms dispersal. Three years later the colt repaid Mrs. Genter gener-ously by powering to victories in the Florida Derby (gr. I), Kentucky Derby, and Breeders' Cup Classic before earning honors as U.S. champion three-year-old male.

Unbridled was never an entirely sound horse as a four-year-old. The mas-sive build inherited from his broodmare sire, *Le Fabuleux, began to take its toll on his ill-constructed forelegs. Nonetheless, the big colt (he officially measured 16.3 hands) showed enough speed to run down champion sprinter Housebuster in the seven-furlong Deputy Minister Handicap and was a respectable third in that year's Breeders' Cup Classic. He retired to stud having won eight of twenty-four starts for earnings of $4,489,475.

Unbridled came from a female line that held some promise of stallion prowess; his dam, Gana Facil, was a half sister to the useful sprint sire Pentelicus (by Fappiano), while his third dam, Magic, was a half sister by Buckpasser to the great Dr. Fager. Standing at Gainesway Farm through the 1996 breeding season and then at Claiborne Farm, Unbridled became the most important of Fappiano's sons at stud before his untimely death from complications of colic at age fourteen. Although not the most consistent of stallions — he got forty-eight stakes winners from 582 foals and often threw progeny troubled by soundness problems — his best were very good indeed.

Unbridled's first crop, foals of 1993, set the stage for the future with three stakes winners — two of which were grade I winners — from thirty-six named foals. Grindstone, who nipped Cavonnier on the line to take the 1996 Kentucky Derby, made Unbridled only the fourth Kentucky Derby winner to sire a similar winner in his first crop, following in the hoofprints of Gallant Fox (Omaha), Pensive (Ponder), and Ponder (Needles). But six days after the Kentucky Derby, Grindstone came up with a knee injury and was retired to Overbrook Farm near Lexington, Kentucky. A smaller, neater type than many of his sire's progeny,

Grindstone has so far sired thirteen stakes winners from 389 foals of racing age including 2004 Belmont and Travers (gr. I) stakes winner Birdstone, now at stud at Gainesway Farm in Kentucky.

Unbridled's Song, the other top colt from Unbridled's 1993 crop, stands in marked contrast to Grindstone in physique. A tall, long-striding, elegant gray who officially stands 17 hands, Unbridled's Song rocketed to early favoritism for the 1996 Kentucky Derby with a game win over Hennessy in the Breeders' Cup Juvenile (gr. I). The big colt's three-year-old campaign was enigmatic, however, and was probably compromised by a push to make the Kentucky Derby despite foot problems. Made the Derby favorite off wins in the Florida Derby (gr. I) and Wood Memorial (gr. II), Unbridled's Song never appeared entirely comfortable while racing in egg-bar shoes (a type of bar shoe in which the shoe forms a complete oval) in the Derby itself and flattened out to finish fifth after taking a brief lead. The colt never seemed to recover his best form following the Derby and was retired as a four-year old, having won five of his twelve starts.

As a stallion, Unbridled's Song has been one of the most popular commercial sires of the early twenty-first century, with seventeen of his yearlings selling for seven figures in his first seven crops. To date, he has sired fifty-two stakes winners from 846 foals of racing age including eight grade I winners. His best daughters so far have been 2001 Breeders' Cup Distaff winner Unbridled Elaine and multiple grade I winner Splendid Blended, while his best sons have been 2002 Wood Memorial Stakes (gr. I) winner Buddha, 2007 Suburban Handicap (gr. I) winner Political Force, and 2001 Fountain of Youth Stakes (gr. I) winner Songandaprayer. The last-named horse has sired six stakes winners — four of them graded — from his first two crops of racing age.

Four stakes winners came out of Unbridled's second crop of forty-three named foals, but his next outstanding runners were both fillies from the 1995 crop: Banshee Breeze, the 1998 U.S. champion three-year-old filly and five-time grade I winner, and Manistique, who had trouble carrying her best form outside California but in that state won the Vanity Handicap (gr. I) and Santa Margarita Invitational Handicap (gr. I) at four and the Santa Maria Handicap (gr. I) in her only start at five. Unfortunately, Banshee Breeze died in 2001 of complications from the Caesarian delivery of her first foal, a colt by Storm Cat, and the colt also did not survive. As for Manistique, she has yet to produce a winner.

Unbridled waited until 1997 to come up with more grade I winners but once again struck gold with a champion. This was Anees, whose lone stakes victory in the Breeders' Cup Juvenile was enough to give him the championship in a year in which no single two-year-old colt managed to put together a consistent record at the top of the class. Anees struggled with physical issues early in his three-year-old season and ended his career with two wins from seven starts after wrenching an ankle during the running of the Kentucky Derby. He was no luckier at stud and had to be humanely destroyed in the spring of 2003 after breaking his left front leg in a paddock accident. His best runner was Coin Silver, winner of the 2005 Lexington Stakes (gr. II).

Unbridled's other grade I winners from the 1997 crop were the gelding Unshaded, winner of the 2000 Travers Stakes (gr. I), and Red Bullet, winner of the Preakness (gr. I). After having won four of his first five starts through the Preakness — his only loss was his second to Fusaichi Pegasus in the Wood Memorial (gr. II) — Red Bullet suffered a series of misfortunes and eventually ended his career as a five-year-old having won six of fourteen starts. He is now at stud at Adena Springs South in Florida and had his first stakes winner on October 20, 2006, when his son Power of Freedom captured the six-furlong Comet Stakes at the Meadowlands.

Broken Vow, another member of the 1997 crop, did not quite measure up to grade I standards on the racetrack but was not far below that level, winning the Philip H. Iselin Handicap (gr. II) and placing in the Gulfstream Park

Handicap (gr. I) in 2001. Retired to stud in 2002, he has so far sired eleven stakes winners, headed by 2007 Acorn Stakes (gr. I) winner Cotton Blossom and 2005 Futurity (gr. II) and Kentucky Jockey Club Stakes (gr. II) winner Private Vow.

Unbridled finally broke the pattern of getting grade I winners only in odd-numbered years by siring Exogenous from his 1998 crop. Winner of the 2001 Gazelle Handicap (gr. I) and Beldame Stakes (gr. I), Exogenous was thought to have a chance of contending for three-year-old filly honors in the Breeders' Cup Distaff but flipped over backward on the way from the paddock to the track and struck her head hard on the pavement. Although she survived the initial injury, brain swelling and spinal trauma forced her humane destruction a few days later.

Less accomplished on the racetrack but more fortunate in other regards is Saarland, a beautifully bred son of multiple grade I winner Versailles Treaty (by Danzig) from Unbridled's 1999 crop. Winner of the Remsen Stakes (gr. II) at two, Saarland turned in the best performance of his career at age four, when he ran eventual champion sprinter Aldebaran to a neck in the 2003 Metropolitan Handicap (gr. I). Saarland was extremely well received by breeders during his first stud season in 2005 at Darby Dan Farm, serving a good-quality book of 120 mares, and as of this writing is considered to be one of the stronger prospects to make a good sire among Unbridled's younger sons.

The year 2000 saw the birth of one of Unbridled's most talented — and controversial — sons. This was Empire Maker, a Juddmonte Farms homebred out of the grade I winner and great producer Toussaud. Impressive wins in the 2003 Florida Derby (gr. I) and Wood Memorial (gr. I) sent him to Churchill Downs as the Kentucky Derby favorite, but a bruised foot suffered during Derby Week cost him a couple of days' training time and may possibly have been the difference in the colt's effort. Never showing the same ease or authority as he had in his earlier races, Empire Maker was well beaten by Funny Cide, whom he had defeated with apparent ease in the Wood, and barely saved the place from his stablemate, Peace Rules.

Following the Derby, trainer Bobby Frankel blamed the foot problem for the colt's defeat and elected to skip the Preakness with him, reserving the colt for the Belmont. In the meantime, Funny Cide scored by nearly ten lengths in the Preakness, immediately becoming a hot favorite to win the Triple Crown. It was now Empire Maker's turn to play spoiler, and spoil the party he did, winning the Belmont Stakes (gr. I) by three-quarters of a length over Ten Most Wanted with Funny Cide another five lengths back in third.

The win immediately raised a firestorm of fans screaming that it was unfair for a horse that had competed in both the previous Triple Crown events to have his chances for completing the sweep spoiled by a horse that had sat out a race, but cooler heads pointed out that every previous Triple Crown winner had faced the challenge of fresh horses and won anyway. In the meantime, Frankel went on with his colt, whose next major target was to be the Travers Stakes.

Empire Maker, however, had other ideas. He had always been a colt whose mental maturity was suspect, and in the Jim Dandy Stakes (gr. II), a lackadaisical attitude until the final hundred yards may well have cost him the race. When he finally decided to get running, he had left himself with too much to do and failed by a neck to make up two lengths on Strong Hope. Then the colt came up with a cough, forcing Frankel to declare him out of the Travers just a few days before the race.

Frankel next decided to point Empire Maker to the Jockey Club Gold Cup (gr. I) as a prep for the Breeders' Cup Classic, but the colt came up with another foot bruise a few days before the race and was declared out. A short time later he was officially retired to Juddmonte, ending a career that had teased at least as much as it had delivered. At year's end he lost another race by a narrow margin as Funny Cide — whom he had beaten in two of their three meetings — rode the strength of his two classic wins to a title as U.S. champion three-year-old male.

While Funny Cide, a gelding, is beginning a new career as a stable pony after being retired from racing in July 2007, Empire Maker served a stellar book of 111 mares in 2004, his first season at stud. His first few crops have been well received in the sale ring, averaging $294,629 for weanlings and $371,273 for yearlings (including a $1.6 million colt at the 2006 Fasig-Tipton Saratoga sale). But the real question is how the Empire Makers will do at the racetrack, a question that got its first hint of an answer on June 18, 2007, when Miss Red Delicious powered to a 13-1/2 length win over 5-1/2 furlongs at Colonial Downs to become her sire's first winner.

The 2003 U.S. champion two-year-old filly Halfbridled, 2004 Queen's Plate winner Niigon, and 2005 Pimlico Special (gr. I) winner Eddington were the stars of Unbridled's 2001 crop, which featured six stakes winners among its 103 foals. So good did Halfbridled look in winning the 2003 Breeders' Cup Juvenile Fillies (gr. I) that many speculated she would take on the colts in the Kentucky Derby, but the filly instead had trouble finding her best form at three and suffered repeated episodes of tying up, one of which kept her out of the Kentucky Oaks (gr. I). A stress fracture suffered in May 2004 kept her away from the races for months, and a similar injury found in November of the same year led her connections to make the decision to retire her. As for Eddington, he entered stud at Claiborne Farm in 2006 and served 121 mares; Niigon was slated to enter stud in Ontario in 2007.

In his 2002 crop, Unbridled sired his final grade I winner and champion in Smuggler, a daughter of 1995 U.S. champion older female Inside Information. Smuggler was crowned champion three-year-old filly in 2005 after winning the Mother Goose Stakes (gr. I) and Coaching Club American Oaks (gr. I) and running second in the Acorn Stakes (gr. I). Unbridled's last son of note was Harlington, a son of 1995 U.S. champion three-year-old filly Serena's Song, who won the 2006 Gulfstream Park Handicap (gr. II).

* * *

Despite the assumption that the move from Kentucky would give him access to better mares, Fappiano never again reached the heights that he had scaled with the 1987 crop and, in fact, was to sire only three more grade/group I winners during the remainder of his career. The first, Cahill Road, was a 1988 full brother to Unbridled. Even taller and more massive than his brother, Cahill Road won the 1991 Wood Memorial Invitational Stakes (gr. I) impressively but bowed a tendon during the running, forcing his retirement. He has had a modest stud career and is currently in Washington. The second, Faaz, became a group I winner in Peru as a four-year-old in 1993 and is now at stud in Chile, while the third, the 1992 Ballerina Stakes (gr. I) winner Serape, is the dam of multiple grade III winner Batique.

In a sad loss for the U.S. breeding industry, Fappiano fractured a hind leg in a stall accident sometime during the night of June 16, 1990 (he was found with the fracture at 3:00 a.m. on June 17), and had to be euthanized on September 3, 1990, due to complications from the injury. His stud career ended with his having sired forty-eight stakes winners from 420 foals, but not before he had founded what to date has been the most classics-oriented branch of the Mr. Prospector line.

Louis Wolfson, *above left*, owner of Raise a Native, chats with Leslie Combs II, breeder of Raise a Native's most important son, Mr. Prospector. Peter Brant, *left center*, and Seth Hancock, *right center*, were responsible for moving Mr. Prospector to Claiborne Farm in Kentucky. Trainer

Jimmy Croll, *below left*, and owner A.I. "Butch" Savin, *right*, with jockey Walter Blum.

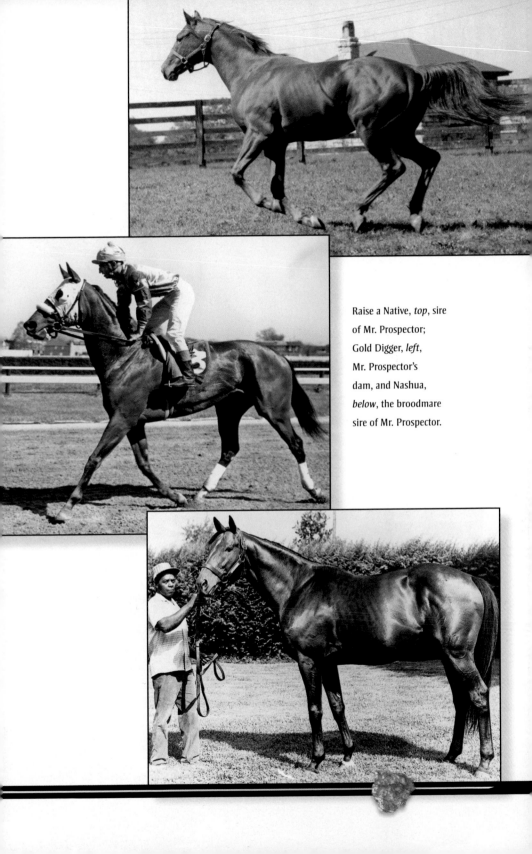

Raise a Native, *top*, sire of Mr. Prospector; Gold Digger, *left*, Mr. Prospector's dam, and Nashua, *below*, the broodmare sire of Mr. Prospector.

Mr. Prospector, *opposite*, as the Keeneland July yearling sale topper in 1971 with Savin, *inset right*, and Croll looking on.

Trainer Jimmy Croll, *top right*, holds his two prime contenders for the 1973 Kentucky Derby: Mr. Prospector, *left*, and Royal and Regal. Mr. Prospector, *right*, capturing the Whirlaway Handicap for his first stakes win. He later added the Gravesend Handicap, *below*, to his resumé.

Mr. Prospector enjoying the sunshine in his paddock at Claiborne Farm in Kentucky.

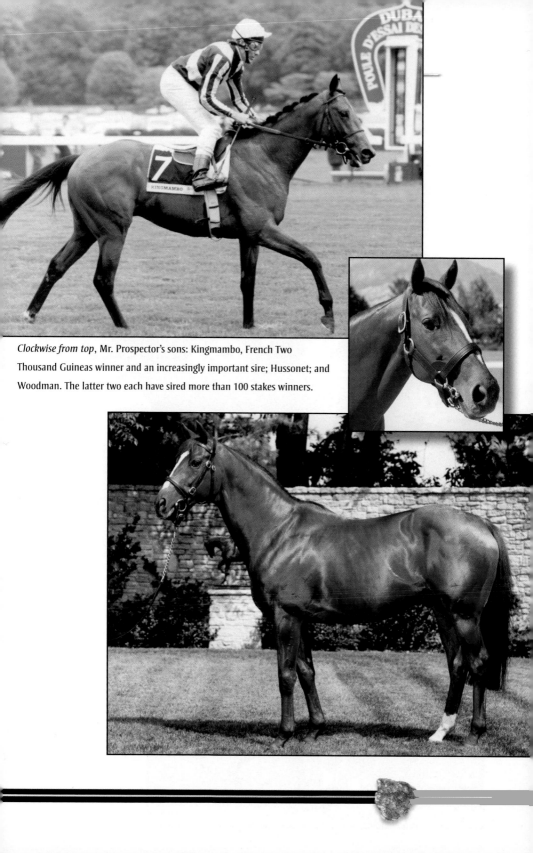

Clockwise from top, Mr. Prospector's sons: Kingmambo, French Two Thousand Guineas winner and an increasingly important sire; Hussonet; and Woodman. The latter two each have sired more than 100 stakes winners.

Mr. Prospector sired a
winner of all three American
classics: Conquistador Cielo,
top, won the 1982 Belmont;
Tank's Prospect, *center*, *outside*, the 1985 Preakness, and
Fusaichi Pegasus, *left*, won
the 2000 Kentucky Derby.

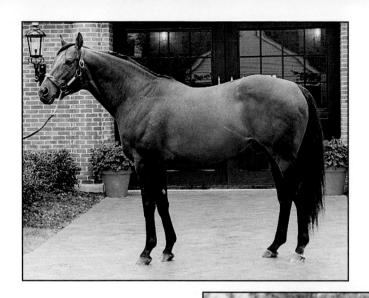

An important branch of the
Mr. Prospector family tree,
Fappiano, *top*, sired such
important stallions
as Quiet American, *right*,
and Unbridled, *below*,
among others.

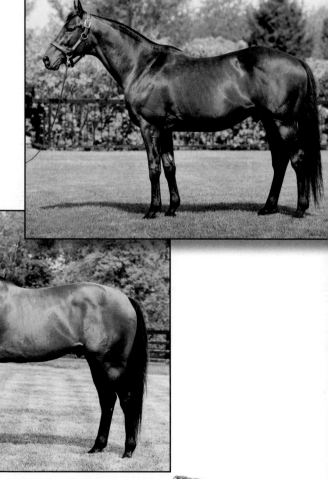

Mr. Prospector's son Forty Niner, rail, eked out a narrow victory over another son of Mr. Prospector, Seeking the Gold, in the 1988 Travers Stakes.

Forty Niner and Seeking the Gold would go on to become important sires, with Forty Niner, *top right*, siring leading stallion Distorted Humor, *above*, and Seeking the Gold, *right*, siring the ill-fated Dubai Millennium, *below*.

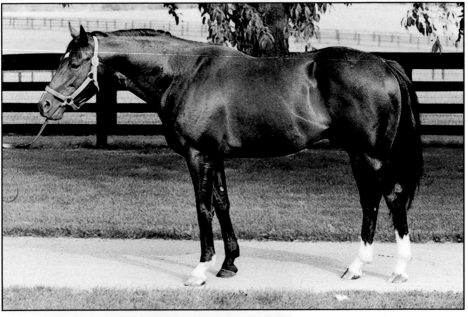

Another important branch of the Mr. Prospector sire line is Gone West, *center*, who has sired two important sons in Mr. Greeley, *top*, and Elusive Quality, *left*.

The 2007 classics were dominated by descendants of Mr. Prospector, whose son Machiavellian, *above*, is the grandsire of Kentucky Derby winner Street Sense, *inset*, while Mr. Prospector's son Smart Strike, *below*, sired Preakness winner Curlin, *bottom inset*, who nosed out Street Sense at the wire.

Mr. Prospector also had his success with his daughters. Ravinella, *above*, was a champion in France, and Queena, *below*, was named champion older mare in the United States.

Golden Attraction, *above*, was named champion two-year-old filly in 1995, and such mares as Prospector's Delite, *below*, have helped Mr. Prospector be leading broodmare sire ten times.

Mr. Prospector at age 28 at Claiborne Farm

Branches From The Tree:
Forty Niner And Gone West

———————————◆———————————

10

Forty Niner retired to Claiborne with high expectations. One of the best racing sons of Mr. Prospector, he met all the criteria that Bull Hancock had established for a good stallion prospect: He had been a top two-year-old, had proved able to stay the American classic distance of ten furlongs, had shown tactical speed, had good conformation with a masculine appearance, had retired sound, and descended from a good female family.

The one question was the ability of Forty Niner's family to produce a top sire. Although he belonged to the same family as Rhodes Scholar, Knightly Manner, and Dignitas, that of Book Law, none had proven more than moderately useful as stallions; Swale, of course, had died before he could go to stud.

In hindsight Forty Niner actually got off to a very good start at stud, getting 129 winners, twenty-seven of them stakes winners, from the 192 foals of his first four crops. But he did not get the precocity that many people hoped for, nor did he at first appear to be getting major stakes horses. By mid-1995, with his fourth crop just getting into its juvenile season, the stallion had been credited with only thirteen individual stakes winners — six of them in graded races — and had not sired a top colt, his best runners to that time being the 1994 Apple Blossom Handicap (gr. I) winner Nine Keys and multiple grade II winner Twining. So when a $10 million offer for the horse came in from Japan, Claiborne was willing to sell. Forty Niner left for his new home at Shizunai Stud after the end of the 1995 breeding season.

With hindsight, Forty Niner's sale was a great loss to North American breeders. The seven crops he sired while at Claiborne eventually yielded forty-two stakes winners from 347 foals. And, as luck would have it, things started happening for Forty Niner almost as soon as he got on the airplane. In 1996 Editor's Note won the Belmont Stakes and the Super Derby (gr. I) to become his sire's first male grade I winner. In the same year, Gold Fever won the NYRA Mile (gr. I) and Roar won the Jim Beam Stakes (gr. II), while the highly regarded Ide won the Southwest (gr. III) and Rebel (gr. III) stakes before having to bow off the Triple Crown trail with an injury.

Banker's Gold and Distorted Humor did their part in 1997 and 1998, each becoming multiple grade II winners while the talented but temperamental Coronado's Quest, a multiple graded stakes winner as a juvenile, won the 1998 Haskell Invitational Handicap (gr. I) and Travers Stakes (gr. I) and three other graded events. The following year Ecton Park won the Super Derby and Marley Vale won the Test Stakes (gr. I), providing two grade I winners from Forty Niner's last Kentucky-sired crop.

None of Forty Niner's grade I-winning sons have lived up to expectations as sires so far though Gold Fever is the sire of four-time Canadian champion A Bit O'Gold (a gelding) and the multiple grade II-winning filly Gold Mover. Coronado's Quest also got one first-rate runner in two-time grade I winner Society Selection before being sent to Japan in 2004 (he died there of a heart attack on March 8, 2006). Lesser sons, however, have made a huge impact, particularly in South America. Among them is Apprentice, a stakes-placed member of Forty Niner's first crop. Standing at Haras Gina-Santa Rosa in Peru, he is the sire of national champions Lady Apprentice, Azucar, Colorina, Sumud, and Madrileno. He led the Peruvian general sire list in 2003.

Luhuk, a group III-placed stakes winner in England, also traveled south of the equator, in his case to Haras La Quebrada in Argentina. His first crop was headed by Guernika, winner of the Polla de Potrancas (Argentine One Thousand Guineas, Arg-I). That attracted the attention of Kentucky horsemen, and Luhuk stood the 2000 through 2005 Northern Hemisphere seasons at Gainesway near Lexington, shuttling to Argentina from 2002 through 2004 before returning to Haras La Quebrada permanently following the 2005 Northern Hemisphere breeding season.

Guernika went on to win the 2001 Gran Premio Estrellas Distaff (Arg-I) and Gran Premio Palermo (Arg-I), earning honors as Argentine champion older female. While Luhuk never became a significant stallion in North America, he continues to enjoy success in Argentina, where he has sired at least twenty-five stakes winners. His one great success in North America has been with his Argentine-bred son Avanzado, who won the 2003 Ancient Title Breeders' Cup Handicap (gr. I) and is now standing at Harris Farms in California. His oldest foals are two-year-olds of 2007.

Rich Man's Gold is another Forty Niner son to do well in South America. Second in the 1995 Rebel Stakes (gr. III) as a three-year-old, he was sent to Chile, where he stood for three years. The stallion was moved to South Africa in 2001 and died there of a heart attack in 2005, but the foals he left behind made him the leading freshman sire in Chile in 1999. The best of them was Lido Palace (Chi), who earned a juvenile championship with his win in the Tanteo de Potrillos (Chi-I). The following year Lido Palace swept the Chilean Triple Crown and was named his country's champion three-year-old and Horse of the Year. Lido Palace also became a multiple grade I winner in the United States at four and five and is now at stud at Lambholm South in Florida. His first foals are juveniles of 2007.

Overall, Rich Man's Gold is known to have sired at least eleven stakes winners in Chile, including Chilean champion three-year-old filly and Horse of the Year Isola Piu Bella, also a two-time grade III winner in North America, and St. Jacques, a Chilean champion as an older horse. Rich Man's Gold's first South African-sired crop came to the races as juveniles of the 2004/05 Southern Hemisphere season.

Jules, from Forty Niner's 1994 crop and winner of the 1996 Nashua Stakes (gr. III), was not a long-lived horse, dying of colic and laminitis in 2003 after having stood in Florida and Brazil. In the latter country he has sired 2003/04 champion miler and three-year-old colt New Famous and the group I winners Must Be Flying, Notificado, Novellista, and Quick Road. In the United States his best-known runner is multiple grade I winner Peace Rules, who entered stud in 2005 at Vinery South in Florida and was bred to 170 mares. A well-balanced, wiry, smallish horse who won fans with the gritty competitiveness that has characterized the best of the Forty Niner tribe, Peace Rules will have his first crop come to the races in 2008.

The best of all of Forty Niner's South American-based sons, however, is indisputably Roar, who beat out nine-time Argentine leading sire Southern Halo to reach the top of the Argentine general sire list in 2004. In doing so, Roar was represented by an incredible twelve group winners of 2004 including four Argentine champions: champion two-year-old filly Forty Greeta, champion two-year-old male Forty Mirage, champion three-year-old filly Forty Marchanta, and champion miler and older male Forty Fabuloso.

Unfortunately for South American breeders, Roar stopped shuttling to Argentina after moving from Lane's End (where he had entered stud in 1997) to Rancho San Miguel, California, for the 2003 Northern Hemisphere breeding season. In North America his best runner has been Roar Emotion, winner of the 2002 Demoiselle Stakes (gr. II) and the 2003 Black-Eyed Susan Stakes (gr. II). Roar is still in service, but fertility issues have led Rancho San Miguel to limit his book; he covered only twenty-five mares in 2006.

All told, Roar has so far been credited with forty-two stakes winners, including seven champions, from the 588 foals of his first eight crops of racing age. In addition to the champions already mentioned, Roar is the sire of 2002/03 Argentine champion two-year-old male and Horse of the Year Little Jim, 2002/03 Argentine champion sprinter Forty Doriana, and three-time Panamanian champion filly Roar Silver.

* * *

In North America, End Sweep gave the first hint that Forty Niner might prove an important sire of sires. Although he was produced from the 1982 Alabama Stakes (gr. I) winner Broom Dance and could reasonably have been expected to stay ten furlongs on pedigree, End Sweep was a confirmed sprinter who scored his biggest win in the 1994 Jersey Shore Budweiser Breeders' Cup Stakes (gr. III) over seven furlongs.

Retired to stud at Mockingbird Farm in Florida, End Sweep created a sensation with his first crop by getting thirty-four individual juvenile winners, a record for a Northern Hemisphere freshman sire. The leader of the 1998 U.S. freshman sire list and the leading American second-crop sire of 1999, End Sweep was sold privately to Arrowfield Stud during the dispersal of Mockingbird's breeding stock and stood the 2000 and 2001 Southern Hemisphere seasons in Australia. Tragically, the stallion fractured his withers while standing the 2002 Northern Hemisphere season at Shadai Stallion Station in Japan and, after failing to respond to treatment, was euthanized on July 12, 2002.

Unlike many other first-crop sire sensations, End Sweep proved a good sire overall, siring the North American grade I winners Trippi, Nany's Sweep, Swept Overboard, and Dark Ending. His New Zealand-bred daughter Clean

Sweep won the 2004 New Zealand Two Thousand Guineas (NZ-I) while his Japanese-bred daughter Sweep Tosho was crowned Japanese champion older female in 2005. Another Japanese-bred daughter, Rhein Kraft, won the 2005 Oka Sho (Japanese One Thousand Guineas, Jpn-I) while his Japanese-bred son Admire Moon proved an international success with victories in the 2007 Dubai Duty Free (UAE-I) and the Takarazuka Kinen (Jpn-I).

End Sweep is represented at stud in the United States by Trippi, who stands at Ocala Stud in Florida and who ranked among the leading second-crop sires in the United States in 2006. As of July 2007, Trippi has seven stakes winners to his credit, headed by 2007 Winning Colors Stakes (gr. III) winner Miss Macy Sue.

But it is Distorted Humor who appears to be the best hope of maintaining Forty Niner's sire line in North America. While it would not be fair to call him a mediocre racehorse as a few have done — he was, after all, a multiple grade II winner — he entered stud overshadowed by such luminaries as 1998 Breeders' Cup Classic winner Awesome Again, 1997 Belmont Stakes winner Touch Gold, 1997 Champagne Stakes (gr. I) winner Grand Slam, and the very fast 1997 King's Bishop Stakes (gr. II) winner Tale of the Cat. If a son of Forty Niner was to make a mark among those stallions standing their first season in 1999, most observers thought it would be Coronado's Quest, not Distorted Humor.

Seven years have told a different tale. Distorted Humor led the 2002 U.S. freshman sire list with four individual stakes winners headed by Spinaway Stakes (gr. I) winner Awesome Humor. Since then, he has gone from strength to strength. In 2003 Funny Cide kept his sire's name in the spotlight by winning the Kentucky Derby and Preakness and narrowly beating out Belmont Stakes winner Empire Maker for the title of U.S. champion three-year-old male. Go Rockin' Robin emerged as another first-crop stakes winner for Distorted Humor, winning the Peter Pan Stakes (gr. II), and Rinky Dink served notice that Distorted Humor could also get good horses in Australia (where he shuttled in 1999 and 2000) by winning the Schweppes Oaks (Aus-I). Finally, Don Dandy became the second champion from Distorted Humor's 2000 crop by earning champion older male honors in Puerto Rico.

Three more grade or group I winners came out of Distorted Humor's second crop. In the United States, Commentator, a very fast but not overly sound gelding, defeated eventual Horse of the Year Saint Liam in the 2005 Whitney Handicap (gr. I), while Fourty Niners Son won the 2005 Clement L. Hirsch Memorial Turf Championship Stakes (gr. IT). Australian-bred Joker Mine won the 2007 Perak Derby, a Malaysian group I race, and the 2001 crop also included Hong Kong group II winner Distorted Halo and multiple Australasian group winner Tirade.

The next star for Distorted Humor was Flower Alley, who developed into one of the better three-year-olds of 2005 with a win in the Travers Stakes (gr. I) and a runner-up finish behind Saint Liam in the 2005 Breeders' Cup Classic. Winner of the 2006 Salvator Mile Stakes (gr. III), Flower Alley stood his first stud season in 2007 at Three Chimneys Farm in Kentucky.

The six stakes winners that have emerged from Distorted Humor's 2003 crop include 2007 Humana Distaff Stakes (gr. I) winner Hystericalady and 2006 Swale Stakes (gr. II) winner Sharp Humor, now at stud at WinStar Farm. The stallion's 2004 crop is the first sired on the better mares attracted by his first-crop successes, and he already has five graded/group stakes winners from this group, headed by 2006 Robert H. Griffin Debutante Stakes (Ire-II) winner Gaudeamus, 2007 Illinois Derby (gr. II) winner Cowtown Cat, and 2007 Dwyer Stakes (gr. II) winner Any Given Saturday.

A muscular, well-balanced, attractive horse who makes his official height of 15.3 hands seem a little generous when seen in person, Distorted Humor throws runners in all shapes and sizes but generally gets a bigger horse than himself even when bred to smallish or average-sized mares. He has done particularly well with mares with the great matron *La Troienne in their pedigrees, especially those who carry *La Troienne through Buckpasser or Seattle Slew. As of July 2, 2007, Distorted Humor has sired fifty-seven stakes winners from 620 foals of racing age — 8 percent — and this percentage is likely to improve on two counts: He is now receiving better mares, and he is no longer shuttling to Australia, where he apparently did not fit the mare population as well as he has in North America. He stood the 2007 season for $225,000, a far cry from the $12,500 of his initial stud fee.

Flower Alley is the first major son of Distorted Humor to retire to stud, but Distorted Humor will doubtless have more retiring to stud in years to come. Further, his later good sons will be more likely to have the strong female families that, combined with good racing performance and the iron will to win so typical of the Distorted Humors, make a horse attractive as a stallion prospect.

Forty Niner has not enjoyed the same level of stud success in Japan as he did in North America but is the sire of Utopia, Meiner Select, and Admire Hope, all Japanese group I winners who should receive reasonable opportunities at stud in their native land or elsewhere. (Utopia, now owned by Godolphin Racing, is still in training as of this writing and won the 2007 Westchester Handicap, gr. III, at Belmont Park.) Another Japanese-bred son of Forty Niner, 2002 Peter Pan Stakes (gr. II) winner Sunday Break, is now at stud at Walmac Farm in Kentucky. Reports from the summer of 2006 indicated that Forty Niner might be experiencing fertility problems, but as of this writing, he remains officially active in Japan.

As a broodmare sire, Forty Niner has also been fairly successful. As of

July 2007, his daughters have produced fifty-four stakes winners from 897 foals, headed by grade/group I winners High Yield, Island Sand, Mass Media, and Big Easy.

* * *

With excellent conformation, a strong pedigree, and a grade I victory under his belt, Gone West was expected to do well as a sire and has fulfilled those expectations. As of July 2007, he has gotten eighty-seven stakes winners from 1,070 foals of racing age and has progeny earnings of more than $67.7 million.

Gone West's first crop was led by the 1993 Nassau County Handicap (gr. I) winner West by West, but the stallion's first real headliner was 1992 English and French champion juvenile Zafonic, who added a title as French champion three-year-old male in 1993. Zafonic also won the 1993 Two Thousand Guineas to give Gone West his first classic winner. Two-time German champion Royal Abjar and 1995 Rothmans Ltd. International Stakes (gr. IT) Lassigny followed in the 1991 crop, and the 1992 crop starred two-time Breeders' Cup Mile (gr. IT) winner Da Hoss.

Although the stakes winners kept on coming, Gone West did not get another top-class runner until 1995, when Grand Slam was foaled. The colt proved to be one of the best juveniles of 1997, winning the Futurity (gr. I) and the Champagne (gr. I), but he suffered a severe hind tendon cut during the Breeders' Cup Juvenile and was eased in the stretch. Amazingly, he came back from that injury well enough to win the 1998 Peter Pan Stakes (gr. II) and finish second in the Breeders' Cup Sprint before retiring to Ashford Stud in 1999.

Commendable, a foal of 1997, won the 2000 Belmont Stakes, netting Gone West his first winner in a Triple Crown race, and 2004 U.S. champion sprinter Speightstown followed from the 1998 crop. But 1999 proved to be the breakout year for Gone West. The stallion was represented by seventeen individual stakes winners from the 1999 crop (which contained seventy-three named foals), including three grade I winners: Came Home, winner of the 2002 Santa Anita Derby against his peers and the Pacific Classic against older males; Johar, dead-heat winner of the 2003 Breeders' Cup Turf and solo winner of the 2002 Hollywood Derby (gr. IT); and Changeintheweather, winner of the 2001 Grey Breeders' Cup Stakes (Can-I).

Rather surprisingly, only in the last few years has Gone West developed an increasing reputation as a sire of sires. West by West and Royal Abjar both proved disappointing and are now in Turkey while Da Hoss is a gelding and now resides at the Kentucky Horse Park's Hall of Champions. Zafonic, although a good stallion with fifty-seven stakes winners to his credit, never quite succeeded in living up to the high expectations placed on him before his death in 2002. His best runner, two-time English champion Xaar, is at stud in Europe while 2003 St. James's Palace Stakes (Eng-I) winner Zafeen is shuttling between Australia (where he entered stud in 2005) and England.

Zamindar, a French group III-winning full brother to Zafonic, stands at stud in England and is now making a name for himself outside of his brother's shadow. After opening his stud career by getting 2002 Poule d'Essai des Pouliches (French One Thousand Guineas, Fr-I) winner Zenda in his first crop, he cooled off quickly. However, he returned to the headlines with the 2007 Poule d'Essai des Pouliches victory of Darjina, who overtook Finsceal Beo in the final strides to win by a head. Another daughter, the Irish-bred Coquerelle, won the 2007 Prix Saint-Alary (Fr-I).

Mr. Greeley has been the first son of Gone West to establish a reputation as an important sire in North America. A cleverly named horse out of the Reviewer mare Long Legend, Mr. Greeley was a three-time grade III winner as a three-year-old of 1995 and ran second in that year's Breeder's

Cup Sprint.

Retired to Dixiana Farm (he later transferred to Spendthrift Farm and is now at Gainesway) in 1996, Mr. Greeley started his stud career with a splash by getting the speedy El Corredor, winner of the 2000 Cigar Mile Handicap (gr. I), in his first Northern Hemisphere crop. He also began shuttling to Australia in 2006 and got off to an equally good start there with Miss Kournikova, winner of the Oakleigh Plate (Aus-I).

The sire of thirty-eight stakes winners as of July 2007, Mr. Greeley has not always been the most consistent of stallions; his stakes winners represent only 4 percent of his named foals. But the ability to get the "big horse" is there. His second crop, foals of 1998, contained the 2003 Sussex Stakes (Eng-I) winner Reel Buddy and the 2002 Distaff Handicap (gr. I) winner Celtic Melody while his third crop produced the 2002 Mother Goose Stakes (gr. I) winner Nonsuch Bay. Whywhywhy (2002 Futurity Stakes, gr. I) headlined the stallion's fourth crop.

Mr. Greeley quieted down a little for a couple of years, but 2006 proved a banner year for the stallion. He was represented by nine individual stakes winners, with the aforementioned Finsceal Beo ("living legend" in Gaelic) being named European champion two-year-old filly at the 2006 Cartier Awards. (The Irish-bred filly went on to score victories in the 2007 One Thousand Guineas and Irish One Thousand Guineas and narrowly missed a historic classic triple when she sandwiched a runner-up finish in the Poule d'Essai des Pouliches in between her classic wins.) In addition, Abraham Champion won the 2006 Derby Mexicano (Mex-I) to become Mr. Greeley's first classic winner; he had previously been the Mexican champion juvenile of 2005.

While it is too early to tell how Mr. Greeley will fare as a sire of sires, both El Corredor and Whywhywhy were well received on retiring to stud.

The former has sired seven stakes winners so far, headed by 2005 Frizette Stakes (gr. I) winner Adieu; the latter, a freshman sire of 2007, stands at Gainesway in Kentucky.

Another son of Gone West to meet with some success at stud has been Elusive Quality. A big, powerful, extremely handsome horse, Elusive Quality clearly possessed exceptional talent but was never quite able to make full use of what he had due to an assortment of minor injuries. Still, he retired to stud as a grade III winner on turf and with the reputation of terrific speed at seven to eight furlongs: He set a course record of 1:20.17 for seven furlongs at Gulfstream Park as a four-year-old in 1997 and the following year won the one-mile Poker Handicap (gr. IIIT) in world-record time of 1:31.60. Those credentials plus a good pedigree (his dam, Touch of Greatness, is a half sister to German and Italian champion Gold and Ivory while his second dam is grade III winner Ivory Wand, one of five stakes winners produced from 1966 Alabama Stakes winner Natashka) were enough to make Elusive Quality an attractive commodity in the commercial stallion market. He covered 101 mares in 1999, his first year at stud.

Elusive Quality sired eleven stakes winners from his first crop of seventy-six named foals, headed by 2002 French champion juvenile male Elusive City. But it was 2004 that vaulted Elusive Quality to the first rank among North American sires. That was Smarty Jones' year.

Produced from the Smile mare I'll Get Along, Smarty Jones (whose catchy name came from the nickname of owner Roy Chapman's mother-in-law) was a restricted stakes winner in Pennsylvania at two but exploded into the Kentucky Derby picture with successive wins in the Count Fleet Stakes, Southwest Stakes, Rebel Stakes, and Arkansas Derby (gr. II). Doubters pointed to the colt's pedigree as a reason for believing he might not get ten furlongs, but over a sopping-wet Churchill Downs track officially rated "sloppy," Smarty Jones splashed past game pacesetter Lion Heart en route to a 2 3/4-lengths victory.

The victory made Smarty Jones the first horse since Seattle Slew to win the Derby while still undefeated. Two weeks later the colt joined a still more exclusive club with a devastating 11 1/2-length score in the Preakness: not only was the margin a new record for the Preakness, but it also made Smarty one of just three colts to enter the third leg of the Triple Crown undefeated. The others were Majestic Prince in 1969 and Seattle Slew in 1977.

Smarty Jones lined up against eight rivals as a heavy favorite for the Belmont Stakes on June 5, 2004. The reasons for the outcome have been debated ever since — whether Smarty was rank and would not settle, whether jockey Stewart Elliott moved too soon, or whether other jockeys sacrificed their mounts to beat Smarty rather than win the race — but the outcome itself is racing history: Birdstone rolled up on the outside, overhauled a dead-game but exhausted Smarty Jones, and won by a length.

As events turned out, the Belmont was Smarty Jones' last race. After minor setbacks derailed possible appearances in the Haskell Invitational Handicap (gr. I) and the Pennsylvania Derby (gr. II), radiographic imaging revealed areas of bruising at the end of all four cannon bones. While the colt could theoretically have returned to racing eventually, his value as a stud prospect plus the high price of insuring him if he continued to race tipped the scales toward retirement. Smarty Jones entered stud at Three Chimneys Farm near Midway, Kentucky, where he served a select book of 113 mares in 2005, his first season at stud. His first crop will come to the races in 2008.

Smarty Jones vaulted Elusive Quality to the top of the 2004 North American general sire list, making Elusive Quality only the second tail-male descendant of Mr. Prospector to head the North American list (the first was Thunder Gulch, who turned the trick in 2001 on the strength of Point Given's championship season). Only one other horse of comparable quality has emerged from Elusive Quality's next three crops of racing age — his Australian-bred daughter Camarilla, winner of the 2007 AJC Sires' Produce Stakes (Aus-I) — but his 396 foals of three years of age and upward have so far produced a respectable 234 winners (59.1 percent) and thirty stakes winners (7.6 percent). Those statistics may well improve as the foals sired from the better mares attracted by Smarty Jones' heroics will begin coming to the races in 2008.

Grand Slam, the third of Gone West's notable sire sons in North America, has been hampered in maintaining consistency by the huge books he has served at Ashford Stud (he has averaged 165 mares a year since entering stud in 1999). Nonetheless, he has thirty-five stakes winners to his credit as of July 2, 2007, headed by 2003 Breeders' Cup Sprint winner Cajun Beat (a gelding) and 2004 Japan Dirt Derby (Jpn-I) winner Cafe Olympus. Grand Slam's best entire son in North America has been multiple grade II winner Limehouse, who stood his first season at stud in 2006 at Vinery in Kentucky. Another multiple grade II winner by Grand Slam, Strong Hope, entered stud at Claiborne Farm in 2005 and will have his first crop come to the races in 2008.

Gone West himself is still active in the stud as of this writing and has several younger sons who are receiving good opportunities as new sires, including 2004 U.S. champion sprinter Speightstown, multiple grade I winners Came Home and Johar, and 2002 Kentucky Derby runner-up Proud Citizen. As of July 2007, Gone West is also the maternal grandsire of forty-three stakes winners, among them 2005 Derby Stakes winner Motivator.

The Golden Girls

11

M r. Prospector has been hailed as the best sire of sires in North America since Northern Dancer's heyday in the 1980s, with reason. But he has been better still as a broodmare sire. For nine of the past ten years, Mr. Prospector has been the unquestioned king of maternal grandsires in the United States; only Dixieland Band in 2004 has stood between him and an uninterrupted ten-year run at the top.

Mr. Prospector's career as a broodmare sire was perhaps a little slower to get off the ground than one might expect in hindsight, given his merit early on as a sire of winners. Many of his Florida-bred daughters, however, came from relatively weak female families; if they lacked strong race records, being bred to sires of modest class often further hampered them.

Even so, there were hints early on that Mr. Prospector's daughters were going to do well as producers. From the stallion's first crop, foals of 1976, Fabulous Prospect, a minor stakes winner out of the Sunglow mare Double Sun, produced 1992 What a Pleasure Stakes (gr. III) winner Sir Pinder (by Baldski). With better opportunities, champion It's in the Air never quite succeeded in reproducing herself but did throw three stakes winners, among them the Criterium de Maisons-Laffitte (Fr-II) winner Bitooh (by Seattle Slew); she is also the granddam of 2003 Poule d'Essai des Pouliches (Fr-I) winner Musical Chimes and of multiple grade/group I winner Storming

Home. Roundelay, a daughter of the *Noholme II mare Tunka Shela who was exported to Venezuela, produced the 1988 Gran Premio Nacional (Ven-I) winner Mcgwire. And, best of all, Prospector's Fire — a daughter of Native Street — produced two grade/group I winners: 1988 Vernons Sprint Cup (Eng-I) winner Dowsing, a son of Riverman, and the Blushing Groom (Fr) filly Fire the Groom, winner of the 1991 Beverly D. Stakes (gr. IT) and dam of the 1999 July Cup (Eng-I) and Nunthorpe Stakes (Eng-I) winner Stravinsky.

From that beginning, Mr. Prospector's daughters have poured out good horses in a golden stream. While space does not permit a complete listing of Mr. Prospector's record as a maternal grandsire, some of the highlights follow:

Aliata (1983, out of Drumtop, by Round Table) won two of four races in England but failed to place in five North American starts. Her produce include Storm Allied, a 2004 gelding by Stormy Atlantic who became a Puerto Rican grade I winner in 2007. More important, however, she is the dam of Storm Boot, a 1989 son of Storm Cat who was only stakes-placed on the track but became a consistent breed-to-race sire before he died May 10, 2007. At the time of his death, he had sired 376 winners (63.4 percent) and forty-six stakes winners (7.8 percent) from 593 foals of racing age.

Blue Jean Baby (1985, Jones Time Machine, by Current Concept) won the 1987 Sorority Stakes (gr. II) and produced multiple stakes winner Denim Yenem to the cover of Ogygian. Blue Jean Baby's 1994 filly by Dixieland Band, Dixieland Blues, failed to win but produced a solid racehorse in multiple grade II winner Limehouse, now at stud at Vinery Kentucky. Dixieland Blues also produced the Honour and Glory colt Blues and Royals, a twelve-length winner of the 2005 UAE Derby (UAE-II), but, unfortunately, he succumbed to colitis and laminitis before he could show his form in the United States.

Chic Shirine (1984, Too Chic, by Blushing Groom [Fr]) won the 1987 Ashland Stakes (gr. I) before producing 1994 Ladies Handicap (gr. II) winner Tara Roma (by Lyphard) and 1995 True North Handicap (gr. II) winner Waldoboro, a full brother to Tara Roma. Tara Roma, in turn, has become the dam of 2001 Go for Wand Handicap (gr. I) winner Serra Lake (by Seattle Slew) and multiple grade III winner Cappuchino (by Capote).

Colour Chart (1987, Rainbow Connection, Halo) won the 1990 Prix de l'Opera (Fr-II) and placed in three grade I events. She produced four stakes winners: multiple group III winner Equerry (by St. Jovite), 2001 U.S. champion juvenile filly Tempera (by A.P. Indy), French stakes winner Ecole d'Art (by Theatrical), and multiple Saudi Arabian stakes winner Chirico (by Danzig).

Coup de Genie (1991, Coup de Folie, by Halo) emulated her full brother Machiavellian by becoming a champion juvenile in France. She is the dam of four stakes winners, headed by multiple grade III winner Snake Mountain (by A.P. Indy) and Denebola. The last-named filly, a 2001 daughter of Storm Cat, used a victory in the 2003 Prix Marcel Boussac (Fr-I) to vault to a title as French champion juvenile filly. Coup de Genie is also the dam of Moonlight's Box (by Nureyev), whose son Bago cemented his position as the best three-year-old colt in France for 2004 by winning that year's Prix de l'Arc de Triomphe (Fr-I).

Doff (1982, Furling, by Hoist the Flag), a winner of half of her ten starts over two years, was exported to Japan in 1991. Before her departure, however, she produced the Private Account colt Brunswick, who won the Whitney Handicap (gr. I) as a four-year-old in 1993. He has been a disappointing sire and is now at stud in Alberta, Canada.

Fantastic Find (1986, Blitey, by Riva Ridge), one of three grade I stakes winners produced from the excellent matron Blitey, won the 1990

Hempstead Handicap. She is the dam of the 2000 Acorn Stakes (gr. I) winner Finder's Fee, a daughter of Storm Cat, and of Freedom of Speech (by Danzig), dam of 2005 National Museum of Racing Hall of Fame Stakes (gr. IIT) winner T. D. Vance.

Garimpeiro (1987, Far Flying, by Far North) failed to win in ten starts in France and the United States. But she struck gold with her first foal, a 1992 colt by Theatrical. Named Geri, the colt won the 1996 Oaklawn Handicap (gr. I). The following year Geri proved his ability on grass by winning the newly instituted Woodbine Mile, now a grade I turf race. Garimpeiro is also the dam of Geri's stakes-winning full brother Clure and of A. P. Arrow (by A.P. Indy), winner of the 2007 Skip Away Handicap (gr. III).

Get Lucky (1988, Dance Number, by Northern Dancer) won the 1992 Affectionately Handicap (gr. III). She is the dam of 1996 Pilgrim Stakes (gr. III) winner Accelerator (by A.P. Indy), 2004 Top Flight Handicap (gr. II) winner Daydreaming (also by A.P. Indy), and Canadian stakes winner Harborage (by Monarchos). Get Lucky also produced She's a Winner, an unraced full sister to Daydreaming and Accelerator who is the dam of 2006 Haskell Invitational Handicap (gr. I) winner Bluegrass Cat.

Champion ***Gold Beauty*** (1979, Stick to Beauty, by Illustrious) produced Maplejinsky as her first foal. A 1985 daughter of Nijinsky II, Maplejinsky won the 1988 Monmouth Oaks (gr. I) and Alabama Stakes (gr. I) before retiring to the paddocks. There, she produced 1994 U.S. champion older female Sky Beauty (by Blushing Groom [Fr]), dam of 2005 Horris Hill Stakes (Eng-III) winner Hurricane Cat, and Our Country Place (by Pleasant Colony), dam of two-time First Flight Handicap (gr. II) winner Country Hideaway and 2005 Breeders' Cup Distaff winner Pleasant Home. Such a debut would be hard to match, let alone outdo, but Gold Beauty's second foal was Dayjur, a son of Danzig who was named English champion sprinter, champion three-year-old male, and Horse of the Year in 1990; he was also the highweight among French sprinters that year.

Here I Go (1996, Shufflin in Seatle, by Seattle Slew) placed twice in grade III events. Her second foal is Summerly, a daughter of Summer Squall who captured the 2005 Kentucky Oaks (gr. I).

Love From Mom (1981, Hoso, by Solo Landing) did not race but produced four graded stakes winners: Dancing Jon (by Gate Dancer; 1992 Board of Governors' Handicap, gr. III), Fight for Love (by Fit to Fight; 1995 Broward Handicap, gr. III), Love That Jazz (by Dixieland Band; 1998 Vernon O. Underwood Stakes, gr. III), and Sea of Secrets (by Storm Cat; 1998 San Vicente Stakes, gr. II). Love That Jazz, in turn, became the dam of multiple grade I winner Society Selection to the cover of Coronado's Quest, while Sea of Secrets is a regional sire in California and got his first graded stakes winner in 2006 Best Pal Stakes (gr. II) victor Principle Secret. All told, Sea of Secrets has sired nine stakes winners as of July 2007.

Love Style (1999, Likeable Style, by Nijinsky II) never raced. Her second foal is the Johannesburg colt Scat Daddy, winner of the 2006 Champagne Stakes (gr. I) and the 2007 Florida Derby (gr. I). Scat Daddy will stand his first season in 2008.

Mine Only (1981, Mono, by Better Self) won one of her eight starts. She produced three graded stakes winners: Academy Award (by Secretariat; 1991 Early Times Manhattan Handicap, gr. IIT), Good Mood (by Devil's Bag; 1991 Miss Grillo Stakes, gr. IIIT), and Statuette (by Pancho Villa; 1993 Nijana Stakes, gr. IIIT). Statuette, in turn, produced 2002 Irish highweighted juvenile male Tomahawk, a son of Seattle Slew. Mine Only is also the dam of Chosen Lady, a full sister to Academy Award who produced 1998 Ashland Stakes (gr. I) winner Well Chosen, 1996 Cherry Hill Stakes (gr. III) winner In Contention, and Lady of Choice, dam of multiple grade III winner Multiple Choice.

Miss Du Bois (1994, Blanche Du Bois, by Green Dancer) failed to win in fifteen starts, but her first foal is 2003 Queen Elizabeth II Challenge Cup Stakes (gr. IT) winner Film Maker (by Dynaformer), twice runner-up and once third in the Breeders' Cup Filly and Mare Turf.

Miss Wildcatter (1980, Elizabeth K., by Third Martini) never raced but hit the jackpot with her fourth foal, the Kris S. mare Hollywood Wildcat. The U.S. champion three-year-old filly of 1993, Hollywood Wildcat is the dam of 2000 Breeders' Cup Mile winner War Chant (by Danzig), 2005 July Stakes (Eng-II) winner Ivan Denisovich (Ire) (by Danehill), and stakes winners Double Cat (by Storm Cat) and Ministers Wild Cat (by Deputy Minister).

Monevassia (1994, Miesque, by Nureyev) managed only one placing in two starts but is a full sister to Kingmambo and to French group III winner Miesque's Son, now the sire of 2006 Breeders' Cup Mile winner Miesque's Approval. In keeping with her regal heritage, Monevassia has become the dam of Rumplestiltskin, a Danehill filly who earned the title of 2005 European champion juvenile filly with wins in the Moyglare Stud Stakes (Ire-I) and Prix Marcel Boussac (Fr-I).

Mr. P's Princess (1993, Anne Campbell, by Never Bend) never raced. Her first foal is Fasliyev (by Nureyev), who won the 1999 Phoenix Stakes (Ire-I) and Prix Morny (Fr-I) on his way to being named European champion juvenile male. Fasliyev created a sensation with his first crop, foals of 2003, by tying the Northern Hemisphere record of thirty-four individual juvenile winners set by End Sweep in 1998. Mr. P's Princess is also the dam of Kamarinskaya (by Storm Cat), winner of the 2006 One Thousand Guineas Trial (Ire-III) at Leopardstown and Dubai to Dubai, a stakes winner in the United Arab Emirates.

Onaga (1994, Savannah Dancer, by Northern Dancer) failed to win in eight starts. Nonetheless, she is the dam of Aragorn (Ire), a 2002 son of

Giant's Causeway. Named after the heroic character in *The Lord of the Rings*, Aragorn won four straight graded stakes in 2006, including the Shoemaker Breeders' Cup Mile (gr. IT) and the Eddie Read Handicap (gr. IT) before falling 2 3/4 lengths short of Miesque's Approval in the Breeders' Cup Mile.

Optimistic Lass (1981, Loveliest, by *Tibaldo) won the 1984 Nassau Stakes (Eng-II) and Musidora Stakes (Eng-III). She is the dam of Golden Opinion, a 1986 daughter of Slew o' Gold who won the 1989 Coronation Stakes (Eng-I).

Preach (1989, Narrate, by Honest Pleasure) won the 1991 Frizette Stakes (gr. I). Her first foal is Pulpit, a son of A.P. Indy, who was among the most highly regarded Kentucky Derby candidates of 1997. After winning the Fountain of Youth Stakes (gr. II), running second in the Florida Derby (gr. I), and winning the Blue Grass Stakes (gr. II), Pulpit finished fourth in the Derby. Now a stallion at Claiborne Farm, Pulpit is one of the more commercially popular sires in the United States and as of July 2007, is the sire of twenty-nine stakes winners from 428 foals of racing age including grade I winners Corinthian, Stroll, Sky Mesa, Purge, and Tapit.

Prime Prospect (1978, Square Generation, by Olden Times) won the 1983 First Lady Handicap. She produced only four foals, none of them stakes winners, but her good allowance-winning daughter by Blushing Groom (Fr), Primal Force, earned U.S. Broodmare of the Year honors in 2000 thanks to the feats of her sons Awesome Again (1998 Breeders' Cup Classic) and Macho Uno (2000 Breeders' Cup Juvenile and U.S. champion juvenile male).

Proflare (1984, Flare Pass, by Buckpasser) was stakes-placed in France. She has produced a remarkable six stakes winners, five of them of graded or group stature. The best of them, two-time grade II winner True Flare (by Capote) has, in turn, produced 2006 Malibu Stakes (gr. I) winner Latent

Heat, 2007 Vagrancy Handicap (gr. II) winner Indian Flare, and French multiple group III winner Art Master.

Propositioning (1980, Stay Over, by Prove It) was group III-placed in France and grade III-placed in the United States. Her first foal, the unraced Key to the Mint mare Questionablevirtue, produced the 1998 Sussex Stakes (Eng-I) winner Among Men to the cover of Zilzal. Prospositioning's second foal, the Northern Baby colt Deposit Ticket, won the 1990 Hopeful Stakes (gr. I) and sired 1996 Canadian champion juvenile male Cash Deposit.

Prospectors Delite (1989, Up the Flagpole, by Hoist the Flag) won the 1992 Ashland and Acorn stakes, both grade I races. All five of her named foals won stakes. Her first, the 1994 A.P. Indy filly Tomisue's Delight, won the 1997 Ruffian Handicap (gr. I) and the 1998 Personal Ensign Handicap (gr. I); the second, Delta Music (by Dixieland Band), won the Straight Deal Breeders' Cup Handicap as a four-year-old in 1999. Monashee Mountain (by Danzig) won the 2000 Tetrarch Stakes (Ire-III) before going to stud at Ashford Stud, Kentucky, while Rock Slide, a 1998 full brother to Tomisue's Delight, was a stakes winner at four and five and is now at stud at Maryland Stallion Station.

Prospectors Delite's last foal, a 1999 colt by A.P. Indy, proved to be best of all. Named Mineshaft, the colt won seven of his nine starts as a four-year-old in 2003 to earn honors as U.S. champion older male and Horse of the Year. He stands at stud at Lane's End in Kentucky and is a freshman sire of 2007.

As mentioned in a previous chapter, **Queena** (1986, Too Chic, by Blushing Groom [Fr]) was U.S. champion older female as a five-year-old in 1991. She is the dam of 2000 Hollywood Derby (gr. IT) winner Brahms (by Danzig), now standing at Vinery Kentucky, and of La Reina (by A.P. Indy), winner of the 2003 Tempted Stakes (gr. III).

Red Carnival (1992, Seaside Attraction, by Seattle Slew) won the 1994 Cherry Hinton Stakes (Eng-III). She is the dam of English and French group III winner Carnival Dancer, 2005 Kelso Breeders' Cup Handicap (gr. IIT) winner Funfair, and 2006 Prix de l'Abbaye (Fr-I) winner Desert Lord.

Silver Valley (1979, Seven Valleys, by Road At Sea) won two minor stakes as a four-year-old. Her first foal, Silver Deputy, showed great promise in winning his first two starts, including the Swynford Stakes in Canada, before falling prey to injury. But as a sire, the son of Deputy Minister has been a consistent stallion just below the top rank. As of July 2007, Silver Deputy has sired seventy stakes winners, seven of them champions, from 924 foals of racing age, headed by two-time U.S. champion filly Silverbulletday. He also has developed a reputation as a solid broodmare sire with thirty-five stakes winners from 673 foals, headed by 2002 Canadian Horse of the Year Wake At Noon and the grade I-winning half brothers El Corredor and Roman Ruler.

Soundings (1983, Ocean's Answer, by Northern Answer) won two of nine starts. She is responsible for four stakes winners, headed by 1994 Poule d'Essai des Poulains winner Green Tune (by Green Dancer) and 1996 Cheveley Park Stakes (Eng-I) winner Pas de Response (by Danzig). Didyme (by Dixieland Band) won the 1992 Prix Robert Papin (Fr-II), and the 1993 Manila filly Ecoute won minor stakes in France and in the United States.

Sue Babe (1978, Sleek Dancer, by Northern Dancer) won two stakes as a juvenile and ran second in the 1980 Sorority Stakes (gr. I). Her second foal, the Alleged colt Sir Harry Lewis, reaped classic glory in 1987 by winning the Budweiser Irish Derby (Ire-I). Sue Babe later produced the restricted stakes winners Sir Richard Lewis (by Carr de Naskra) and Cyrano (by Seattle Slew). Sir Harry Lewis' full sister Champagne Babe is the dam of Champagneforashley, winner of the 1989 Nashua Stakes (gr. III).

Tacha (1992, Savannah Dancer, by Northern Dancer) won one of nine starts. She is the dam of One Cool Cat, a 2001 Storm Cat colt who was named European champion two-year-old male of 2003 following victories in the Phoenix Stakes (Ire-I) and National Stakes (Ire-I). He is now at stud at Coolmore Ireland.

French champion ***Tersa*** (1986, Peacefully, by Jacinto) seemed a disappointing broodmare until her eighth foal, a 2001 colt by Kris S. Named Rock Hard Ten, the physically imposing colt took some time gaining the mental maturity to match his handsome physique but swept through the 2004-2005 Santa Anita winter meeting with wins in the 2004 Malibu Stakes (gr. I), 2005 Strub Stakes (gr. II), and 2005 Santa Anita Handicap (gr. I) before retiring to stud at Lane's End in 2006.

Vue (1989, Harbor Flag, by Hoist the Flag) placed in two stakes as a three-year-old. Her first foal, the Known Fact filly Oath, won the 1996 Spinaway Stakes (gr. I).

Wayage (1984, Waya [Fr], Faraway Son) could not win in twelve starts in France but produced 1992 Italian highweighted two-year-old filly Secrage (by Secreto) as her second foal. Secrage, in turn, is the dam of 1997 Royal Lodge Stakes (Eng-II) winner Teapot Row. Wayage also produced the 2002 Diadem Stakes (Eng-II) winner Crystal Castle, a 1998 gelding by Gilded Time.

Witwatersrand (1981, Sleek Belle, by *Vaguely Noble) won the 1984 Pucker Up Stakes (gr. III). While in the United States, she produced Nelson, a late-developing son of Seattle Slew who won the 1994 Ark-La-Tex Handicap (gr. III) as a seven-year-old. Following the 1989 breeding season, Witwatersrand was exported to Japan, where her daughter Chokai Carol (by Brian's Time) won the 1994 Yushun Himba (Japanese Oaks). Another daughter of Witwatersrand, group II-placed Blushing Storm (by Blushing Groom

[Fr]), is the dam of 1999 Yorkshire Cup (Eng-II) winner Churlish Charm to the cover of Niniski.

Yarn (1987, Narrate, by Honest Pleasure) won one of six starts. She produced two fast horses in Tale of the Cat (1994, Storm Cat) and Minardi (1998, Boundary). Tale of the Cat won the 1997 King's Bishop Stakes (gr. II) and placed in three grade I events before retiring to Ashford Stud, where he has sired multiple grade I winner Lion Heart; Minardi won the 2000 Phoenix Stakes (Ire-I) and Middle Park Stakes (Eng-I). Yarn is also the dam of Spunoutacontrol, a 1996 Wild Again filly, who won the restricted Singing Beauty Stakes as a four-year-old before producing Spun Silk (by A.P. Indy), likewise a restricted stakes winner.

Myth, a 1993 daughter of Yarn by Ogygian, managed only one win from sixteen starts but has atoned richly for her deficiencies as a racer by producing Johannesburg as her first foal. Rated the champion juvenile in both Europe and the United States in 2001 after wins in the Phoenix Stakes (Ire-I), Middle Park Stakes (Eng-I), Prix Morny (Fr-I), and Breeders' Cup Juvenile, Johannesburg entered stud at Ashford Stud in 2003. His first crop to race, two-year-olds of 2006, has yielded eight stakes winners, headed by multiple grade I winner Scat Daddy.

***

All told, Mr. Prospector has 331 stakes winners to his credit as a maternal grandsire, and the list likely will continue growing for some time. Given that Mr. Prospector's youngest daughters are foals of 2000, it is not impossible that Mr. Prospector may match or even surpass *Sir Gallahad III's record of twelve U.S. broodmare sire titles, which would be a stellar feat indeed.

As can be seen from the list above, Mr. Prospector daughters have thrown good horses to sires of many sire lines but have been particularly productive with sires from the Northern Dancer male line and with A.P. Indy.

They have thrown everything from top juveniles to older champions, dirt runners to grass runners, sprinters to stayers, and their influence is likely to continue for decades. Even if Mr. Prospector's male line eventually fails, his daughters will ensure his name remains prominent in pedigrees well into the twenty-first century.

King Of The Ring

12

M r. Prospector came into his own as a major commercial sire following the collapse of the North American bloodstock market in 1987, an event that ensured his progeny would never command the heady prices rung up for Northern Dancer's top auction yearlings. The most expensive yearling he ever had, Shah Jehan, seems positively inexpensive at $4.4 million compared to Snaafi Dancer, a Northern Dancer colt who went for $10.2 million in 1983 after a tense bidding duel between Robert Sangster's Coolmore conglomerate and Sheikh Mohammed bid Rashid al Maktoum; in fact, seven other Northern Dancer colts sold for higher prices than Shah Jehan. Further, the Northern Dancer sire line has continued to dominate the list of highest-priced sales yearlings with Nijinsky II's son Seattle Dancer, sold in 1985, still holding the all-time record of $13.1 million.

Although a number of the Mr. Prospector tribe have done well on turf, the general perception of the Mr. Prospector was (and is) that his offspring excel primarily on dirt, which has limited their appeal to European, Arab, and Japanese buyers. The notable exceptions among Mr. Prospector's sons have been Machiavellian, who spent his entire stud career in England, and Kingmambo, who has paralleled Northern Dancer and many of the Dancer's top sons by having his primary stud successes in Europe while remaining physically based in Kentucky. Both Machiavellian and Kingmambo, however, have female lines suggesting potential

Gold Rush

turf ability and had proven themselves on the grass in Europe. Mr. Prospector himself, as well as most of his other sons, have appealed primarily to the North American market.

In fact, although the ripple effect from the 1987 U.S. stock market correction negatively impacted financial markets around the world, the rise of Mr. Prospector and his sons, combined with the pensioning of Northern Dancer and the aging of his best sire sons, may have contributed just as much to the reduction in foreign participation in the American yearling market during the late 1980s and early 1990s. Within the parameters of the market he inherited, however, Mr. Prospector's feats have been just as remarkable as those of Northern Dancer. Consider the following:

• Mr. Prospector dominated the elite Keeneland July yearling sale through the 1990s and up to the sale's final year in 2003. He had the highest yearling average of any stallion at the sale from 1992 through 1995, in 1998, and in 2000. Further, he sired the sales topper in 1992, 1993, 1994, 1995, 1998, and 2000.

• At the Keeneland September yearling sale, which rose into increasing prominence during the late 1990s and is now the premier sale for elite yearlings in the United States, Mr. Prospector had the sales topper in 1997 and 1998 and led all sires by yearling sales average in 1991 and 1999.

• Mr. Prospector is credited with siring forty-nine yearlings that sold for seven figures during his career. While this does not equal the fifty-two such yearlings sired by Northern Dancer or the eighty such that Storm Cat has to date, one must remember that Mr. Prospector had many of his best-bred yearlings pass through the ring during the depressed bloodstock market between the crash of 1987 and the recovery of the mid-1990s.

• For nine consecutive years (1992–2000), Mr. Prospector led all North American sires by yearling sales average throughout the year; he had been second in 1990 and 1991 and with his final crop in 2001 was second to Storm Cat. Only Northern Dancer has been the continent's leading sire of yearlings for as many years, and his nine years (1978, 1980–1984, and 1986–1988) were not consecutive.

• Mr. Prospector sired the top overall North American sales yearling in 1994, 1995, and 1997. He sired the top overall North American sales weanling in 1995 and had the highest-priced weanling filly in 1996.

• The $4 million paid for Fusaichi Pegasus in 1998 marked the highest price paid for a yearling at auction since 1985, when Seattle Dancer set a world record at $13.1 million at Keeneland July and the Nijinsky II—Crimson Saint colt Laa Etab went for $7 million later in the same sale.

• Mr. Prospector's 367 yearlings sold at auction totaled more than $218 million, a world record for any sire through 2001.

• Over the course of his career, Mr. Prospector's yearling average climbed from $42,500 in 1977 to $1,327,500 in 2001, the year that his last youngsters passed through the ring.

• Mr. Prospector was the leading covering sire by average for mares sold at North American auctions in 1995. He would probably have led the list more frequently save that he usually did not have the minimum of three mares sold to be considered for the rankings.

Mr. Prospector, in fact, came to epitomize the modern North American commercial market. A brilliantly fast horse of questionable soundness (though, as we have seen, perhaps not wholly due to inherent factors), he consistently sired what the market wanted: a precocious, speedy, medium- to large-sized horse that could usually stay a mile and with the right distaff pedigree had the potential of going nine or ten furlongs. Once it was found that his sons often turned out to be good sires, Mr. Prospector was on his way to becoming the dominant commercial sire of the 1990s.

The commercial market has historically swung between emphasizing pedigree and conformation in its valuations of yearlings. During Mr. Prospector's heyday, the pendulum swung more toward pedigree, in no small part because buyers learned what faults could be tolerated in Mr. Prospector's youngsters. While the stallion was commonly criticized for siring foals with leg faults, particularly turning out on the right foreleg, the fact remained that most of them could run; in fact, more than 83 percent of Mr. Prospector's foals eventually got to the races and more than 63 percent became winners.

Unlike Northern Dancer, Mr. Prospector never sired sons that threatened his own dominance of the market; Fappiano did not live long enough to mount a serious challenge to his sire, and while other Mr. Prospector sons have done very well, none have had records comparable to Nijinsky II, Lyphard, Danzig, or Nureyev. Still, Mr. Prospector remains a major influence in North American commercial breeding. In 2006, the great sire had eight sons and grandsons among the top twenty sires of yearlings by sales average, headed by third-place Kingmambo, whose twenty yearlings (with a boost from the $11.7 million Keeneland September sales topper) sold averaged $960,633. Only Danzig ($1,465,833) and Storm Cat ($1,255,400) had higher sales averages. The other Mr. Prospector-line stallions among the 2006 sales leaders were Seeking the Gold (fourth, $574,778), Unbridled's Song (seventh, $421,465), Empire Maker (eighth, $379,125), Gone West (twelfth, $305,004), Distorted Humor (fourteenth, $281,635), Mr. Greeley (sixteenth, $253,702), and Machiavellian (seventeenth, $246,483).

Not only do offspring of sons and male-line descendants of Mr. Prospector continue to do well in the sales ring, but progeny of Mr. Prospector's daughters and granddaughters are a force in the market — not to mention that those daughters and granddaughters themselves are valuable commodities when they become available. All told, the heritage of Mr. Prospector appears likely to remain a force in American commercial breeding for a long time to come.

A Legacy Of Gold

13

A t first glance, Mr. Prospector does not appear to rank as one of the epochal sires of the Thoroughbred breed. Unlike stallions such as Herod, Phalaris, or Northern Dancer, Mr. Prospector's contribution appears to be more that of establishing a solid branch of the mainstream of the breed rather than redirecting the stream itself.

For the time being, the future of Mr. Prospector's male line seems secure. Fappiano and Forty Niner have established clear branches of their own; Gone West appears to be at the head of an emerging branch, and lines such as those of Gulch through Thunder Gulch and Point Given, Two Punch through Smoke Glacken, and Seeking the Gold through Mutakddim and through Dubai Millennium and Dubawi have a chance of survival. In addition, younger sons of Mr. Prospector such as Smart Strike, Kingmambo, and Fusaichi Pegasus are receiving opportunities that suggest a good chance that they will manage to get one or more good sire sons.

North America and Argentina have become the main strongholds of the Mr. Prospector line; not coincidentally, these are also the regions in which dirt racing is predominant. In 2006, thirty sons or descendants of Mr. Prospector ranked among the top one hundred North American sires, headed by Distorted Humor in sixth. Likewise, eight sons or descendants of Mr. Prospector rank among the current top twenty Argentine sires.

Change is in the wind, however. With the increasing prevalence of all-weather surfaces such as Polytrack in North America, the American Thoroughbred is entering a transitional period in which various bloodlines' stock may rise or fall depending on their ability to adapt to the new racing conditions. This is not necessarily bad news for the Mr. Prospector line, which has always had a fair share of individuals that could adapt to turf and presumably also will have a reasonable share of individuals that take well to all-weather surfaces. The changes may, however, tend to shift dominance back toward bloodlines that have traditionally performed well on turf, a surface that many all-weather surfaces appear to resemble more than dirt.

A more difficult challenge for the Mr. Prospector male line to weather may spring from within itself. Not only has Mr. Prospector proven a great broodmare sire, but sons and descendants such as Woodman, Crafty Prospector, Carson City, Conquistador Cielo, Miswaki, Seeking the Gold, Afleet, Forty Niner, and Unbridled are also establishing reputations as good broodmare sires. As most North American breeders do not care to inbreed closer than 3x3 and many will not do so closer than 3x4 or 4x4, the increasing prevalence of Mr. Prospector in many good mares' pedigrees reduces the pool of mates available to the great sire's sons and descendants. Further, good stallions produced from Mr. Prospector's daughters and those of his sons also will be competing for the same mares.

While it seems unlikely that Mr. Prospector's male line is likely to decline into extinction any time during this century, his primary legacy may not be through his sons but through his daughters. As already discussed in Chapter 12, daughters of Mr. Prospector continue to churn out high-class winners in a steady stream, and their daughters appear to be breeding on as well. It may be that in time Mr. Prospector will be remembered less as a great sire of sires than as a great broodmare sire in the class of *Sir Gallahad III or *Princequillo and, in so doing, will carry on what has been one of Claiborne Farm's greatest legacies to the American Thoroughbred.

There is no question that Mr. Prospector's success as a sire has far outstripped anything that might have been expected based on a bare reading of his racing career. Had he not become a great stallion, he would be only one small footnote in the annals of the 1970 North American foal crop, remembered primarily on Gulfstream Park programs as the co-holder of the six-furlong track record.

Yet there are tantalizing hints that he could have been far more. Perhaps if he had not unveiled his blazing speed in quite so spectacular a fashion, he might not have been rushed toward the Kentucky Derby and might never have suffered the injuries that, in trainer Jimmy Croll's opinion, compromised him for the rest of his career. But for one shining moment in March 1973, he was the fastest colt in

America, and that moment both defined him and, perhaps, destroyed the racehorse he might have been.

According to racing legend, an old Kentucky groom was once asked what made a good horse. "Speed, suh," the old man replied. And when asked "What else?" by his questioner, the old groom replied, "More speed, suh, more speed — dat's what makes a good horse."

That old groom would have loved Mr. Prospector.

Appendix

Contents

Appendix notes:

The inbreeding noted on the lists of Mr. Prospector's stakes winners (page 150) and his stakes winners as broodmare sire (page 162) reflects inbreeding between sire and dam only.

Stakes winners of Mr. Prospector's leading sons begin on page 190. For stallions with progeny still racing, the lists are current through July 11, 2007.

Pedigree: Mr. Prospector

	Native Dancer, 1950
Raise a Native, 1961	
	Raise You, 1946
MR. PROSPECTOR	
	Nashua, 1952
Gold Digger, 1962	
	Sequence, 1946

Polynesian, 1942	Unbreakable, 1935	Sickle Blue Glass
	Black Polly, 1936	Polymelian Black Queen
Geisha, 1943	Discovery, 1931	Display Ariadne
	Miyako, 1935	John P. Grier La Chica
Case Ace, 1934	**Teddy**, 1913	Ajax Rondeau
	Sweetheart, 1920	Ultimus Humanity
Lady Glory, 1934	American Flag, 1922	Man o' War Lady Comfey
	Beloved, 1927	Whisk Broom Bill and Coo
*Nasrullah, 1940	Nearco, 1935	Pharos Nogara
	Mumtaz Begum, 1932	Blenheim II Mumtaz Mahal
Segula, 1942	Johnstown, 1936	Jamestown La France
	Sekhmet, 1929	Sardanapale Prosopopee
Count Fleet, 1940	Reigh Count, 1925	Sunreigh Contessina
	Quickly, 1930	Haste Stephanie
Miss Dogwood, 1939	Bull Dog, 1927	**Teddy** Plucky Liege
	Myrtlewood, 1932	Blue Larkspur Frizeur

HORSE	COLOR	S	YEAR	DAM	BROODMARE SIRE	STATUS
Fine Prospect	b	f	1976	First Nominee	Rough'n Tumble	
It's in the Air	b	f	1976	A Wind Is Rising	Francis S.	G1
Northern Prospect	b	c	1976	Sleek Dancer	Northern Dancer	
Patience Worth	ch	f	1976	Dark Duet	Spy Song	
Antique Gold	b	c	1977	Old Love	Olden Times	
Arisen	ch	f	1977	Rosy Alibhai	Your Alibhai	
Fabulous Prospect	ch	f	1977	Double Sun	Sun Glow	
Fappiano	b	c	1977	Killaloe	Dr. Fager	G1
Fast Prospect	dk b/br	c	1977	Jetaway	Polly's Jet	
Favorite Prospect	b	f	1977	Valiant Queen	Bold Ruler	
Gold Stage	dk b/br	c	1977	Stage Princess	Cornish Prince	G2
Hello Gorgeous	ch	c	1977	Bonny Jet	Jet Jewel	G1
Rare Performer	b	c	1977	Mono	Better Self	
Speedy Prospect	ch	c	1977	Rapidly	Nashua	
Stutz Blackhawk	b	c	1977	Sunny Morning	Amber Morn	
Count Prospector	ch	c	1978	Countess Nita	One Count	
Derby	ch	c	1978	Deck Stewardess	Deck Hand	
Diamond Prospect	b	c	1978	Sociable Angel	Social Climber	
Miswaki	ch	c	1978	Hopespringseternal	Buckpasser	G1
Prime Prospect	b	f	1978	Square Generation	Olden Times	
Seeker's Gold	b	f	1978	I Understand	Dr. Fager	G3
Star Valentine	ch	f	1978	Bold Linstar	Bold Monarch	
Sue Babe	b	f	1978	Sleek Dancer	Northern Dancer	
Conquistador Cielo	b	c	1979	K D Princess	Bold Commander	G1
Distinctive Pro	dk b/br	c	1979	Well Done	Distinctive	G3
Fast Gold	dk b/br	c	1979	Flack Attack	Ack Ack	G2
Furry Prospector	b	f	1979	Furry Road	Hasty Road	
Gnome's Gold	b	c	1979	Gnome Home	Noholme II	
Gold Beauty	b	f	1979	Stick to Beauty	Illustrious	G2
Main Prospect	b	f	1979	Main Pleasure	What a Pleasure	
Silver Valley	ch	f	1979	Seven Valleys	Road At Sea	

INBREEDING MALE	INBREEDING FEMALE
Teddy 5x5; Bull Dog 5x4	
Nasrullah 4x3; Nearco 5x4x4	Mumtaz Begum 5 (Nasrullah) x 5 (Sun Princess) x 4 (Nasrullah)
Native Dancer 3x4; Unbreakable 5x4; Nearco 5x4	
none	
Nasrullah 4x4	
none	
Teddy 5x5x4	
Bull Dog 5x5	
Polynesian 4x3; Case Ace 4x4	
Nasrullah 4x3; Discovery 5x4; Reigh Count 5x4	Quickly 5 (Count Fleet) x 4 (Count Speed)
Nasrullah 4x4; Discovery 5x5; Bull Dog 5x5	
none	Myrtlewood 5 (Miss Dogwood) x 4 (Crepe Myrtle)
Teddy 5x5	
Nashua 3x2	
Teddy 5x5	
Case Ace 4x4; Count Fleet 4x3; Teddy 5x5x5	
Polynesian 4x4; Nasrullah 4x5	
none	
Nasrullah 4x4; Bull Dog 5x5	
Count Fleet 4x4	
Native Dancer 3x3; Bull Dog 5x5	
Nasrullah 4x4; Discovery 5x5; Bull Dog 5x5	
Native Dancer 3x4; Unbreakable 5x4; Nearco 5x4	
Nasrullah 4x4; Discovery 5x5; Nearco 5x5x5	
Discovery 5x5; Bull Dog 5x5	
Count Fleet 4x5	
Discovery 5x4; Teddy 5x5; Nearco 5x5	
none	
Nasrullah 4x4	
Native Dancer 3x4; Nasrullah 4x4; Discovery 5x5	
Nasrullah 4x4	

HORSE	COLOR	S	YEAR	DAM	BROODMARE SIRE	STATUS
Sleek Gold	b	c	1979	Sleek Belle	Vaguely Noble	
Vain Gold	b	f	1979	Chancy Dance	Bold Reason	G3
Chic Belle	dk b/br	f	1980	Sleek Belle	Vaguely Noble	
Eillo	ch	c	1980	Barbs Dancer	Northern Dancer	G1
My Dear Lady	b	f	1980	My Dear Girl	Rough'n Tumble	
North Prospect	ch	c	1980	Lady Northcraft	Northern Dancer	
Proclaim	b	c	1980	Maybellene	Fleet Nasrullah	G3
Shawnee Creek	dk b/br	f	1980	Back Ack	Ack Ack	
Strike Gold	dk b/br	c	1980	Newchance Lady	Roi Dagobert	G3
Unreal Zeal	dk b/br	c	1980	Quick Nurse	Dr. Fager	
Widaad	dk b/br	f	1980	Attache Case	Diplomat Way	G2
Allusion	b	f	1981	Touch	Herbager	
Athenia	ch	f	1981	Bonavista	Dead Ahead	
Capture Him	b	c	1981	A Streaker	Dr. Fager	
Optimistic Lass	b	f	1981	Loveliest	Tibaldo	G2
Pleasant Prospect	ch	c	1981	Foresight Princess	Reviewer	
Procida	dk b/br	c	1981	With Distinction	Distinctive	G1
Proskona	b	f	1981	Konafa	Damascus	G2
Witwatersrand	b	f	1981	Sleek Belle	Vaguely Noble	G3
Damister	b	c	1982	Batucada	Roman Line	G2
Gold Crest	dk b/br	c	1982	Northernette	Northern Dancer	G2
Kohaylan	ch	c	1982	Delray Dancer	Chateaugay	
Raise a Prospector	b	f	1982	Hoso	Solo Landing	
Tank's Prospect	b	c	1982	Midnight Pumpkin	Pretense	G1
Varick	dk b/br	c	1982	Fleeing Partner	Fleet Nasrullah	
Boom and Bust	b	f	1983	Belle Gallante	Gallant Man	
Gold Alert	ch	c	1983	Croquis	Arts and Letters	G3
Gold Carat	b	c	1983	Gaite	Tom Rolfe	
Mogambo	ch	c	1983	Lakeville Miss	Rainy Lake	G1
Mr. Nutcracker	b	c	1983	Christmas Wishes	Northern Dancer	
Scoot	dk b/br	f	1983	Northernette	Northern Dancer	G1
Two Punch	ro	c	1983	Heavenly Cause	Grey Dawn II	

	INBREEDING MALE	INBREEDING FEMALE
	Native Dancer 3x5; Unbreakable 5x5; Nearco 5x4x5	
	none	
	Native Dancer 3x5; Unbreakable 5x5; Nearco 5x4x5	
	Native Dancer 3x4; Polynesian 4x5x4; Nearco 5x4; Bull Dog 5x5	
	Teddy 5x5; Bull Dog 5x4	
	Native Dancer 3x4; Nearco 5x4	
	Nasrullah 4x3; Count Fleet 4x4; Bull Dog 5x5x5	
	Count Fleet 4x5	
	none	
	Bull Dog 5x5	
	Nashua 4x4	
	none	
	Nearco 5x5; Bull Dog 5x5	
	Nasrullah 4x4; Bull Dog 5x5	
	Count Fleet 4x4; Reigh Count 5x5x5	
	Nasrullah 4x4; Discovery 5x5	
	Nasrullah 4x4; Bull Dog 5x5x5	
	Native Dancer 3x5; Nearco 5x5	
	Native Dancer 3x5; Unbreakable 5x5; Nearco 5x4x5	
	Teddy 5x5; Bull Dog 5x5	
	Native Dancer 3x4; Nearco 5x4	
	Native Dancer 3x3; Polynesian 4x4x4	
	Nasrullah 4x4	
	Bull Dog 5x5	
	Nasrullah 4x3; Count Fleet 4x4; Bull Dog 5x5x5	
	none	
	none	
	none	
	Case Ace 4x5; Nearco 5x4	Mumtaz Begum 5 (Nasrullah) x 5 (Sun Princess)
	Native Dancer 3x4; Nearco 5x4; Reigh Count 5x5	
	Native Dancer 3x4; Nearco 5x4	
	Nasrullah 4x4	

APPENDIX: MR. PROSPECTOR'S STAKES WINNERS

HORSE	COLOR	S	YEAR	DAM	BROODMARE SIRE	STATUS
Woodman	ch	c	1983	Playmate	Buckpasser	G1
Afleet	ch	c	1984	Polite Lady	Venetian Jester	G1
Art's Prospector	b	f	1984	No Duplicate	Arts and Letters	
At Risk	gr	f	1984	Misgivings	Cyane	G3
Chic Shirine	b	f	1984	Too Chic	Blushing Groom (Fr)	G1
Gone West	b	c	1984	Secrettame	Secretariat	G1
Gulch	b	c	1984	Jameela	Rambunctious	G1
Homebuilder	ch	c	1984	Smart Heiress	Vaguely Noble	G2
Jade Hunter	ch	c	1984	Jadana	Pharly	G1
Mining	ch	c	1984	I Pass	Buckpasser	G1
Stutz Goldrush	b	f	1984	Sunny Morning	Amber Morn	
Blue Jean Baby	b	f	1985	Jones Time Machine	Current Concept	G2
Claim	b	c	1985	Santiago Lassie	Vertex	
Classic Crown	dk b/br	f	1985	Six Crowns	Secretariat	G1
Forty Niner	ch	c	1985	File	Tom Rolfe	G1
Lake Valley	dk b/br	f	1985	La Vue	Reviewer	
Lost Lode	ch	f	1985	Past Forgetting	Messenger of Song	
Over All	ch	f	1985	Full Tigress	El Tigre Grand	G1
Ravinella	dk b/br	f	1985	Really Lucky	Northern Dancer	G1
Seeking the Gold	b	c	1985	Con Game	Buckpasser	G1
Smackover Creek	b	c	1985	Grand Luxe	Sir Ivor	
Cascading Gold	b	f	1986	Cascapedia	Chieftain	G3
Ebros	b	c	1986	Scuff	Forli	G2
Fantastic Find	dk b/br	f	1986	Blitey	Riva Ridge	G1
Gild	ch	f	1986	Veroushka	Nijinsky II	G2
Gold Seam	b	c	1986	Ballare	Nijinsky II	G3
Idabel	b	c	1986	Impetuous Gal	Briartic	G3
Inca Chief	dk b/br	c	1986	Katonka	Minnesota Mac	
Queena	b	f	1986	Too Chic	Blushing Groom (Fr)	G1
Reine Maid	b	f	1986	Rivermaid (Fr)	Riverman	

INBREEDING MALE	INBREEDING FEMALE
Nasrullah 4x4; Bull Dog 5x5	
Nasrullah 4x5; Bull Dog 5x5	
Nearco 5x5	
Native Dancer 3x4; Nearco 5x5	
Nasrullah 4x4	
Nasrullah 4x4; Discovery 5x5	
none	
Nearco 5x4	
none	
Raise a Native 2x4; Bull Dog 5x5	
Teddy 5x5	
Nasrullah 4x5x4x5; Count Fleet 4x5	
Case Ace 4x4; Nearco 5x5	
Nasrullah 4x4; Discovery 5x5; Bull Dog 5x5	
Nasrullah 4x4	
Nasrullah 4x4; Discovery 5x5	
Native Dancer 3x5; Nasrullah 4x5	
Nasrullah 4x5x5	
Native Dancer 3x4; Nearco 5x4	
Discovery 5x5; Bull Dog 5x5	
Native Dancer 3x5; Nearco 5x5	
Nasrullah 4x4; Discovery 5x5	
Nasrullah 4x4	
none	
Native Dancer 3x5; Nearco 5x5	
Native Dancer 3x5; Nasrullah 4x4; Nearco 5x5x5	
Discovery 5x5; Nearco 5x4	
Nasrullah 4x5; Bull Dog 5x5	
Nasrullah 4x4	
Nasrullah 4x4; Nearco 5x5x5	

APPENDIX: MR. PROSPECTOR'S STAKES WINNERS

HORSE	COLOR	S	YEAR	DAM	BROODMARE SIRE	STATUS
Tersa	dk b/br	f	1986	Peacefully	Jacinto	G1
Carson City	ch	c	1987	Blushing Promise	Blushing Groom (Fr)	G2
Colour Chart	b	f	1987	Rainbow Connection	Halo	G2
Golden Reef	b	f	1987	Virginia Reef (Ire)	Mill Reef	G2
Jade Robbery	dk b/br	c	1987	Number	Nijinsky II	G1
Jarraar	dk b/br	c	1987	Awaasif	Snow Knight	G3
Machiavellian	dk b/br	c	1987	Coup de Folie	Halo	G1
Manlove	b	c	1987	Thirty Flags	Hoist the Flag	
Maximilian	b	c	1987	Mystery Mood	Night Invader	G3
Rhythm	b	c	1987	Dance Number	Northern Dancer	G1
Search	dk b/br	g	1987	Loan	Buckfinder	
Arrowtown	dk b/br	c	1988	Born a Lady	Tentam	
Barkerville	b	c	1988	Euryanthe	Nijinsky II	G2
Cuddles	b	f	1988	Stellarette	Tentam	G1
Dodge	dk b/br	c	1988	Storm Star	Storm Bird	G3
Get Lucky	b	f	1988	Dance Number	Northern Dancer	G3
Lycius	ch	c	1988	Lypatia (Fr)	Lyphard	G1
Man From Eldorado	b	c	1988	Promising Girl	Youth	G2
Scan	b	c	1988	Video	Nijinsky II	G1
Sha Tha	dk b/br	f	1988	Savannah Dancer	Northern Dancer	G2
Withallprobability	b	f	1988	Sulemeif	Northern Dancer	G2
Line In The Sand	ch	c	1989	Really Lucky	Northern Dancer	G3
Lion Cavern	ch	c	1989	Secrettame	Secretariat	G2
Mineral Wells	b	c	1989	Lantana Lady	Vice Regent	G3
Portroe	dk b/br	c	1989	Killaloe	Dr. Fager	G3
Preach	b	f	1989	Narrate	Honest Pleasure	G1
Prospectors Delite	ch	f	1989	Up the Flagpole	Hoist the Flag	G1
Steinbeck	b	c	1989	Femme Elite	Northjet	G3
Educated Risk	b	f	1990	Pure Profit	Key to the Mint	G1
Elizabeth Bay	b	f	1990	Life At the Top	Seattle Slew	G3

INBREEDING MALE	INBREEDING FEMALE
Nasrullah 4x4; Discovery 5x5	
Nasrullah 4x4	
none	
Nasrullah 4x4x5; Count Fleet 4x5	
Native Dancer 3x5; Nasrullah 4x5; Nearco 5x5	
Native Dancer 3x5; Nearco 5x5	
Native Dancer 3x4	
Nasrullah 4x5	
Discovery 5x4; Bull Dog 5x5	
Native Dancer 3x4; Nasrullah 4x5; Nearco 5x4	
Native Dancer 3x4x5; Nasrullah 4x5; Nearco 5x5	
Native Dancer 3x3; Discovery 5x5x5	
Native Dancer 3x5; Count Fleet 4x4; Nearco 5x5	
Discovery 5x5; Nearco 5x5	
Native Dancer 3x5; Nasrullah 4x5; Nearco 5x5	
Native Dancer 3x4; Nasrullah 4x5; Nearco 5x4	
Native Dancer 3x5; Nasrullah 4x5; Nearco 5x5	
none	
Native Dancer 3x5; Nearco 5x5	
Native Dancer 3x4; Nearco 5x4	
Native Dancer 3x4; Nasrullah 4x5; Nearco 5x4; Bull Dog 5x5	
Native Dancer 3x4; Nearco 5x4	
Nasrullah 4x4; Discovery 5x5	
Native Dancer 3x5; Nearco 5x5	
Bull Dog 5x5	
Nasrullah 4x5	
Nasrullah 4x5	
none	
Nasrullah 4x4; Discovery 5x5	
none	

APPENDIX: MR. PROSPECTOR'S STAKES WINNERS

HORSE	COLOR	S	YEAR	DAM	BROODMARE SIRE	STATUS
Faltaat	b	c	1990	Epitome	Summing	
Fort Chaffee	ch	c	1990	Till Eternity	Nijinsky II	
Kingmambo	b	c	1990	Miesque	Nureyev	G1
Miner's Mark	b	c	1990	Personal Ensign	Private Account	G1
Namaqualand	dk b/br	c	1990	Courtly Dee	Storm Bird	G3
Placerville	b	c	1990	Classy Cathy	Private Account	G2
Tenga	dk b/br	f	1990	Royal Strait Flush	Seattle Slew	
Coup de Genie	b	f	1991	Coup de Folie	Halo	G1
Dance With Grace	b	f	1991	Dancing Tribute	Nureyev	
Distant View	b	c	1991	Seven Springs	Irish River (Fr)	G1
Numerous	b	c	1991	Number	Nijinsky II	G3
Syourinomegami	dk b/br	f	1991	Cinegita	Secretariat	G3
Always a Rainbow	ch	c	1992	Rainbow Connection	Halo	
Chequer	dk b/br	c	1992	Number	Nijinsky II	G3
Faygo	dk b/br	c	1992	Shocker T.	Nodouble	
Kayrawan	b	c	1992	Muhbubh	Blushing Groom (Fr)	G2
Macoumba	b	f	1992	Maximova (Fr)	Green Dancer	G1
Miesque's Son	dk b/br	c	1992	Miesque	Nureyev	G3
Red Carnival	b	f	1992	Seaside Attraction	Seattle Slew	G3
Shake Hand	b	f	1992	Dancing Tribute	Nureyev	G2
Smart Strike	b	c	1992	Classy 'n Smart	Smarten	G1
Tereshkova	b	f	1992	Lypatia (Fr)	Lyphard	G3
Canyon Creek (Ire)	b	c	1993	River Memories	Riverman	
Cat's Career	b	c	1993	Comical Cat	Exceller	G3
Dance Sequence	ch	f	1993	Dancing Tribute	Nureyev	G2
Delta Love	dk b/br	f	1993	Love's Exchange	Key to the Mint	
Gold Token	b	c	1993	Connie's Gift	Nijinsky II	
Golden Attraction	b	f	1993	Seaside Attraction	Seattle Slew	G1
Race Artist	b	f	1993	So Divine	Staff Writer	G3
Ta Rib	ch	f	1993	Madame Secretary	Secretariat	G1
Wall Street	ch	c	1993	Wajd	Northern Dancer	G3

	INBREEDING MALE	INBREEDING FEMALE
	Nashua 3x5	
	Native Dancer 3x5; Nasrullah 4x5; Nearco 5x5	
	Native Dancer 3x5; Nearco 5x5	
	none	
	Native Dancer 3x5; Nasrullah 4x4; Nearco 5x5x5	
	none	
	Nasrullah 4x5	
	Native Dancer 3x4	
	Native Dancer 3x5; Nearco 5x5	
	Nasrullah 4x5	
	Native Dancer 3x5; Nasrullah 4x5; Nearco 5x5	
	Nasrullah 4x4; Discovery 5x5	
	none	
	Native Dancer 3x5; Nasrullah 4x5; Nearco 5x5	
	Nashua 3x4	
	Nasrullah 4x4	
	none	
	Native Dancer 3x5; Nearco 5x5	
	none	
	Native Dancer 3x5; Nearco 5x5	
	Nasrullah 4x5	
	Native Dancer 3x5; Nasrullah 4x5; Nearco 5x5	
	Nasrullah 4x4; Nearco 5x5x5	
	Native Dancer 3x5; Nasrullah 4x5; Nearco 5x5x5	
	Native Dancer 3x5; Nearco 5x5	
	Nasrullah 4x5	
	Native Dancer 3x5; Nasrullah 4x5; Nearco 5x5	
	none	
	Native Dancer 3x5; Nearco 5x5	
	Nasrullah 4x4; Discovery 5x5	
	Native Dancer 3x4; Nearco 5x4x5	

HORSE	COLOR	S	YEAR	DAM	BROODMARE SIRE	STATUS
Alpha Plus	dk b/br	c	1994	Danzante	Danzig	
Classy Prospector	ch	c	1994	Fantastic Look	Green Dancer	
Family Calling	b	c	1994	Sense of Unity	Northern Dancer	
Sahm	dk b/br	c	1994	Salsabil	Sadler's Wells	G2
Sarayir	b	f	1994	Height of Fashion (GB)	Bustino	
Siyadah	ch	f	1994	Roseate Tern (GB)	Blakeney	
Chester House	dk b/br	c	1995	Toussaud	El Gran Senor	G1
Diamond	ch	c	1995	Pure Profit	Key to the Mint	
Ikhteyaar	dk b/br	f	1995	Linda's Magic	Far North	
Souvenir Copy	dk b/br	c	1995	Dancing Tribute	Nureyev	G2
Strategic Mission	dk b/br	c	1995	Sultry Sun	Buckfinder	G3
Cape Canaveral	dk b/br	c	1996	Seaside Attraction	Seattle Slew	G3
Insinuate	ch	f	1996	All At Sea	Riverman	
Fusaichi Pegasus	b	c	1997	Angel Fever	Danzig	G1
Moon Driver	dk b/br	f	1997	East of the Moon	Private Account	G3
Ocean of Wisdom	b	c	1997	Coup de Folie	Halo	G3
Scatter the Gold	dk b/br	c	1997	Dance Smartly	Danzig	
Strike Smartly	b	c	1997	Classy 'n Smart	Smarten	G2
Traditionally	ch	c	1997	Personal Ensign	Private Account	G1
Aldebaran	b	c	1998	Chimes of Freedom	Private Account	G1
Dancethruthedawn	dk b/br	f	1998	Dance Smartly	Danzig	G1
E Dubai	b	c	1998	Words of War	Lord At War (Arg)	G2
Full of Wonder	dk b/br	c	1998	Classy 'n Smart	Smarten	G1
Pyrus	dk b/br	c	1998	Most Precious	Nureyev	G2
Serena's Tune	b	f	1998	Serena's Song	Rahy	
Golden Sonata	dk b/br	f	1999	Elissa Beethoven (GB)	Royal Academy	G3
Subsidy	b	g	2000	Foreign Aid	Danzig	G3

INBREEDING MALE	INBREEDING FEMALE
Native Dancer 3x5x4; Polynesian 4x5x5; Nasrullah 4x5; Count Fleet 4x5; Nearco 5x5	
none	
Native Dancer 3x4; Nearco 5x4	
Native Dancer 3x5; Nearco 5x5	
none	
none	
Native Dancer 3x5; Nearco 5x5	
Nasrullah 4x4; Discovery 5x5	
Native Dancer 3x5; Nasrullah 4x5; Nearco 5x5	
Native Dancer 3x5; Nearco 5x5	
Native Dancer 3x4	
none	
Nasrullah 4x4	
Native Dancer 3x5; Nearco 5x5	
none	
Native Dancer 3x4	
Native Dancer 3x5; Nearco 5x5	
Nasrullah 4x5	
none	
none	
Native Dancer 3x5; Nearco 5x5	
Nasrullah 4x5	
Nasrullah 4x5	
Native Dancer 3x5; Nearco 5x5	
Native Dancer 3x5; Nasrullah 4x5	
none	
Native Dancer 3x5; Nasrullah 4x5; Nearco 5x5	

HORSE	COLOR	SEX	YEAR	SIRE	DAM	STATUS
True and Blue	b	g	1985	Hurry Up Blue	A Real Native	
Bountiful Native	b	f	1988	Pirate's Bounty	A Real Native	G3
Forty Nine Deeds	b	g	1999	Alydeed	Abrade	
Storm Allied	b	g	2004	Stormy Atlantic	Aliata	G3
Bag	ch	c	1989	Devil's Bag	Allusion	
Intidab	dk b/br	c	1993	Phone Trick	Alqwani	G2
Lahan (GB)	b	f	1997	Unfuwain	Amanah	G1
No Reason (Jpn)	b	c	1999	Brian's Time	Ambrosine	G1
Great Journey (Jpn)	dk b/br	c	2001	Sunday Silence	Ambrosine	G3
Victory Piper	ch	c	1987	Nijinsky II	Arisen	G2
Athenia Green (GB)	ch	g	1986	Green Dancer	Athenia	G3
Suteki Shinsukekun	b	c	2003	Danzig	Autumn Moon	G3
Salmon Ladder	b	c	1992	Bering (GB)	Ballerina Princess	G3
Areed Al Ola	b	c	1993	Chief's Crown	Ballerina Princess	
Capote's Prospect	b	c	1994	Capote	Ballerina Princess	
Pico Teneriffe	b	f	1996	Red Ransom	Ballerina Princess	G3
Natural Nine (Jpn)	dk b/br	c	2000	Tokai Teio (Jpn)	Bazilia	
Away	ch	f	1997	Dixieland Band	Be a Prospector	
Rich Find	b	f	2001	Exploit	Be a Prospector	
Tenshino Kiseki (Jpn)	ch	f	1998	Fuji Kiseki (Jpn)	Be Bop a Lu	G3
Big Gold (Jpn)	b	c	1998	Brian's Time	Beautiful Gold	G3
Hopedale O.	dk b/br	c	1984	For The Moment	Beautiful Prospect	
Really Quick	ch	f	1988	In Reality	Beautiful Prospect	G2
Crimson Road	ch	f	1993	Strawberry Road (Aus)	Bejat	
Glick	dk b/br	c	1996	Theatrical (Ire)	Bejat	G3

INBREEDING MALE	INBREEDING FEMALE
Nasrullah 5x5	
Nashua 4x4	
Raise a Native 4x3	Continue 5 (Continuation) x 3 (File)
none	Rough Shod II 5 (Moccasin) x 5 (Gambetta)
Herbager 3x3; Mahmoud 5x5x5	
Native Dancer 5x4	
Northern Dancer 2x5; Native Dancer 4x4	
Nashua 4x4; Nasrullah 5x5x5	
none	
Native Dancer 4x4	
Native Dancer 5x4	
Northern Dancer2x4; Native Dancer 4x4; Hyperion 5x5	
Northern Dancer 4x3; Naative Dancer 5x4x5	Almahmoud 4 (Bubbling Beauty) x 5 (Natalma)
Northern Dancer 3x3; Native Dancer 5x4x5; Nasrullah 5x5; Princequillo 5x5	
Nasrullah 4x5x5; Nearco 5x5	
Nashua 4x4; Nearctic 4x4	
Northern Dancer 4x5	
Native Dancer 4x4x5	
none	
none	
Nashua 4x4x5	
Nasrullah 4x5	
Bull Dog 5x5	
Nasrullah 5x5x5	
Native Dancer 5x4	

APPENDIX: MR. PROSPECTOR'S STAKES WINNERS AS BROODMARE SIRE

HORSE	COLOR	SEX	YEAR	SIRE	DAM	STATUS
My Vet Peter	ch	c	1987	North Pole	Bernice of Winloc	
Blazing Rate	ch	c	2003	Exchange Rate	Blazing Alarmiss	
Brave Tin Soldier	b	c	2004	Storm Cat	Bless	
Denim Yenem	ch	c	1992	Ogygian	Blue Jean Baby	
Tokai Wild (Jpn)	dk b/br	c	2002	Sunday Silence	Bob's Dilemma	G2
Land Boom	b	c	1994	Dixieland Band	Boom and Bust	
Dancehall	b	c	1986	Assert (Ire)	Cancan Madame	G1
Sabana Perdida (Ire)	b	f	2003	Cape Cross (Ire)	Capriola	
Tara Roma	b	f	1990	Lyphard	Chic Shirine	G2
Waldoboro	dk b/br	c	1991	Lyphard	Chic Shirine	G2
Chimes Band	b	f	1988	Dixieland Band	Chimes	G2
Lady Dixie	b	f	1995	Dixieland Band	Chimes	
Christina Czarina	b	f	1988	Czaravich	Christines Pixie	
Event of the Year	dk b/br	c	1995	Seattle Slew	Classic Event	G2
Eightsome	ch	c	1987	Sharpen Up (GB)	Clever Dancer	
Latin American	b	c	1988	Riverman	Clever Dancer	G1
Chirico	b	c	1993	Danzig	Colour Chart	
Equerry	dk b/br	c	1998	St. Jovite	Colour Chart	G3
Tempera	dk b/br	f	1999	A.P. Indy	Colour Chart	G1
Ecole d'Art	b	c	2001	Theatrical (Ire)	Colour Chart	
Tap Routine	ch	f	1989	Fred Astaire	Composing	
Steaming Home	b	f	1999	Salt Lake	County Fair	
Snake Mountain	ch	g	1998	A.P. Indy	Coup de Genie	G3
Glia	b	f	1999	A.P. Indy	Coup de Genie	
Loving Kindness	dk b/br	f	2000	Seattle Slew	Coup de Genie	G3
Denebola	dk b/br	f	2001	Storm Cat	Coup de Genie	G1

164

INBREEDING MALE	INBREEDING FEMALE
Native Dancer 4x4	
Mr. Prospector 4x2; Native Dancer 5x4	
Northern Dancer 3x4; Native Dancer 5x4; Nasrullah 5x5	
none	0
Turn-to 4x4	
Native Dancer 4x4; Mahmoud 5x5	
Native Dancer 5x5x4; Sicambre 5x5	
Sir Gaylord 5x4	
Native Dancer 4x4	
Native Dancer 4x4	
Native Dancer 4x4; Mahmoud 5x5	
Native Dancer 4x4; Mahmoud 5x5	
Native Dancer 5x4; Hyperion 5x5	
Nasrullah 5x5x5; Polynesian 5x5	
Native Dancer 3x4x5	
Nasrullah 3x5; Nearco 4x5; Princequillo 4x5; Count Fleet 5x5	
Native Dancer 4x4	Almahmoud 4 (Natalma) x 5 (Cosmah)
none	
Hail to Reason 5x4; Nasrullah 5x5	
Hail to Reason 4x4; Native Dancer 5x4	Almahmoud 5 (Natalma) x 5 (Cosmah)
Northern Dancer 3x3; Native Dancer 5x4x5	
none	
Hail to Reason 5x4; Nasrullah 5x5	
Hail to Reason 5x4; Nasrullah 5x5	
Hail to Reason 4x4; Nasrullah 5x5x5; Polynesian 5x5	
Native Dancer 5x4x5Nasrullah 5x5	Natalma 4 (Northern Dancer) x 4 (Raise the Standard); Almahmoud 5 (Natalma) x 5 (Cosmah) x5 (Natalma)

APPENDIX: MR. PROSPECTOR'S STAKES WINNERS AS BROODMARE SIRE

HORSE	COLOR	SEX	YEAR	SIRE	DAM	STATUS
Clear Destiny	ch	f	1999	Deputy Minister	Crystal Shard	
Katz Me If You Can	dk b/br	f	1997	Storm Cat	Cuddles	G2
Country Romance	dk b/br	f	2000	Saint Ballado	Cuddles	
Catienus	dk b/br	c	1994	Storm Cat	Diamond City	
Wafayt (Ire)	b	c	1991	Danehill	Diamond Field	
New Frontier (Ire)	b	c	1994	Sadler's Wells	Diamond Field	G3
Brunswick	b	c	1989	Private Account	Doff	G1
Season's Greetings (Ire)	dk b/br	f	1998	Ezzoud (Ire)	Dream Season	
Strategy	b	f	2001	A.P. Indy	Educated Risk	
Bayeux	b	g	2001	Red Ransom	Elizabeth Bay	G3
Boston Common	b	g	1999	Boston Harbor	Especially	G2
Storm Surge	dk b/br	c	2002	Storm Cat	Especially	G3
Faiza (Aus)	b	f	1998	Danehill	Excellent Prospect	G3
Sir Pinder	dk b/br	c	1989	Baldski	Fabulous Prospect	G3
Casperoo	gr	c	1992	Silver Buck	Fabulous Prospect	
Glorious Reason	dk b/br	f	1981	Hall of Reason	Fager's Glory	
Glory Forever	gr	c	1984	Forever Casting	Fager's Glory	G3
Finder's Fee	dk b/br	f	1997	Storm Cat	Fantastic Find	G1
Aramram	b	c	1999	Danzig	Fleawnah	
Discover	b	c	1988	Cox's Ridge	Find	G3
Calistay	b	f	1988	Spend a Buck	Fine Prospect	
Fighting K	b	g	1989	Island Whirl	Fine Prospect	
Hayworth (Brz)	b	f	1996	Minstrel Glory	Flash Prancer	
Saintly Prospector	ch	c	1990	Sunny's Halo	Foolish Gold	G3
Furioso (Jpn)	ch	f	2004	Brian's Time	Fursa	G1
Love Conquers All	ch	f	1988	Romeo	Ganadora	
Geri	ch	c	1992	Theatrical (Ire)	Garimpeiro	G1
Clure	ch	c	1993	Theatrical (Ire)	Garimpeiro	
Reactress	ch	f	1983	Sharpen Up (GB)	Geiger Countess	

INBREEDING MALE	INBREEDING FEMALE
Northern Dancer 3x3; Native Dancer 5x4x5; Polynesian 5x5	
Nearctic 4x5; Native Dancer 5x4; Nasrullah 5x5	
Cohoes 4x5	
Native Dancer 5x4; Nasrullah 5x5	
Nearco 5x5; Native Dancer 5x5x4	
Nearco 4x5; Native Dancer 4x4;	Rough Shod II 5 (Thong) x 5 (Gambetta)
War Admiral 5x5; Nasrullah 5x5x5	
Nasrullah 5x5	
Bold Ruler 5x4x4; Nasrullah 5x5x5; Princequillo 5x5	
Nashua 4x4	
Nasrullah 5x5	
Native Dancer 5x4; Nasrullah 5x5	
Northern Dancer 3x5; Buckpasser 4x4; Native Dancer 5x5x4	
Nasrullah 4x5x5; Native Dancer 5x4;	
none	
Nasrullah 5x5	
none	
Native Dancer 5x4; Nasrullah 5x5	
Native Dancer 4x4	
none	
Nasrullah 5x5	
Native Dancer 4x4	
Native Dancer 5x4; Polynesian 5x5; Nasrullah 5x5x5	
Sun Again 5x5; Count Fleet 5x5	
Hail to Reason 3x5; Nashua 4x4	
Nasrullah 4x5	
Northern Dancer 3x4; Native Dancer 5x4	
Northern Dancer 3x4; Native Dancer 5x4	
Native Dancer 3x4x4	

HORSE	COLOR	SEX	YEAR	SIRE	DAM	STATUS
Diamond Knight	dk b/br	c	1984	Native Charger	Gem in the Rough	
Accelerator	dk b/br	c	1994	A.P. Indy	Get Lucky	G3
Daydreaming	b	f	2001	A.P. Indy	Get Lucky	G2
Harborage	dk b/br	c	2003	Monarchos	Get Lucky	
Poker Brad	b	g	1998	Go for Gin	Gild	
Valentine Dancer	b	f	2000	In Excess (Ire)	Gilded Dancer	
Sallysay	dk b/br	f	1989	Oh Say	Glittering Legend	G3
Spring Meadow	ch	f	1999	Meadowlake	Go for It Lady	G3
Maplejinsky	b	f	1985	Nijinsky II	Gold Beauty	G1
Dayjur	dk b/br	c	1987	Danzig	Gold Beauty	G1
Shotgun	b	c	1988	Pancho Villa	Gold Heist	
Heister	b	f	1989	Air Forbes Won	Gold Heist	
Avie's Shadow	dk b/br	f	1990	Lord Avie	Gold Shadow	
Nastassja	b	f	1993	Seattle Dancer	Gold Shadow	
Keys to the Heart	dk b/br	f	1999	Wild Again	Gold Shadow	G3
Golden Gale	b	f	1993	Summer Squall	Gold Whirl	G2
Gold Trader	dk b/br	c	1998	Storm Cat	Golden Attrac-tion	
Cheerful Smile (Jpn)	dk b/br	f	2000	Sunday Silence	Golden Colors	G3
Naheef (Ire)	b	g	1999	Marju (Ire)	Golden Digger	G3
Lotus Pool	b	c	1987	Spectacular Bid	Golden Petal	G3
October Gold	b	c	1989	Ogygian	Golden Petal	
Cherokee Reef	b	f	1994	Cherokee Colony	Golden Reef	
Chanting	b	f	2004	Danehill	Golden Reef	
Kyowa Happiness (Jpn)	b	f	2001	Oath (Ire)	Good Looks	G3
Straw Hat	dk b/br	c	2002	Dixie Union	Grass Skirt	
Waquaas (GB)	b	g	1996	Green Desert	Hamaya	G3
Lord Pergrine	b	c	1984	Regal and Royal	Hawkeye's Girl	
Stalker	dk b/br	c	1987	Stalwart	Hawkeye's Girl	
Cash Road	b	g	1988	Smile	Hawkeye's Girl	

INBREEDING MALE	INBREEDING FEMALE
Native Dancer 2x4x4	
Buckpasser 4x4; Nasrullah 5x5	Glamour 5 (Poker) x 5 (Intriguing)
Buckpasser 4x4; Nasrullah 5x5	Gamour 5 (Poker) x 5 (Intriguing)
Northern Dancer 4x3; Buckpasser 5x4	
Nasrullah 5x5; Polynesian 5x5	
none	
none	
Raise a Native 3x3; Native Dancer 4x4x5	
Native Dancer 4x4	
Native Dancer 4x4	
Nasrullah 4x5x4	
Nasrullah 5x5x4	
none	
Native Dancer 5x4; Nasrullah 5x5	
Native Dancer 4x4	
Nearco 5x5; Native Dancer 5x4; Nasrullah 5x5x5	
Native Dancer 5x4; Nasrullah 5x5	
none	
Round Table 4x4; Buckpasser 5x3	
Nasrullah 4x5	
War Admiral 5x5	
none	
Native Dancer 5x5x4	
Nearctic 4x5; Native Dancer 5x4	
Northern Dancer 3x4; Mr. Prospector 4x2; Native Dancer 5x4	
Never Bend 4x4; Native Dancer 5x4; Nasrullah 5x5x5	
Native Dancer 3x4	
Narulllah 5x5	
Nasrullah 5x5; Polynesian 5x5	

HORSE	COLOR	SEX	YEAR	SIRE	DAM	STATUS
Plano Pleasure	b	c	1990	Dixieland Band	Headin' West	
Summerly	ch	f	2002	Summer Squall	Here I Go	G1
Jazz Club	b	c	1995	Dixieland Band	Hidden Garden	G3
Philanthropist	ch	c	2001	Kris S.	Hidden Reserve	G3
Defer	b	c	2002	Danzig	Hidden Reserve	G3
Quintons Gold Rush	ch	c	2001	Wild Rush	Hollywood Gold	G2
Apollo Cat	dk b/br	f	1997	Storm Cat	Hopesprings-forever	
Belle of Perintown	b	f	2000	Dehere	Hot Match	G2
Patsyprospect	b	c	1991	Personal Flag	Im a Star Prospect	
Terreavigne	ch	f	1995	Belong to Me	Im a Star Prospect	
Stronghold (GB)	b	c	2002	Danehill	Insinuate	
Iktitaf (Ire)	b	c	2001	Alhaarth (Ire)	Istibshar	
Air Dancer	b	f	1983	Northern Dancer	It's in the Air	
Bitooh (GB)	b	f	1985	Seattle Slew	It's in theAir	G2
Monaassabaat	ch	f	1991	Zilzal	I'ts in the Air	
Green Light	b	f	1994	Sheikh Albadou (GB)	Jade Jewel	
Jade Quest (Ire)	ch	c	2000	Rainbow Quest	Jade Jewel	
Iflookscouldkill (Ind)	b	g	1998	Don't Forget Me	Keep Looking	G2
Four Corners	b	g	1999	Salt Lake	Kettle Ridge	
Love n' Kiss S.	dk b/br	f	1998	Kris S.	Key to My Heart	G3
Judge Connelly	b	c	1990	Hero's Honor	Kind Prospect	
Soldera	b	f	2000	Polish Numbers	La Pepite	
Batuka	dk b/br	f	1996	Bates Motel	Lady Is a Tramp (Ire)	G1
Copper Carnival (GB)	ch	c	1996	Petit Loup	Lailati	
Lailani (GB)	b	f	1998	Unfuwain	Lailati	G1
Prussian Blue	b	c	1992	Polish Navy	Lit'l Rose	G2
Handsome Hunk	ch	c	1999	Hennessy	Lit'l Rose	

INBREEDING MALE	INBREEDING FEMALE
Native Dancer 4x4; Traffic Judge 4x4	
Native Dancer 5x4; Nasrullah 5x5	
Native Dancer 4x4	
Princequillo 3x5; Nashua 4x4	
Native Dancer 4x4; Mahmoud 5x5	
Native Dancer 5x4	
Native Dancer 5x4; Nasrullah 5x5x5; Princequillo 5x4	
Northern Dancer 4x4; Nasrullah 5x5	
Tom Fool 5x5	
Raise a Native 4x3; Native Dancer 5x5x4	
Native Dancer 5x5x4	
Northern Dancer 3x4; Native Dancer 5x4; Never Bend 5x4	
Nearco 3x5x5; Native Dancer 3x4	
Nasrullah 5x5x5x4; Polynesian 5x5	
Nearco 5x5x5; Native Dancer 5x4	
Northern Dancer 4x5	
Nasrullah 4x5; Raise a Native 4x3	
Tudor Minstrel 5x5	
none	
Nashua 4x4	
Nearco 4x5; Native Dancer 4x4;	
Northern Dancer 3x3; Native Dancer 5x4x5; Nasrullah 5x5	
Nasrullah 5x5; Count Fleet 5x5	
Native Dancer 5x4	
Native Dancer 4x4	
Native Dancer 5x4	
none	

HORSE	COLOR	SEX	YEAR	SIRE	DAM	STATUS
Macau Prospect (Ven)	dk b/br	c	2001	Macau	Lively Prospect	
Morocoto (Ven)	b	c	2002	Macau	Lively Prospect	
Find the Treasure	dk b/br	c	1993	Housebuster	Lost Lode	
Diplomatic Bag	b	c	2000	Devil's Bag	Louis d'Or	G2
Dancing Jon	dk b/br	g	1988	Gate Dancer	Love From Mom	G3
Fight for Love	dk b/br	g	1990	Fit to Fight	Love From Mom	G3
Love That Jazz	b	f	1994	Dixieland Band	Love From Mom	G3
Sea of Secrets	b	c	1995	Storm Cat	Love From Mom	G2
Scat Daddy		c	2004	Johannesburg	Love Style	G2
Lord Joe	b	g	1988	Lord At War (Arg)	Madame Gold	G3
Gold Bet	dk b/br	g	1991	Lord At War (Arg)	Madame Gold	
Mr. Doubledown	b	g	1994	Alwuhush	Madame Gold	G3
Mighty	dk b/br	c	1997	Lord At War (Arg)	Madame Gold	G2
Irish Osprey	dk b/br	g	2003	Arch	Maiden Voyage	
Main Slew	dk b/br	f	1992	Slew o' Gold	Main Prospect	
Nid d'Abeilles (Ire)	b	c	2002	Green Desert	Massarossa (GB)	
Belmont Beach (Jpn)	b	f	1998	Adjudicating	Matisse	G3
Star of Broadway	dk b/br	f	1995	Broad Brush	Meteor Miner	G2
Scudan	ch	c	1989	Ogygian	Michelky	
Creaseinherjeans	dk b/br	f	1997	Pleasant Tap	Middle Prospect	
Look Honey (Ire)	b	c	2000	Sadler's Wells	Middle Prospect	G2
Academy Award	ch	c	1986	Secretariat	Mine Only	G2
Good Mood	ch	f	1989	Devil's Bag	Mine Only	G3
Statuette	b	f	1990	Pancho Villa	Mine Only	G3
Survivalist	dk b/br	c	2002	Danzig	Miner's Game	G3
Film Maker	dk b/br	f	2000	Dynaformer	Miss Du Bois	G1
Hollywood Wildcat	dk b/br	f	1990	Kris S.	Miss Wildcatter	G1
Coast Line	b	g	2001	Boston Harbor	Mission Pass	
Rumplestiltskin (Ire)	b	f	2003	Danehill	Monevassia	G1

INBREEDING MALE	INBREEDING FEMALE
none	
none	
Nasrullah 5x5	
Turn-to 4x5; Swaps 5x5	
Native Dancer 5x4; Nasrullah 5x5x5	
Nasrullah 4x5x5; Count Fleet 4x5; Case Ace 5x5	
Native Dancer 4x4	
Native Dancer 5x4; Nasrullah 5x5x5	
Mr. Prospector 4x2; Northern Dancer 5x4	
none	
none	
Nearco 5x5; Native Dancer 5x4; Nasrullah 5x5x4	
none	
Northern Dancer 4x5; Nashua 5x4; Raise a Native 5x3; Never Bend 5x4	
Bold Ruler 5x4	
Northern Dancer 3x4; Native Dancer 5x4; Nasrullah 5x5	
Nearco 5x5; Native Dancer 5x4; Nasrullah 5x5x4	
none	
none	
Stage Door Johnny 3x3; Nasrullah 5x5; Polynesian 5x5	
Native Dancer 4x4	
Nasrullah 3x5	
none	
Nasrullah 4x5	
Native Dancer 4x4	
Nashua 4x4	
Nashua 4x4	
Northern Dancer 4x4; Nasrullah 5x5	
Northern Dancer 3x4; Native Dancer 5x5x4	Natalma 4 (Northern Dancer) x 4 (Spring Adieu) x 5 (Northern Dancer)

HORSE	COLOR	SEX	YEAR	SIRE	DAM	STATUS
Fasliyev	b	c	1997	Nureyev	Mr. P's Princess	G1
Kamarinskaya	dk b/br	f	2003	Storm Cat	Mr. P's Princess	G3
Thunderdome	dk b/br	f	1983	Lyphard	Mr. P.'s Girl	
Nisswa	ch	c	1985	Irish River (Fr)	My Dear Lady	
My Dear Frances	ch	f	1986	Caro (Ire)	My Dear Lady	
Albarahin	b	c	1995	Silver Hawk	My Dear Lady	G2
Flower Forest	dk b/br	f	2000	Kris S.	Nortena	
Bluebell Dancer	b	f	1994	Sovereign Dancer	O My Darling	
Shy Contessa	b	f	1980	Cutlass	O. Jackie	
Jacque l'Heureux	b	c	1982	L'Heureux	O. Jackie	
Semarang (GB)	b	c	2002	Hernando (Fr)	Obscura	
Viva La Paz (Ven)	b	f	1991	Sauce Boat	Odessa	G2
First Final	dk b/br	f	1997	Hadif	On Final	
Aragorn (Ire)	ch	c	2002	Giant's Causeway	Onaga	G1
Bet Twice Princess	b	f	1993	Bet Twice	One Tough Lady	
Golden Opinion	ch	f	1986	Slew o' Gold	Optimistic Lass	G1
Hustler	b	c	1995	Strawberry Road (Aus)	Over All	
For All We Know	ch	f	2002	Stephen Got Even	Over All	G2
Carpan (Arg)	dk b/br	c	1996	Careafolie (Ire)	Pan D'Ore	G2
Buff	b	g	1995	Pleasant Tap	Pedicure	
Second Performance	dk b/br	c	2001	Theatrical (Ire)	Pedicure	
Pentagonal	dk b/br	c	1997	Dynaformer	Pent	
Tokio Perfect	dk b/br	c	1995	Rahy	Perfect Probe	G3
Perfect Cat	b	c	1997	Tabasco Cat	Perfect Probe	G3
Key Timing	b	g	1987	Mr. Leader	Platinum Princess	
Wish Dream	ch	c	1989	Lyphard's Wish (Fr)	Platinum Princess	G3
Hookipa Wave (Jpn)	dk b/br	c	2001	Carnegie (Ire)	Platinum Wave	G2
Congrats	b	c	2000	A.P. Indy	Praise	G2
Pulpit	b	c	1994	A.P. Indy	Preach	G2
True Flare	b	f	1993	Capote	Proflare	G2

INBREEDING MALE	INBREEDING FEMALE
Nearco 4x5; Native Dancer 4x4; Nasrullah 5x5x4	
Nearco 5x5; Native Dancer 5x4; Nasrullah 5x5x4	
Native Dancer 4x4x3	
Nasrullah 4x5	
Nasrullah 4x5; War Relic 5x4	
Nashua 4x 4	
Nashua 4x4	
Native Dancer 4x4; Nasrullah 4x5; Hyperion 5x5	
none	
none	
Mr. Prospector 4x2; Northern Dancer 4x5x4	
none	
Native Dancer 5x4; Nasrullah 5x5x5	
Northern Dancer 4x3	
Nasrullah 5x5x5x5	
none	
Nasrullah 5x5	
Poker 5x4; Turn-to 5x5	
none	
Nasrullah 5x5; Polynesian 5x5	
Northern Dancer 3x4; Native Dancer 5x4	
Nashua 4x4	
Nasrullah 4x5	
Northern Dancer 4x4; Polynesian 5x5	
Royal Charger 4x5	
Native Dancer 5x4	
Native Dancer 5x4; Nasrullah 5x5	
Hail to Reason 5x5; Nasrullah 5x5	
Bold Ruler 5x4x5; Nsrullah 5x5; Princequillo 5x5	
Nasrullah 4x5x5	

HORSE	COLOR	SEX	YEAR	SIRE	DAM	STATUS
River Flare	ch	f	1995	Riverman	Proflare	
Apple of Kent	dk b/br	f	1996	Kris S.	Proflare	G2
Capital Secret	dk b/br	g	1997	Capote	Proflare	G3
War Zone	b	c	1999	Danzig	Proflare	G3
Set Alight	b	c	2003	Hennessy	Proflare	G3
Deposit Ticket	b	c	1988	Northern Baby	Propositioning	G1
Calista (GB)	b	f	1998	Caerleon	Proskona	G2
Lermontov	dk b/br	g	1997	Alleged	Prospect Dalia	G3
Famous Digger	b	f	1994	Quest for Fame (GB)	Prospect Digger	G1
Way West (Aus)	b	c	2001	Danehill	Prospect Fever	G3
Primary	b	c	2003	Giant's Causeway	Prospective	G3
Deputy Shaw	ch	g	1985	Deputy Minister	Prospective Lady	
Prost Line	ch	c	1989	Mt. Livermore	Prospective Lady	G3
Political Wife	b	f	1998	Dehere	Prospective Wife	
Superb Prospect	dk b/br	f	1984	Superbity	Prospector's Charm	
Gold Digs	b	g	1987	Regal and Royal	Prospector's Charm	
Dowsing	dk b/br	c	1984	Riverman	Prospector's Fire	G1
Fire the Groom	dk b/br	f	1987	Blushing Groom (Fr)	Prospector's Fire	G1
Faradawn	b	f	1987	Regal and Royal	Prospector's First	
Southern Rhythm	ch	c	1991	Dixieland Band	Prospector's Queen	G2
Totostar (GB)	b	f	1992	Mtoto (GB)	Prospector's Star	
La Gandilie (Fr)	gr/ro	f	1997	Highest Honor (Fr)	Prospector's Star	
Tomisue's Delight	ch	f	1994	A.P. Indy	Prospectors Delite	G1
Delta Music	dk b/br	f	1995	Dixieland Band	Prospectors Delite	
Monashee Mountain	b	c	1997	Danzig	Prospectors Delite	G3

INBREEDING MALE	INBREEDING FEMALE
Nasrullah 3x5; Count Fleet 5x5	
Nashua 4x4	
Nasrullah 4x5x5	
Native Dancer 4x4	
Tom Fool 5x4	
Native Dancer 4x4	
Northern Dancer 3x4; Native Dancer 5x4	
Count Fleet 5x5	
Nasrullah 5x5; Vandale 5x5; Raise a Native 5x3	
Northern Dancer 3x4; Native Dancer 5x5x4	Natalma 4 (Northern Dancer) x 4 (Spring Adieu) x 5 (Northern Dancer)
none	
Native Dancer 5x4; Polynesian 5x5	
Nasrullah 4x5	
Nasrullah 5x5; Princequillo 5x5	
none	
Native Dancer 3x4; Nearco 4x5	
Nasrullah 3x5; Djebel 5x5; Count Fleet 5x5	
Nasrullah 5x5	
Vaguely Noble 2x3; Native Dancer 3x4	
Native Dancer 4x4; Mahmoud 5x5	
none	
Nasrullah 5x5x5	
Nasrullah 5x5	
Native Dancer 4x4	
Native Dancer 4x4	

HORSE	COLOR	SEX	YEAR	SIRE	DAM	STATUS
Rock Slide	b	c	1998	A.P. Indy	Prospectors Delite	
Mineshaft	dk b/br	c	1999	A.P. Indy	Prospectors Delite	G1
Piranesi	dk b/br	f	1988	Sportin' Life	Prospectress	
Spin Control	dk b/br	f	2000	A.P. Indy	Prospinsky	
Brahms	dk b/br	c	1997	Danzig	Queena	G1
La Reina	ch	f	2001	A.P. Indy	Queena	G3
Cherokee Girl	dk b/br	f	1999	Cherokee Run	Race Artist	
Admiralofthefleet	dk b/br	c	2004	Danehill	Rafina	G2
Fairlee Wild	b	f	1988	Wild Again	Raise Me	
Prince Randi	dk b/br	c	1986	Caveat	Randi's Queen	
Haint	dk b/br	c	1994	Devil's Bag	Realm	
Northern Lombardi	b	f	1989	Lombardi	Reckless Star	
Carnival Dancer (GB)	b	c	1998	Sadler's Wells	Red Carnival	G3
Funfair (GB)	b	g	1999	Singspiel (Ire)	Red Carnival	G2
Desert Lord (GB)	b	g	2000	Green Desert	Red Carnival	G1
Crustaceo	ch	c	2002	Royal Anthem	Regal Grant	G1
Mar Mar	dk b/br	f	1984	Forever Casting	Retospector	G3
Brilliant Prospect	ro	f	1991	Marine Bras	Ridan Prospect	
Snowberg	b	f	1995	Seattle Sleet	Ridan Prospect	
San Nicolas	dk b/br	c	1998	Go for Gin	Riffle	
Flying Spur (Aus)	b	c	1992	Danehill	Rolls	G1
Mcgwire		c	1985	White Face (Arg)	Roundelay	G1
Holy Holy Holy	dk b/br	f	1986	Lord of All	Roxie Turpin	
Gallant Talent	b	c	1992	Local Talent	Rub al Khali	
Resounder	b	g	1993	Explodent	Rub al Khali	
Fusaichi Airedale (Jpn)	dk b/br	f	1996	Sunday Silence	Rustic Belle	G2
Bellagio (Jpn)	b	c	1999	Mejiro Ryan (Jpn)	Rustic Belle	

INBREEDING MALE	INBREEDING FEMALE
Nasrullah 5x5	
Nasrullah 5x5	
Nasrullah 4x5; Native Dancer 5x4x5	
Nasrullah 5x5x5	
Native Dancer 4x4	
Nasrullah 5x5x5	
Nasrullah 5x5x5	
Native Dancer 5x5x4x5	Natalma 4 (Northern Dancer) x 4 (Spring Adieu) x 4 (Raise the Standard); Almahmoud 5 (Natalma), x 5 (Natalma) x 5 (Cosmah) x 5 (Natalma)
Nearco 4x5x5; Native Dancer 4x4x5;	
Nasrullah 5x5	
none	
Nearco 4x5x5; Native Dancer 4x4; Nasrullah 5x5x4	
Native Dancer 4x4	
none	
Native Dancer 5x4; Nasrullah 5x5x5	
Turn-to 5x5; Bold Ruler 5x5	
none	
Princequillo 4x5	
Round Table 5x4	
Nasrullah 5x5; Polynesian 5x5	
Northern Dancer 3x4; Native Dancer 5x5x4	Natalma 4 (Northern Dancer) x 4 (Spring Adieu) x 5 (Northern Dancer)
Colombo 3x5	
Native Dancer 4x4x4; Jet Action 5x4	
Native Dancer 4x4x5; Nasrullah 5x5	
none	
Royal Charger 5x4	
none	

APPENDIX: MR. PROSPECTOR'S STAKES WINNERS AS BROODMARE SIRE

HORSE	COLOR	SEX	YEAR	SIRE	DAM	STATUS
Battlin Prospect	dk b/br	g	1985	Ribet	Ryan's Prospect	
I've Decided	dk b/br	g	1997	Bertrando	Ryn	
Sensation	b	f	2003	Dixie Union	Ryn	G3
Welcome Home	b	f	2001	Dixieland Band	Safe Return	
Walayef	b	f	2000	Danzig	Sayedat Alhadh	G3
Ulfah	b	f	2001	Danzig	Sayedat Alhadh	
Iron Gavel	ch	g	1990	Time for a Change	Sealed Bid	G2
Divine Task	ch	c	1998	Irish River (Fr)	Set in Motion	G3
State Shinto	dk b/br	g	1996	Pleasant Colony	Sha Tha	G2
Raft Trip	b	c	1986	Assert (Ire)	Shawnee Creek	G2
Rose Violet	b	f	1990	Alleged	Shawnee Creek	
Storm Creek	dk b/br	c	1993	Storm Cat	Shawnee Creek	G3
She's Tops	dk b/br	f	1989	Capote	She's a Talent	G2
Early Colony	dk b/br	c	1994	Pleasant Colony	She's a Talent	
Agog (Ire)	ch	c	1999	Singspiel (Ire)	Shining Eyes	
Silver Deputy	b	c	1985	Deputy Minister	Silver Valley	
Buzzy's Gold	ch	c	2000	Touch Gold	Silver Valley	
Six Zero (Fr)	gr/ro	c	1994	Linamix (Fr)	Six Love	
Bint Allayl (GB)	b	f	1996	Green Desert	Society Lady	G2
Kheleyf	dk b/br	c	2001	Green Desert	Society Lady	G3
Lake William	dk b/br	c	1996	Salt Lake	Sol de Terre	G3
Dixieland Diamond	dk b/br	c	1997	Dixieland Band	Sometimesadia-mond	
Didyme	b	c	1990	Dixieland Band	Soundings	G2
Green Tune	ch	c	1991	Green Dancer	Soundings	G1
Ecoute	b	f	1993	Manila	Soundings	
Pas de Reponse	b	f	1994	Danzig	Soundings	G1
Special Broad	dk b/br	f	1990	Broad Brush	Special Strike	G3
Beware Avalanche	b	g	1996	Mt. Livermore	Special Strike	
Astro	dk b/br	c	1986	Five Star Flight	Stone Rock	

INBREEDING MALE	INBREEDING FEMALE
Native Dancer 4x4	
Native Dancer 5x4	
Northern Dancer 3x4; Mr. Prospector 4x2; Native Dancer 5x4	
Native Dancer 4x4	
Native Dancer 4x4	
Native Dancer 4x4	
Nasrullah 5x5	
Nasrullah 4x5	
Nasrullah 5x5	
Native Dancer 5x5x4	
Count Fleet 5x5	
Native Dancer 5x4; Nasrullah 5x5	
Nasrullah 4x5x5x5; Bold Ruler 5x4	
Nasrullah 5x5x5	
Northern Dancer 4x4	
Native Dancer 5x4; Polynesian 5x5	
none	
Northern Dancer 5x4	
Northern Dancer 3x4; Native Dancer 5x4; Nasrullah 5x5	
Northern Dancer 3x4; Native Dancer 5x4; Nasrullah 5x5	
none	
Nearctic 3x5; Native Dancer 4x4	
Northern Dancer 2x4; Native Dancer 4x4	
Northern Dancer 3x4; Bull Page 4x5; Native Dancer 5x4	
Northern Dancer 3x4; Native Dancer 5x4; Nasrullah 5x5	
Northern Dancer 2x4; Native Dancer 4x4	
none	
Nasrullah 4x5	
Nasrullah 4x5	

APPENDIX: MR. PROSPECTOR'S STAKES WINNERS AS BROODMARE SIRE

HORSE	COLOR	SEX	YEAR	SIRE	DAM	STATUS
Sleek World	ro	g	1991	Will Win	Street Native	
Identical Prospect	dk b/br	f	1986	Verbatim	Stretch Prospector	
Sky Chariot	ch	g	1996	Sky Classic	Stutz Goldrush	
Sir Harry Lewis	b	c	1984	Alleged	Sue Babe	G1
Sir Richard Lews	b	c	1987	Carr de Naskra	Sue Babe	
Cyrano	b	c	1992	Seattle Slew	Sue Babe	
Vamos Al Oro	dk b/b	c	1984	Forli	Sugar Gold	
Kechi	sb	g	1986	Pappa Riccio	Sugar Gold	
Prospector's Flag	dk b/br	c	1990	Personal Flag	Sugar Gold	G3
Under the Rug	b	f	1995	Lord At War (Arg)	Sweepings	
One Cool Cat	dk b/br	c	2001	Storm Cat	Tacha	G1
Crystal Symphony	b	f	1996	Red Ransom	Tappity Tap	G3
Silver Colours	dk b/br	f	1997	Silver Hawk	Team Colors	
God of Chance (Jpn)	b	c	1998	Cozzene	Team Colors	G2
Carnegie Daian (Jpn)	dk b/br	c	1997	Carnegie (Ire)	Teibun Angel	G3
Startac	b	c	1998	Theatrical (Ire)	Tenga	G1
Rock Hard Ten	dk b/br	c	2001	Kris S.	Tersa	G1
Daiwa Bandit	b	c	2001	Boston Harbor	Texas Robbery	G3
Thirst for Peace	b	f	1989	Time for a Change	Thirst for Gold	G2
Reallyaroan	dk b/br	f	1993	Imperial Falcon	Tiz a Looker	
Twenty Four Hours	dk b/br	g	1987	Moonsplash	Twenty Four Carats	
Sundrenched (Ire)	ch	f	1999	Desert King (Ire)	Utr	
Phantom Jet	b	c	1984	Tri Jet	Vain Gold	G3
Behind the Mask (Jpn)	b	f	1996	White Muzzle (GB)	Vain Gold	G2
Wasseema	b	f	2003	Danzig	Vantive	
Visionary (Fr)	gr/ro	c	1994	Linamix (Fr)	Visor	
Visorama (Ire)	gr/ro	f	2000	Linamix (Fr)	Visor	G3
Visindar (GB)	ch	c	2003	Sinndar (Ire)	Visor	G2

INBREEDING MALE	INBREEDING FEMALE
Raise a Native 2x3; Native Dancer 3x4x5	
Nasrullah 4x5x5; Count Fleet 5x5	
Native Dancer 5x4; Nasrullah 5x5	
Count Fleet 5x5	
Nasrullah 5x5x5	
Nasrullah 5x5x5; Polynesian 5x5	
none	
Nashua 2x4; Nasrullah 3x5x5x5; Raise a Native 3x3	
none	
none	
Northern Dancer 3x3; Native Dancer 5x4; Nasrullah 5x5	
Nashua 4x4; Nearco 5x5	
Nashua 4x4	
Nasrullah 5x5; Count Fleet 5x5	
Native Dancer 5x4; Hail to Reason 5x3; Nasrullah 5x5x5	
Native Dancer 5x4	Pange 4 (Sensibility) x 4 (Strip Poker)
Hail to Reeason 3x4; Nashua 4x4; Nasrullah 5x5x5	
Nasrullah 5x5x5	
Nasrullah 5x5	
Native Dancer 4x4	
Nasrullah 4x5x5; Polynesian 4x5	
none	
none	
none	
Native Dancer 4x4	
none	
none	
none	

APPENDIX: MR. PROSPECTOR'S STAKES WINNERS AS BROODMARE SIRE

HORSE	COLOR	SEX	YEAR	SIRE	DAM	STATUS
Oath	dk b/br	f	1994	Known Fact	Vue	G1
Secrage	b	f	1990	Secreto	Wayage	G3
Crystal Castle	b	g	1998	Gilded Time	Wayage	G2
Three Peat	ch	g	1989	Magesterial	Whatsoraire	G2
Tahdeed	ch	c	1990	Shadeed	Widaad	
Deed of Love	dk b/br	c	1993	Shadeed	Widaad	
Oriental Fashion (Ire)	b	f	1996	Marju (Ire)	Wijdan	G2
Makderah (Ire)	b	f	2003	Danehill	Wijdan	
Capable Capers	dk b/br	c	1999	Native Factor	Wind Capers	
Winzalot	b	c	2003	Forest Wildcat	Winze	
Always Friendly (GB)	ch	f	1988	High Line (GB)	Wise Specula-tion	G3
With Ability	b	f	1998	A.P. Indy	Withallprob-ability	G3
Nelson	b	c	1987	Seattle Slew	Witwatersrand	G3
Chokai Carol	ch	f	1991	Brian's Time	Witwatersrand	G1
Tale of the Cat	dk b/br	c	1994	Storm Cat	Yarn	G2
Spunoutacontrol	dk b/br	f	1996	Wild Again	Yarn	
Minardi	dk b/br	c	1998	Boundary	Yarn	G1
Anna Karenina (Ire)	b	f	2003	Green Desert	Simaat	
Sopran Promo (Ire)	b	c	2004	Montjeu (Ire)	Middle Prospect	
Massuese	dk b/br	f	2002	Dynaformer	Pedicure	G3
Hiraboku Royal (Jpn)	dk b/br	c	2004	Tanino Gimlet (Jpn)	Mars Violet	
A. P. Arrow	ch	c	2002	A.P. Indy	Garimpeiro	G3
Helion (Arg)	b	g	2002	Riton (Fr)	Tiz a Looker	G2
Dubai to Dubai	dk b/br	c	1998	Kris S.	Mr. P's Princess	
Heathcote (GB)	b	g	2002	Unfuwain	Chere Amie	
Sydenham	b	c	1998	A.P. Indy	Crystal Shard	

INBREEDING MALE	INBREEDING FEMALE
none	
Native Dancer 4x4; Nasrullah 5x5; Princequillo 5x5x5	
Native Dancer 4x4; Princequillo 4x5; Count Fleet 5x5; Nasrullah 5x5	
Native Dancer 4x4x4; Bold Ruler 4x4; Mahmoud 5x5; Nasrullah 5x5x5	Grey Flight 5 (Misty Morn) x 4 (What a Pleasure)
Native Dancer 5x4	
Native Dancer 5x4	
Crepello 5x5	
Native Dancer 5x5x4	
Bold Ruler 4x4; Nashua 4x4; Nasrullah 5x5x5x5x5	
Northern Dancer 4x4; Raise a Native 4x3	
none	
Nasrullah 5x5	
Nasrullah 5x5x5; Polynesian 5x5	
Nashua 4x4	
Northern Dancer 3x5; Bold Ruler 4x5; Native Dancer 5x4; Nasrullah 5x5; Princequillo 5x5	
Native Dancer 4x4	
Northern Dancer 3x5; Native Dancer 5x4; Princequillo 5x5; Bold Ruler 5x5	Knight's Daughter 5 (Round Table) x 5 (Monarchy)
Native Dancer 5x4; Crafty Admiral 5x5; Nasrullah 5x5	
Native Dancer 5x4	
Nashua 4x4	
Turn-to 5x5; Nashua 5x4	
Nasrullah 5x5	
none	
Nashua 4x4; Nasrullah 5x5x4	
Northern Dancer 2x5; Native Dancer 4x4	
Nasrullah 5x5	

APPENDIX: MR. PROSPECTOR'S MILLION-DOLLAR YEARLINGS

HORSE	COLOR	SEX	YEAR	DAM
Shah Jehan	dk b/br	c	1999	Voodoo Lily
Fusaichi Pegasus	b	c	1997	Angel Fever
Hoyer	dk b/br	c	2000	Destination Mir
Born Perfect	b	f	1999	Molly Girl
Act of Duty	ch	c	2000	Nuryette
Woodman	ch	c	1983	Playmate
Royal Walk	dk b/br	c	2000	Stone Flower
Ochoco	b	c	1998	Eaves
Al Zawbaah	b	c	1982	Ocean's Answer
Apuron	dk b/br	c	1982	Regal Line
Holt	dk b/br	c	1999	Fineza
Tagish	dk b/br	c	1986	Waya (Fr)
Sasha's Prospect	gr	c	1996	Missy's Mirage
Shan Fara	dk b/br	c	1998	Sheer Elegance
Pelican Island	ch	f	2000	Lady Madonna
Hardy	b	c	1997	Korveya
Sharp Breeze	dk b/br	g	2000	Windy Mindy
Hushood	dk b/br	c	2000	Princess Mitterand
Gone West	dk b/br	c	1984	Secrettame
Shakeel	b	c	1988	Mom's Command
Renoir	dk b/br	c	1997	Foreign Aid
Numerous	b	c	1991	Number
Suitably Discreet	b	f	1998	Alywow
Videographic	b	c	1997	Video
Paynes Bay	b	c	1998	Embellished

BROODMARE SIRE	PRICE	STATUS
Baldski	4,400,000	G3sp
Danzig	4,000,000	G1
Cherokee Colony	3,800,000	unraced
Seattle Slew	3,600,000	unraced
Nureyev	3,600,000	placed
Buckpasser	3,000,000	G3
Storm Bird	3,000,000	runner
Cox's Ridge	3,000,000	winner
Northern Answer	2,700,000	winner
Prince John	2,600,000	winner
Lypheor (GB)	2,450,000	winner
Faraway Son	2,400,000	winner
Stop the Music	2,300,000	winner
Capote	2,250,000	runner
Chief's Crown	2,100,000	winner
Riverman	2,100,000	winner
Honey Jay	1,900,000	winner
Seattle Slew	1,900,000	placed
Secretariat	1,900,000	G1
Top Command	1,800,000	winner
Danzig	1,700,000	winner
Nijinsky II	1,700,000	G3
Alysheba	1,635,960	unraced
Niinsky II	1,600,000	runner
Seattle Slew	1,600,000	winner

APPENDIX: MR. PROSPECTOR'S MILLION-DOLLAR YEARLINGS

HORSE	COLOR	SEX	YEAR	DAM
Mashaarif	ch	f	1987	Larida
Kasparov	b	c	1999	Sovereign Kitty
Secret Pond	dk b/br	c	1999	Golden Pond (Ire)
Graphite	dk b/br	f	1984	Stellarette
Golden Voyager	b	c	1987	La Voyageuse
Gallant Prospect	dk b/br	c	1987	Jadana (Ire)
E Dubai	b	c	1998	Words of War
Team Colors	b	f	1988	Private Colors
Laabity	b	c	1991	Bound
Constant Wish	b	f	1994	Daring Bidder
La Lupe	b	f	1989	Larida
Istibshar	b	c	1991	Namaqua
Barkerville	b	c	1988	Euryanthe
Al Sakkab	dk b/br	c	1999	Fit to Scout
True Panache	b	c	1985	Durtal (Ire)
Excavate	ch	c	1988	Anne Campbell
Pompion	dk b/br	c	1989	Midnight Pumpkin
Golden Legend	b	c	1992	Reminiscing
Golden Colors	b	f	1993	Winning Colors
Wayward Bound	dk b/br	f	1990	Really Lucky
unnamed	b	c	1998	Angel Fever
Serena's Tune	b	f	1998	Serena's Song
Kingsland	ch	f	1998	Fit for a Queen
Elizabeth Bay	b	f	1990	Life at the Top

BROODMARE SIRE	PRICE	STATUS
Northern Dancer	1,500,000	unraced
Sovereign Dancer	1,500,000	winner
Don't Forget Me (Ire)	1,400,000	unraced
Tentam	1,400,000	winner
Tentam	1,400,000	winner
Pharly (Fr)	1,400,000	unraced
Lord At War (Arg)	1,350,000	G2
Private Account	1,325,000	unraced
Nijinsky II	1,300,000	winner
Bold Bidder	1,250,000	unraced
Northern Dancer	1,200,000	winner
Storm Bird	1,200,000	winner
Nijinsky II	1,200,000	G2
Fit to Fight	1,200,000	runner
Lyphard	1,150,000	winner
Never Bend	1,100,000	G2sp
Pretense	1,050,000	placed
Never Bend	1,050,000	runner
Caro (Ire)	1,050,000	G3sp
Northern Dancer	1,000,000	winner
Danzig	1,000,000	unraced
Rahy	1,000,000	SW
Fit to Fight	1,000,000	G2sp
Seattle Slew	1,000,000	G3

HORSE	C	S	YEAR	DAM	BROODMARE SIRE	STATUS
Chalk Sound	gr	c	1988	Floating Taler	Verbatim	
Diablo Amigo	ch	g	1988	Made in America	Explodent	
Hansel	b	c	1988	Count On Bonnie	Dancing Count	G1
Hector Protector	ch	c	1988	Korveya	Riverman	G1
Inspired Prospect	b	c	1988	Inspire	Tell	
Mujtahid	ch	c	1988	Mesmerize (Ire)	Mill Reef	G2
Our Woodman	b	g	1989	Fedora	Exceller	
Andromaque	ch	f	1990	Heaven's Mine	Graustark	G2
Brankman	gr	g	1990	The Branks	Hold Your Peace	
Saw Mill	ch	c	1990	Reina Real (Arg)	Escudo Real (Arg)	
Woods of Windsor	b	c	1990	Cyane's Slippers	Cyane	G3
Wootton Rivers	ch	c	1990	Mount Holyoke (Ire)	Golden Fleece	G2
Bound by Honor	b	c	1991	Jody G.	Roberto	G3
First Flag	gr	f	1991	Hoist Her Flag	Aferd	
Honest Advice	b	g	1991	Don't Honey Me	Triple Bend	
Lahint	c	c	1991	Count On Bonnie	Dancing Count	G3
Mahogany Hall	ch	c	1991	Glimpse of Heaven	Majestic Light	G1
Saltgrass	b	c	1991	Papochino	Apalachee	
Who's John Galt	dk b/ br	c	1991	Faint Heart	Baldski	
Wood of Binn	b	f	1991	The Way It's Binn	Peterhof	G3
Chadayed	dk b/ br	c	1992	Chaudennay	Assert (Ire)	

HORSE	C	S	YEAR	DAM	BROODMARE SIRE	STATUS
Gay Gallanta	ch	f	1992	Gallanta (Fr)	Nureyev	G1
Genovefa	b	f	1992	Reigning Countess	Far North	G3
Golden Orb (Ire)	ch	f	1992	Katie May (GB)	Busted (GB)	
Heart of Oak	ch	c	1992	L'On Vite	Secretariat	
Hishi Akebono	dk b/br	c	1992	Mysteries	Seattle Slew	G1
Kathie's Colleen	ch	f	1992	Royal Colleen	Viceregal	G2
Mr. Woodman	b	c	1992	Jardiniere (Ire)	Nijinsky II	
Passionnee	b	f	1992	Pallanza	Lyphard	
Timber Country	ch	c	1992	Fall Aspen	Pretense	G1
Bosra Sham	ch	f	1993	Korveya	Riverman	G1
Ethyl Mae	ch	f	1993	Diane Suzanne	Compliance	
Favorable Ruling	ch	c	1993	Halo Reply	Halo	
Fleur de Nuit	ch	f	1993	Pearl Bracelet	Lyphard	G3
Moon Is Up	b	f	1993	Miesque	Nureyev	
Woodborough	ch	c	1993	Performing Arts (Ire)	The Minstrel	G3
Woodyoubelieveit	b	f	1993	Tricky Fingers	Clever Trick	
Young and Daring	b	f	1993	Youthful Lady	Youth	
Bahhare	b	c	1994	Wasnah	Nijinsky II	G2
Bint Albaadiya	ch	f	1994	Pixie Erin (Ire)	Golden Fleece	
Deodar	b	c	1994	Dhaka	Icecapade	
Dr Johnson	ch	c	1994	Russian Ballet	Nijinsky II	
Holzmeister	ch	c	1994	Harbour Club	Danzig	
Mingling Glances	b	f	1994	Last Glance	Storm Bird	

HORSE	C	S	YEAR	DAM	BROODMARE SIRE	STATUS
Raise Suzuran	ch	c	1994	Sintanous	Danzig	G2
Shell Ginger (Ire)	ch	f	1994	Truly Bound	In Reality	G3
Speed World	gr/ro	c	1994	Gray Tab	Zulu Tom	G3
Woodman's Classic	ch	f	1994	Doubling Time	Timeless Moment	
Wouldn't We All	ch	c	1994	Dream Launch	Relaunch	
Campo Catino (Ire)	br	c	1995	Karri Valley	Storm Bird	
Gypsy Passion (Ire)	ch	c	1995	Rua d'Oro	El Gran Senor	
Hariymi (Ire)	gr	c	1995	Harouniya (Ire)	Siberian Express	
Inspiring Story	b	c	1995	Looking Brill (GB)	Sadler's Wells	
Loon	ch	f	1995	Water Bird	Golden Eagle	
Lord Ax	ch	c	1995	Perl	Graustark	G3
Perfectly Clear	ch	f	1995	Crystal Cream	Secretariat	
Woodland Melody	b	f	1995	Eloquent Minister	Deputy Minister	G3
Franc	b	g	1996	Adventur-ous Di	Private Account	
Hula Angel	b	f	1996	Jode	Danzig	G1
Magic of Sunrise	b	f	1996	Country Cruise	Riverman	
Major Force	b	c	1996	Ready for Action	Riverman	G3
Patience Game	dk b/br	c	1996	Starboard Tack	Seattle Slew	G3
Queen of Norway	ch	f	1996	Qena	The Minstrel	
Tuscania	ch	f	1996	Excitable	Nijinsky II	
Way of Light	dk b/br	c	1996	Salchow	Nijinsky II	G1
Wonneberg	dk b/br	c	1996	Sweet Briar Too	Briartic	

HORSE	C	S	YEAR	DAM	BROODMARE SIRE	STATUS
Woodcarver	gr/ro	c	1996	Sharpening Up	Sharpen Up (GB)	
Airline	dk b/br	f	1997	Action Francaise	Nureyev	
Ciro	ch	c	1997	Gioconda	Nijinsky II	G1
Hataab	ch	c	1997	Miss Mistle-toes (Ire)	The Minstrel	
Kathir	ch	c	1997	Alcando (Ire)	Alzao	G1
Runspastum	b	c	1997	Erandel	Danzig	G3
Coral Salute (NZ)	ch	g	1998	Ethnic (GB)	Rainbow Quest	G3
First Fleet	ch	f	1998	Frankova	Nureyev	
Golden Fawn (Aus)	ch	g	1998	Marscay's Dream (Aus)	Marscay (Aus)	
Illusioned	ch	d	1998	Undeniably	In Reality	G3
Lord Prevail	ch	c	1998	Dance Play (GB)	The Minstrel	
Quiet Ruler	ch	g	1998	Rivermorn	Riverman	
Sheraton (Aus)	ch	g	1998	Bint Mars-cay (Aus)	Marscay (Aus)	G3
Taimana (NZ)	br	f	1998	Abbaye (Aus)	Ahonoora (GB)	G2
Timber Trader (NZ)	b	c	1998	Glenview	Sir Tristram (Ire)	G1
Translucid	dk b/br	c	1998	Gossamer	Seattle Slew	
Wood Sprite	b	f	1998	Long Silence	Alleged	
Wooden Doll	ch	f	1998	Kingscote (Ire)	Kings Lake	
Woodmoon	ch	g	1998	Laramie Moon (Arg)	Swaps	
Allodial Land	b	c	1999	Min Elreeh	Danzig	
Bush Honey (Aus)	br	f	1999	Saving (NZ)	Pevero (Ire)	G3
Chiselling	b	f	1999	Toussaud	El Gran Senor	G1
Civil (Aus)	ch	g	1999	Lihir (NZ)	Grosvenor (NZ)	

HORSE	C	S	YEAR	DAM	BROODMARE SIRE	STATUS
Conspectus (Aus)	ch	g	1999	Planet Hollywood (Aus)	Star Watch (Aus)	
Crianca (Aus)	ch	f	1999	Supermodel (Aus)	Bletchingly (Aus)	G3
Hawk Wing	b	c	1999	La Lorgnette	Val de l'Orne (Fr)	G1
Imtiyaz	gr/ro	c	1999	Shadayid	Shadeed	
Redwood Falls (Aus)	ch	c	1999	Only a Lady	Sir Tristram (Ire)	G1
Zero Engagement (Aus)	b	g	1999	Dateless (NZ)	Grosvenor (NZ)	
Forest Shadows	ch	f	2000	Dance of Sunshine	Sunshine Forever	
Lismore Knight	b	g	2000	Lismore Lady	Ogygian	G2
Shawklit Man	ch	c	2000	Shawklit	Groshawk	
Sue's Good News	ch	f	2000	Montera	Easy Goer	G3
Kelliewood (Aus)	b	f	2000	Welsh Treasure	Sir Ivor	
Mermaid's Flannel (Aus)	b	f	2001	Royal Accord (Aus)	Imperial Prince (Ire)	
Quartier Latin	dk b/br	c	2001	Qui Bid	Spectacular Bid	
Silverpoint (Aus)	ch	g	2001	Early Song (GB)	Precocious (GB)	G2
Sujimoto	ch	g	2001	Slew of Comfort	Seattle Slew	
Fishy Advice	ch	c	2002	Lady Skywalker	Skywalker	
Where Woody Bea	ch	f	2002	Maratha	Devil's Bag	
Fenice (Ire)	gr	c	2003	Venize (Ire)	Kaldoun (Fr)	G3
Grigorieva (Ire)	ch	f	2003	Elbaaha (GB)	Arazi	

HORSE	C	S	YEAR	DAM	BROODMARE SIRE	STATUS
Athenea (Chi)	ch	f	1995	Impuesta	L'Avalanche	G1
Byblos	ch	g	1995	Brittany's Dream	Worldwatch	G1
Desert Fight (Chi)	b	f	2003	Mozinha (Chi)	Mocito Feliz (Chi)	G1
Domaine (Chi)	b	f	2001	Walkabout (Chi)	Worldwatch	G1
El Cumbres (Chi)	b	c	2002	Mascara Roja	Cresta Rider	G1
Franbulo (Chi)	dk b/ br	g	1996	Seminola	Mr. Long	G1
Host (Chi)	ch	c	2000	Colonna Trajana (Chi)	Roy	G1
Hush Money (Chi)	ch	f	2003	Westminster Cathedral (Chi)	Wagon Master (Fr)	G1
Husson (Arg)	ch	c	2003	Villa Elisa (Chi)	Roy	G1
La Chiflota (Chi)	b	f	2002	Single Bet (Arg)	Lorenzoni	G1
Lhiz (Chi)	dk b/ br	f	1998	Dinasty (Chi)	Cresta Rider	G1
Mail Coach (Chi)	dk b/ br	c	1995	Whisper Loud	Worldwatch	G1
Mar De Kara (Chi)	b	f	1997	Urania (Arg)	El Azar (Arg)	G1
Marzuk (Chi)	b	c	1998	Daga (Chi)	Lake Erie (Ire)	G1
National Park (Chi)	b	c	1999	Piazza Venezia (Chi)	Roy	G1
Pecoiquen (Chi)	ch	g	2001	Tonquie (Chi)	Big Play	G1
Penamacor (Chi)	ch	c	1997	Rama (Chi)	Northern Disciple	G1
Perssonet (Chi)	b	g	1995	Percepcion (Chi)	Lake Erie (Ire)	G1
Printemps(Chi)	ch	f	1997	Wrist (Chi)	Worldwatch	G1
River Café (Chi)	ch	c	1998	Rhitza	Royal Danzig	G1

HORSE	C	S	YEAR	DAM	BROODMARE SIRE	STATUS
Shapira (Chi)	ch	f	2003	Shadhia (Chi)	Royal Danzig	G1
Spontaneous (Chi)	gr/ro	f	2003	Galoise (Chi)	Smooth Performance	G1
Trotamondo (Chi)	ch	c	2001	Movie Producer	Give Me Strength	G1
Wild Spirit (Chi)	dk b/br	f	1999	Wild Princess	Wild Again	G1
Arrowfield	b	f	2002	Clasical Lady	Clasico (Fr)	G2
Conservatorio (Chi)	b	g	2001	Carriole (Chi)	Worldwatch	G2
Dime (Chi)	ch	c	1996	Dafar (Chi)	Farnesio (Arg)	G2
Douce (Chi)	b	f	1998	Middle Class (Chi)	Worldwatch	G2
Grand Latour (Chi)		f	2003	Vilinsky (Chi)	Nijinsky Model	G2
Ivory (Chi)	ch	f	1995	White Night (Chi)	Worldwatch	G2
Petit Paris (Chi)	ch	c	2000	Petite France (Chi)	Roy	G2
Se Vera (Chi)	ch	f	1998	Senora Bonita	Stately Form (Ire)	G2
Seinne (Chi)	b	c	1997	White Lady (Chi)	Worldwatch	G2
Tifone (Chi)	ch	c	2003	Dona Oli	Settlement Day	G2
Tilbury (Chi)	b	g	1995	Wabira	Worldwatch	G2
Wild Storm (Chi)	b	f	2000	Wildwind	Worldwatch	G2
Amiral Medina (Chi)	ch	c	2001	Medina Sedonia (Chi)	Winning	G3
Anick (Chi)	ch	f	2000	Navy Blue (Chi)	Kazaroun	G3
Bollinger (Chi)	b	c	2001	Whisper Loud	Worldwatch	G3
Budha (Chi)	ch	c	2002	Cindyrella	Royal Danzig	G3

HORSE	C	S	YEAR	DAM	BROODMARE SIRE	STATUS
Ile St. Louis (Chi)	ch	c	1997	Middle Class (Chi)	Worldwatch	G3
Madour (Chi)	b	f	2001	Dona Oli	Settlement Day	G3
Mar Hondo (Chi)	b	c	2000	Sea Exhibition (Ire)	Tate Gallery	G3
Melancolique (Chi)	b	f	1997	Patsy (Chi)	Parisianne	G3
D'Yquem (Chi)	b	g	1999	Wei-Hai (Chi)	Worldwatch	
Ericeira (Chi)	ch	f	1997	Petite Ball	Settlement Day	
Gelderland (Chi)	gr/ro	f	1996	Watchme	Worldwatch	
Hospitably (Chi)	b	f	2002	Diamant (Chi)	Smooth Performance	
Husserl (Chi)	ch	g	1996	Sensitive	Maribeau	
La Tour (Chi)	b	f	1999	Vilinksy (Chi)	Nijinsky Model	
Mondrian (Chi)	ch	g	1996	Melle Katrine	Maribeau	
Perfect Match (Chi)	ch	f	2001	Brittany's Dream	Worldwatch	
Pitucaza (Chi)	b	f	1997	Wicha (Chi)	Worldwatch	
Ponte Leccia (Chi)	ch	f	1999	Petit Point	Manos de Piedra	
Alma Guerrera (Chi)	ch	f	2001	Tawila (Chi)	Roy	
Altea (Chi)	ch	f	1996	Fancy Way (Chi)	Settlement Day	
Anatole France (Chi)	ch	c	2000	Wahiana (Chi)	Worldwatch	
Aravis (Chi)	b	f	2001	Endearing Way	Conquistador Cielo	
Bay Beach (Chi)	b	f	2003	Teresa Bay (Arg)	Lode	
Beau Sarrasin (Chi)	b	c	2002	L'Eclipse	Smooth Performance	
Beduina Dorada (Chi)	ch	f	2001	House Party (Chi)	Roy	
Byn Shaddad (Chi)	b	g	1998	Colombina (Chi)	Kazaroun	
Canzona (Chi)	ch	f	1999	Johnny's Secretary	Secretariat	

APPENDIX: HUSSONET'S STAKES WINNERS

HORSE	C	S	YEAR	DAM	BROODMARE SIRE	STATUS
Capitan Cook (Chi)	ch	g	1997	Fibrana	Balconaje	
Champ de Mars (Chi)	gr/ro	c	1997	War Wind	Worldwatch	
Chariot (Chi)	ch	g	2001	Middle Class (Chi)	Worldwatch	
Cremroyal (Chi)	ch	f	2003	Cremcara-mel (Chi)	Roy	
Dionysius (Chi)	ch	c	2001	D'Hannis	Domineau	
Fiance (Chi)	gr/ro	c	1997	Claswat (Chi)	Clasico (Fr)	
First Morning (Chi)	ch	c	2001	Rosetta (Chi)	The Great Shark	
Galanteada (Chi)	ch	f	2002	Galia Cisal-pina (Chi)	Edgy Diplomat	
Gentile (Chi)	ch	f	1999	Gran Mineria	Maribeau	
Gig (Chi)	b	g	1995	Wake	Worldwatch	
Habib Adfl Medina (Chi)	ch	c	2000	Medina Sedonia (Chi)	Winning	
Hackney (Chi)	ch	c	1996	Cossifan-tutte (Chi)	Clasico (Fr)	
Haraldo (Chi)	ch	c	2002	Marisette (Chi)	Memo (Chi)	
Hassun Spor (Chi)	ch	g	1999	Ladera	Laguardia	
Hearty (Chi)	b	f	2000	Chiavetta (Arg)	Forlitano (Arg)	
Heroic (Chi)	b	c	2000	Moon Bride	Procida	
Hi Honey (Chi)	b	f	2000	Middle Class (Chi)	Worldwatch	
High Tech (Chi)	b	c	2000	Walia	Worldwatch	
Hinna (Chi)	ch	f	2002	Marbella (Chi)	Mocito Guapo (Arg)	
Hipocrite (Chi)	ch	f	2000	Wild Figure	Worldwatch	
Hivy (Chi)	b	f	2002	Marinola	Mocito Guapo (Arg)	
Holland (Chi)	dk b/br	f	2000	Amandita (Chi)	Roy	

HORSE	C	S	YEAR	DAM	BROODMARE SIRE	STATUS
Holsteiner (Chi)	b	g	1996	White Lady (Chi)	Worldwatch	
Hortense (Chi)	b	f	2000	Carriole (Chi)	Worldwatch	
Hueyusca (Chi)	b	f	2002	Walkabout (Chi)	Worldwatch	
Hutzy (Chi)	ch	f	1997	Rhitza	Royal Danzig	
L'Ete (Chi)	b	f	2001	Wrist (Chi)	Worldwatch	
L'Hiver (Chi)	ch	f	2002	Wrist (Chi)	Worldwatch	
Lagrezette (Chi)	b	f	2003	La Gaffeleire (Chi)	Worldwatch	
Le Yaca (Chi)	b	f	2003	Villa Torlonia	Roy	
Luna Caprese (Chi)	ch	f	2002	Politzer (Chi)	Northair	
Mac Donald (Chi)	dk b/ br	g	1999	Morena Alegre (Chi)	Rusty Anchor	
Maw Hub (Chi)	b	c	2000	Fluroistrada (Chi)	Roy	
Mozo Alegre (Chi)	b	c	1996	Mocita Joven	Mocito Guapo (Arg)	
Noche Oscura (Chi)	dk b/ br	f	2002	Nasty	Three Brothers	G2
Oldenburg (Chi)	b	g	1996	Urania (Arg)	El Azar (Arg)	
Petit Pierrot (Chi)	b	g	1999	L'Eclipse	Smooth Performance	
Reignac (Chi)	b	c	2003	Walia	Worldwatch	
Visconte (Chi)	ch	c	2002	Tallahassee (Chi)	Thornton Hill	
Yaapo (Chi)	b	f	2001	Wei-Hai (Chi)	Worldwatch	
Yildirim (Chi)	ch	c	2003	Madame Ivette (Chi)	Great Regent	
Husson Lightning (Aus)	b	c	2004	Snip Snip (Aus)	Snippets (Aus)	G3

HORSE	C	S	YEAR	DAM	BROODMARE SIRE	STATUS
Ailsa	ch	f	1985	Picture Pretty	Crimson Satan	
Crafty Wife	ch	f	1985	Wife Mistress	Secretariat	
Greg At Bat	ch	g	1985	Nearly a Princess	Prince John	
Prospectors Gamble	ro	c	1985	Fannie C.	Sunny South	G2
Cojinx	b	f	1986	Jinxed	Recaptured	
Crafty Ridan	dk b/br	c	1986	Lady Ridani-lustros	Illustrious	
Crafty Cash	ch	g	1987	Marsh Maid	Coastal	
Crafty Ember	dk b/br	f	1987	Autumn Ember	Gallant Man	
Crafty Gus	ch	g	1987	Honey Witch	Honey Jay	
Crafty Tenderoni	dk b/br	f	1987	Wonderous Steffie	Steve's Friend	
Music Prospector	b	c	1987	Think Music	Stop the Music	
Robyn Dancer	ro	c	1987	Double Dancer	Sword Dancer	G3
Crafty Alfel	ch	g	1988	Regal Lady Hour	Regal and Royal	
Crafty El	ch	f	1988	Sound of the El	Forgotten Dreams	
Infernos Reality	ch	f	1988	Temperature Hot	Believe It	
Topanga Mike	ch	g	1988	Salla Rose (Ire)	Sallust (GB)	
Win Crafty Lady	ch	f	1988	Honeytab	Al Hattab	G3
Crafty Dude	b	c	1989	Torsion Belle	Torsion	
Goldminer's Dream	ch	g	1989	Twelve Tribes	Fifth Marine	
Lonesome Train	ch	g	1989	Alaki Miss	Olden Times	
Looking for a Win	ch	f	1989	Delightful Spring	Francis S.	
Pas by Pas	b	c	1989	Pas Who	Pas Seul	

HORSE	C	S	YEAR	DAM	BROODMARE SIRE	STATUS
Sneaky Solicitor	ch	c	1989	Narrow Escape	Exceller	G3
Sublte Dancer	ch	f	1989	Agony	L'Enjoleur	
Winnie D.	ro	f	1989	Sharon Brown	Al Hattab	
Air Craft	ch	g	1990	We Believe in You	Vent du Nord	
Crafty	ch	c	1990	Tribal to Do	Restless Native	
Crafty Chris	dk b/br	g	1990	Key to My Dream	Key to the Mint	
For All Seasons	ch	f	1990	Religiosity	Irish Tower	
Sigrun	b	f	1990	April Dawn Marie	Baldski	
Smokin Joe Blow	dk b/br	g	1990	Cornish Art	Cornish Prince	
Chasin Gold	dk b/br	g	1991	Quick Results	Icecapade	
Dylan's Crafty	ch	f	1991	Dylan's Delight	One for All	
Lucky Pisces	ch	f	1991	Wig Hill	Cougar II	
Miss Prospector	ch	f	1991	Eternal Vow	Nasty and Bold	
Mr. Bluebird	b	g	1991	Glorious Calling	Nijinsky II	G2
Princess Joanne	ch	f	1991	Illustrious Joanne	Illustrious	
Yecein	ch	f	1991	Lady Val	Quiet Fling	G3
Boundless Moment	ch	g	1992	Mysterious Gift	Great Mystery	
Devious Course	b	c	1992	Saucy Deb	Mr. Leader	G1
Higher Desire	ch	g	1992	Desirous	Exclusive Era	
I'm Lucky	dk b/br	c	1992	Lucky Brook	What Luck	
Miss Golden Circle	ch	f	1992	River Missy	Riverman	G2
Prospect Bay	b	c	1992	Baltic Sea	Danzig	G2
Royal C.	b	c	1992	Landsgirl (Ger)	Rocket (GB)	G1

HORSE	C	S	YEAR	DAM	BROODMARE SIRE	STATUS
Crafty But Sweet	ch	f	1993	Keys Special	Chieftain	G3
Crafty Friend	ch	c	1993	Companion-ship	Princely Native	G2
Don Serafin	ch	c	1993	Fairy's Frolic	Coastal	G1
Gold Memory	ch	c	1993	Sweet Nostalgia	Mr. Redoy	
Goldminer's Gold	ch	c	1993	Miss Secreto	Secreto	
Inquisitive Look	b	f	1993	Illustrious Joanne	Illustrious	G3
Kool Krafty	dk b/br	g	1993	Cincinnity	Shareef Dancer	
Laredo	b	g	1993	La Grandeza	El Gran Senor	
Really Crafty	b	g	1993	Chez Chez Chez	Caucasus	
Reddogsprospector	ch	g	1993	Keep It Legal	Silent Screen	
Stone Stepper	dk b/br	c	1993	Cassadaga	Cassaleria	G3
Tri Line	b	c	1993	Great Birdie	Proud Birdie	
Amarillo	b	f	1994	Popachee	Apalachee	G3
Capture the Gold	ch	c	1994	Countess B. B.	King Emperor	
Crafty Buzz	b	f	1994	Intently	Drone	
Crafty Oak	dk b/br	f	1994	Oak Blossom	Tarleton Oak	G3
Crafty One	b	g	1994	Bonnie Partner	Full Partner	
Golden Cherry	ch	f	1994	A Kiss for Luck	Reflected Glory	G3
Liberty Gold	ch	c	1994	Restless Colony	Pleasant Colony	G3
Mr. Groush	ch	c	1994	Clint's Sec	Secretariat	G3
Phil the Grip	b	g	1994	Ionian Bride	Icecapade	G3
Vegas Prospector	gr/ro	f	1994	Hill Billy Dancer	Never Down Hill	G3
Crafty Toast	gr/ro	f	1995	Give a Toast	Storm Bird	

HORSE	C	S	YEAR	DAM	BROODMARE SIRE	STATUS
Lady Stella	ch	f	1995	Maggie J. Jones	Angle Light	G3
Steal a Heart	b	f	1995	Ransomed Bride	Private Account	
Crafty Number	ch	c	1996	Opposite Number	Secretariat	
Crafty Star	dk b/br	g	1996	Popular Tune	Stop the Music	
Dream for a Moment	ch	f	1996	A Thrilling Moment	Lydian	
Go to the Ink	b	f	1996	Pas Who	Pas Seul	
Agnes Digital	ch	c	1997	Chancey Squaw	Chief's Crown	G1
Golden Sunray	ch	f	1997	Aspenelle	Vice Regent	
Highway Prospector	dk b/br	g	1997	Highway Queen	Wavering Monarch	
Crafty C.T.	ch	c	1998	Andriana B.	Far North	G2
Crafty Shaw	ch	c	1998	Her She Shawklit	Air Forbes Won	G3
Interest Only	b	f	1998	Clever Tide	Clever Trick	
More Crafty	b	c	1998	Morepheme	Rahy	
Rose Frances	b	f	1998	Far Flying	Far North	
That's It Doc	gr/ ro	f	1998	I Fell for It	Hagley	
Crafty Schemer	b	g	1999	Scheme Away	Saratoga Six	
Crafty Guy	ch	g	2000	Sheepish Grin	Our Native	
R. Associate	b	g	2000	Letty's Pennant	Bold Forbes	G3
Crypto's Prospect	ch	g	2001	Crypto's Redjet	Cryptoclearance	
Pies Prospect	ch	c	2001	Hot Pillow	Bates Motel	G3
Chief What It Is	b	g	2003	Grey Matter	Housebuster	

APPENDIX: GONE WEST'S STAKES WINNERS

HORSE	CR	S	YEAR	DAM	BROODMARE SIRE	STATUS
Torrey Canyon	dk b/br	c	1989	Tovalop	Northern Dancer	
West by West	b	c	1989	West Turn	Cox's Ridge	G1
Western Approach	dk b/br	f	1989	Devon Diva	The Minstrel	
Double Sixes	dk b/br	f	1990	Cast the Die	Olden Times	G3
Elkhart	dk b/br	g	1990	Elvia	Roberto	
Gone Prospecting	b	c	1990	Kalista (GB)	Bellypha (Ire)	
Link River	ch	f	1990	Connecting Link	Linkage	G1
Mrs. West	dk b/br	d	1990	Mrs. Hat (GB)	Sharpen Up (GB)	
Mythical Hunter	b	c	1990	Mystery Mood	Night Invader	
Pacific West	b	g	1990	Brackish	Alleged	
Pembroke	b	c	1990	College Bold	Boldnesian	
Way West (Fr)	b	c	1990	Greenway (Fr)	Targowice	
Western Scout	dk b/br	g	1990	Best Dastilles	Storm Bird	
Zafonic	b	c	1990	Zaizafon	The Minstrel	G1
Aboline	ch	c	1991	Constantina	Petrone	G2
Defer West	dk b/br	f	1991	Defer	Damascus	
Gold Land	b	g	1991	Lajna (GB)	Be My Guest	G3
Gone for Real	dk b/br	c	1991	Intently	Drone	G3
Lassigny	ch	c	1991	Love Potion (Brz)	Rio Bravo	G1
Royal Abjar	ch	c	1991	Encorelle (Fr)	Arctic Tern	G2
West Man	dk b/br	c	1991	Belka (Fr)	Riverman	G3
Da Hoss	b	g	1992	Jolly Saint (Ire)	Welsh Saint (GB)	G1

HORSE	CR	S	YEAR	DAM	BROODMARE SIRE	STATUS
Legendary Priness	ch	f	1992	Halo Dotty	Halo	
Mr. Greeley	ch	c	1992	Long Legend	Reviewer	G3
Old Tascosa	dk b/br	g	1992	Chicken Delight	Cornish Prince	G2
Raah Algharb	b	c	1992	Pharlette (Fr)	Pharly (Fr)	G2
Supremo	b	c	1992	Personal Glory	Danzig	G2
Tamayaz	dk b/br	c	1992	Minstrelsy	The Minstrel	G3
Western Fame	b	c	1992	Fariedah	Topsider	
Western Larla	dk b/br	c	1992	Larla	Singh	G3
Western Winter	dk b/br	c	1992	Chilly Hostess	Vice Regent	
Elusive Quality	b	c	1993	Touch of Greatness	Hero's Honor	G3
Tossup	dk b/br	f	1993	Tovalop	Northern Dancer	
Western Dreamer	ch	f	1993	Dream Launch	Relaunch	
Zafolia	ch	c	1993	Gambling Fool	Majestic Light	G3
Dance Parade	ch	f	1994	River Jig	Irish River	G2
Dazzle (GB)	b	f	1994	Belle Et Deluree	The Minstrel	G2
Out West	dk b/br	f	1994	Chellingoua	Sharpen Up (GB)	
Western Borders	dk b/br	c	1994	Ruby Green	J. O. Tobin	
Zamindar	b	c	1994	Zaizafon	The Minstrel	G3
Double Honor	dk b/br	c	1995	Holiday Snow	Storm Bird	G3
Grand Slam	dk b/br	c	1995	Bright Candles	El Gran Senor	G1
Pulsatilla	b	f	1995	Peggibonsi	Proud Truth	
Blue Snake	dk b/br	c	1996	Dabaweyaa (Ire)	Shareef Dancer	G3

HORSE	CR	S	YEAR	DAM	BROODMARE SIRE	STATUS
Muqtarib	b	c	1996	Shicklah	The Minstrel	G2
Mythical Girl	b	f	1996	Yousefia	Danzig	G3
Commendable	ch	c	1997	Bought Twice	In Reality	G1
Dance Master	ch	c	1997	Nijinsky's Lover	Nijinsky II	G2
Performing Magic	ch	c	1997	Performing Arts (Ire)	The Minstrel	G2
Precious Feather	dk b/br	f	1997	Last Feather	Vaguely Noble	
Promontory Gold	ch	c	1997	Possibly Perfect	Northern Baby	G3
Race Leader	dk b/br	c	1997	Dubian (GB)	High Line (GB)	
Sweet Orchid	dk b/br	f	1997	Kenbu (Fr)	Kenmare (Fr)	G3
Trajectory	dk b/br	c	1997	Dream Launch	Relaunch	
Wacky Becky	dk b/br	f	1997	Lady Becker	Nijinsky II	
Conroy	ch	g	1998	Crystal Gazing	El Gran Senor	G3
East Is East	b	f	1998	Grease (Ire)	Filiberto	
Goncharova	b	f	1998	Pure Grain (GB)	Polish Precedent	G3
Hejaziah	dk b/br	f	1998	Top Trestle	Nijinsky II	
Love Kiss	b	f	1998	Hero's Love	Hero's Honor	
Mugharreb	b	c	1998	Marling (Ire)	Lomond	
Scoop	dk b/br	f	1998	Til Forbid	Temperence Hill	G3
Speightstown	ch	c	1998	Silken Cat	Storm Cat	G1
Zghorta	b	f	1998	Miss Alleged	Alleged	
Alienated	dk b/br	f	1999	Extrater-restral	Storm Bird	
Came Home	dk b/br	c	1999	Nice Assay	Clever Trick	G1

HORSE	CR	S	YEAR	DAM	BROODMARE SIRE	STATUS
Canadian Frontier	b	c	1999	Borodislew	Seattle Slew	G3
Castle Gandolfo	ch	c	1999	Golden Oriole	Northern Dancer	G3
Changeinthe-weather	b	c	1999	Meteor Colony	Pleasant Colony	G1
Foregone	dk b/br	c	1999	Adorned	Val de l'Orne	
Johar	b	c	1999	Windsharp	Lear Fan	G1
Proud Citizen	b	c	1999	Drums Of Freedom	Green Forest	G2
Saddad	ch	c	1999	Lite Light	Majestic Light	G2
Surging River	b	c	2000	Classic Slew	Seattle Slew	
Westerly Breeze	dk b/br	f	2000	On the Brink	Cox's Ridge	G2
Conditional	b	g	2001	Given Mo-ment	Diesis (GB)	
Madhya	b	f	2001	Khumba Mela (Ire)	Hero's Honor	
Move West	b	g	2001	Ristna (GB)	Kris (GB)	G1
Outlaw Kid	b	c	2001	Bounteous (Ire)	Last Tycoon (Ire)	
Pearl Grey (GB)	gr	f	2001	Zelanda (Ire)	Night Shift	
Smart Growth	dk b/br	c	2001	Ratings	Caveat	
Istan	b	c	2002	Ronda (GB)	Bluebird	
Last Best Place	ch	c	2003	Belle Cherie	Sovereign Edition	
Marsh Side	b	c	2003	Colonial Play	Pleasant Colony	
Stalwartly	dk b/br	c	2003	Dream Team	Cox's Ridge	
Union Avenue	b	c	2003	Miss Union Avenue	Steinlen	G2
Top Cross	dk b/br	c	2004	Top Order	Dayjur	

APPENDIX: MISWAKI'S STAKES WINNERS

HORSE	C	S	YEAR	DAM	BROODMARE SIRE	STATUS
Grande Couture	b	f	1983	Grande Vogue	Vaguely Noble	
Le Belvedere	b	c	1983	Louisville (Fr)	Val de l'Orne (Fr)	G2
Miscrown	dk b/br	c	1983	Sainera	Stop the Music	G3
Papal Power	ch	c	1983	Papal Decree	Noble Decree	G1
Playlist	b	f	1983	Night Light	Northern Dancer	
Endormir	ch	c	1984	Let Me Sleep	Cyane	
Liswaki	ch	f	1984	Thank You Note	Crème dela Crème	
Midyan	b	c	1984	Country Dream	Ribot	G3
Miss Tawpie	dk b/br	f	1984	Tawpie	In Reality	
Sweet Run	ch	f	1984	Sweetbidder	Bold Bidder	
Whakilyric	b	f	1984	Lyrism	Lyphard	G3
Balawaki	ch	f	1985	Balakhna (Fr)	Tyrant	G2
Miswaki Tern	ch	c	1985	Angela Serra (GB)	Arctic Tern	G2
Mr. Importance	ch	g	1985	Sugary Mist	Nijinsky II	
Waki River (Fr)	dk b/br	c	1985	River Reef (Fr)	Mill Reef	G1
Aliocha	b	c	1986	Chatter Box II	Ribot	G3
Bionic Prospect	ch	c	1986	Bionic Babe	Best Turn	
Black Tie Affair (Ire)	gr/ro	c	1986	Hat Tab Girl	Al Hattab	G1
Conductrice	ch	f	1986	Petit Axe	Outing Class	
Exploding Prospect	b	c	1986	Seasons Past	Explodent	G3
Flying Frippery	ch	f	1986	Delta June	Hawaii	
Miss Walkie Talkie	ch	f	1986	Charming Pan (Fr)	Trepan (Fr)	
Miss Waukesha	ch	f	1986	One and Only	Victor's Pride	
Mistaurian	ro	f	1986	Lady Taurian Peace	Peace Corps	G3
Pookette	b	f	1986	Pensioner	Irish Stronghold	

HORSE	C	S	YEAR	DAM	BROODMARE SIRE	STATUS
Wacky Princess	ch	f	1986	Cornish Princess	Cornish Prince	
Able Express	ch	c	1987	Ms. Balding	Sir Ivor	G2
Avec Les Bleus	ch	g	1987	Ave France	Seattle Slew	
Casey's Romance	b	f	1987	Zippy Do	Hilarious	
Fast Gin Fizz	ch	f	1987	Gin and Juice	Northjet	
Gervazy	dk b/br	c	1987	Ruby Green	J. O. Tobin	
Look n Good Darlin	ch	f	1987	One and Only	Victor's Pride	
Lucky Delight	b	f	1987	Lucky Ole Queen	King's Bishop	
Now Listen	b	c	1987	Nowanna	Envoy	G3
Raj Waki	b	c	1987	Script Approval	Silent Screen	
Spring Flight	b	f	1987	Coco La Investment	Coco La Terreur	
Wakia	b	f	1987	Rascal Rascal	Ack Ack	
Misil	ro	c	1988	April Edge	The Axe II	G1
Serapide	b	f	1988	Simply Divine	Danzig	
Umatilla (NZ)	b	c	1988	Dancing Show	Nijinsky II	G1
Daltawa (Ire)	gr	f	1989	Damana (Fr)	Crystal Palace	
Mister Slippers	ch	c	1989	Chaussons Roses	Lyphard	
Ninja Dancer	b	c	1989	Professional Dance	Nijinsky II	
Red Monsoon	ch	g	1989	Charlotte Amalie (Fr)	Gay Mecene	
Urban Sea	ch	f	1989	Allegretta (GB)	Lombard	G1
Waki Warrior	b	c	1989	Ecole d'Humanite	Bold Forbes	
Aisla	ch	f	1990	Angela Serra (GB)	Arctic Tern	
In Her Glory	dk b/br	f	1990	Forever Waving	Hoist the Flag	
Marvelous Crown	ch	g	1990	Maurita (NZ)	Harbor Prince	G1

HORSE	C	S	YEAR	DAM	BROODMARE SIRE	STATUS
Pont de Sevres	ch	c	1990	Place des Ternes (Ire)	Arctic Tern	
Bay Barrister	b	f	1991	Pas Who	Pas Seul	
Exotic Moves	ch	f	1991	Syrian Dancer	Damascus	
Grafin	ch	f	1991	Reigning Countess	Far North	G3
In My Heart	gr	f	1991	Party Bonnet	The Axe II	
Porto Varas	ch	c	1991	Angela Serra (GB)	Arctic Tern	G3
Showering	b	f	1991	Rain Shower	Bold Forbes	
Takeawakatlove	ch	g	1991	Love From the Air	Deputy Minister	
Another Felix	ch	g	1992	Give Her the Gun	Le Fabuleux	
Because I'm Gold	ch	f	1992	Why So Much	Northern Baby	
Mane Ingredient	b	c	1992	Lady of the North	Northern Baby	
Misnomer	b	c	1992	Danzig Darling	Danzig	
My Son Bill	dk b/br	g	1992	Friendly Face	Star de Naskra	
Allied Forces	ch	c	1993	Mangala	Sharpen Up (GB)	G2
Daylight Come	ch	f	1993	Lady Winner (Fr)	Fabulous Dancer	
Diligence	gr/ro	c	1993	Honeytab	Al Hattab	G2
Fly Fishing	ch	g	1993	Sharp Flick	Sharpen Up (GB)	
Kistena (Fr)	gr/ro	f	1993	Mabrova (GB)	Prince Mab (Fr)	G1
Abou Zouz	b	c	1994	Bold Jessie (GB)	Never So Bold (Ire)	G2
Hurricane State	ch	c	1994	Regal State	Affirmed	G3
Magellano	dk b/br	c	1994	Mount Holyoke (Ire)	Golden Fleece	G3
Set to Sizzle	dk b/br	g	1994	Smiling Neatly	Neater	
Arnaqueur	b	c	1995	All Along (Fr)	Targowice (Fr)	

HORSE	C	S	YEAR	DAM	BROODMARE SIRE	STATUS
Black Mystery	b	f	1995	Miss Secreto	Secreto	
Inexplicable	ch	c	1995	Mythomania	Nureyev	G3
Misty Hour	b	f	1995	Our Tina Marie	Nijinsky II	
Tertullian	ch	c	1995	Turbaine	Trempolino	G3
Cubism	b	c	1996	Seattle Kat	Seattle Song	
Taiki Treasure	b	c	1996	Royal Bride	Blushing Groom (Fr)	G3
Golden Indigo	ch	c	1997	Curl and Set	Nijinsky II	
Misty Mission	ch	f	1997	Hangin On a Star	Vice Regent	
Rossini	b	c	1997	Touch of Greatness	Hero's Honor	G2
Solaia	ch	f	1997	Indian Fashion	General Holme	
Tough Speed	b	c	1997	Nature's Magic	Nijinsky II	G3
Jentzen	b	g	1998	Bold Jessie (GB)	Never So Bold (Ire)	
Le Carre	gr/ ro	c	1998	Dibs	Spectacular Bid	
Panis	b	c	1998	Political Parody	Doonesbury	G3
Posadas	ch	f	1998	Portugal	Topsider	
Smart Timing	ch	f	1998	Sunrise Sonata	Track Barron	
Brown Eyed Beauty	b	f	1999	Stephie Brown Eyes	Explodent	
Kia Ora (Ind)	b	f	1999	Free Thinker	Shadeed	G2
Perfect Touch	b	f	1999	Glen Kate (Ire)	Glenstal	G3
Anani	ch	c	2000	Mystery Rays	Nijinsky II	
Etoile Montante	ch	f	2000	Willstar	Nureyev	G1
Miss Confusion	ch	f	2000	Carol	Jaklin Klugman	
Tarhundas (Tur)	b	f	2000	Royal Welcome (Ire)	Royal Academy	
Bachelor Duke	b	c	2001	Gossamer	Seattle Slew	G1
Sir Shackleton	ch	c	2001	Naskra Colors	Star de Naskra	G2
Zal's Pal	b	g	2001	Token's Pride		

Mr. Prospector's U.S. Classics Connections

This chart shows Mr. Prospector's generational influence on the U.S. classics. Starting with his sons, each indent represents the next generation.

Fappiano
  Cryptoclearance
    Victory Gallop .... 1998 Belmont S.
  Quiet American
    Real Quiet .... 1998 Kentucky Derby, Preakness S.
  Unbridled .... 1990 Kentucky Derby
    Grindstone ....1996 Kentucky Derby
      Birdstone .... 2004 Belmont S.
    Red Bullet .... 2000 Preakness S.
    Empire Maker .... 2003 Belmont S.
  Conquistador Cielo .... 1982 Belmont S.
  Tank's Prospect .... 1985 Preakness S.
Woodman
  Hansel .... 1991 Preakness S., Belmont S.
  Timber Country .... 1995 Preakness S.
Afleet
  Northern Afleet
    Afleet Alex .... 2005 Preakness S., Belmont S.

Gone West

   Elusive Quality

      Smarty Jones .... 2004 Kentucky Derby, Preakness S.

      Commendable .... 2000 Belmont S.

Gulch

      Thunder Gulch ....1995 Kentucky Derby, Belmont S.

      Point Given .... 2001 Preakness S., Belmont S.

Forty Niner

   Distorted Humor

      Funny Cide ...... 2003 Kentucky Derby, Preakness S.

      Editor's Note .... 1996 Belmont S.

Seeking the Gold

      Jazil .... 2006 Belmont S.

Machiavellian

   Street Cry (Ire)

      Street Sense .... 2007 Kentucky Derby

Kingmambo

      Lemon Drop Kid .... 1999 Belmont S.

Our Emblem

      War Emblem .... 2002 Kentucky Derby, Preakness S.

Smart Strike

      Curlin .... 2007 Preakness S.

Fusaichi Pegasus .... 2000 Kentucky Derby

Mr. Prospector's champions/highweights:

It's in the Air .... 1978 U.S. co-champion 2yo filly

Conquistador Cielo .... 1982 U.S. champion 3yo male and

Horse of the Year

Gold Beauty .... 1982 U.S. champion sprinter

Eillo .... 1984 U.S. champion sprinter

Proskona .... 1984 Italian champion 3yo filly

Woodman .... 1985 Irish champion 2yo male

Forty Niner .... 1987 U.S. champion 2yo male

Afleet .... 1987 Canadian champion 3yo male and Horse of the Year

Ravinella .... 1987 English and French champion 2yo filly;

1988 French and European highweight

3yo filly (1,400–1,900 meters)

Gulch .... 1988 U.S. champion sprinter

Tersa .... 1988 French and European champion 2yo filly

Machiavellian ....1989 French champion 2yo male

Rhythm ....1989 U.S. champion 2yo male

Maximilian .... 1990 German highweight 3yo (1,400–1,900 meters)

Queena.. 1991 U.S. champion older female

Coup de Genie ....1993 French champion 2yo filly

Distant View ....1994 English and European highweight

3yo (1,400–1,900 meters)

Faltaat ....1995 UAE highweight older male (1,000–1,400 meters)

Golden Attraction ....1995 U.S. champion 2yo filly

Desert Symphony .... 1996 Scandinavian highweight older male

Dancethruthedawn ....2001 Canadian champion 3yo filly

Aldebaran .... 2003 U.S. champion sprinter

Index

Photo Credits

Page 1:   Mr. Prospector in Florida (Louise Reinagel)

Page 2:   Louis Wolfson & Leslie Combs (Milt Toby)

Peter Brant (Anne M. Eberhardt)

Seth Hancock (Shigeki Kikkawa)

Jimmy Croll, Walter Blum, Butch Savin (The Blood-Horse)

Page 3:   Raise a Native (The Blood-Horse)

Gold Digger (Pimlico Race Course)

Nashua (The Blood-Horse)

Page 4:   Croll & Savin at 1971 Keeneland yearling sale

(John C. Wyatt)

Mr. Prospector in ring at Keeneland yearling sale

(John C. Wyatt)

Page 5:   Croll with Mr. P and Royal and Regal (Jim Raftery/Turfotos)

Mr. Prospector winning Whirlaway H. (Turfotos)

Mr. Prospector winning Gravesend H. (NYRA)

Page 6:   Mr. Prospector in paddock at Claiborne (Dell Hancock)

Page 7:   Kingmambo (John Crofts)

Hussonet (Dan Liebman)

Woodman (Tony Leonard)

Acknowledgments

If modesty is the hallmark of the great, then Hall of Fame trainer Jimmy Croll surely belongs in that class. His accomplishments speak for themselves, yet, generously, he has been willing to share his time and memories. This book would not be what it is without him.

I would also like to thank Hall of Fame jockey Walter Blum, who answered my questions about his rides on Mr. Prospector with patience, and the staff at Claiborne Farm, who helped round out the picture of Mr. Prospector as a stallion. Once again, the members of the Pedigree Query message board were invaluable, and, of course, this book could not have been written without the continued encouragement and support of my husband.

As usual, the editing staff at Eclipse Press has been wonderful to work with. And no list of acknowledgments would ever be complete without remembering God and his many gifts — to Him be the glory.

Avalyn Hunter
July 2007

About the Author

AVALYN HUNTER

One of the first pedigree books Avalyn Hunter can recall reading is Sir Charles Leicester's classic work *Bloodstock Breeding*, which later served as a model and inspiration for Hunter's first book, *American Classic Pedigrees 1914–2002.* Covering the race records, antecedents, and descendants of the winners of the American Triple Crown races plus the Kentucky Oaks and Coaching Club American Oaks for fillies, the massive work took some two years to write. It was published in 2003 by Eclipse Press. In 2006 Hunter fin-ished *The Kingmaker*, a work that looks at the life and the dynastic influence of the great Northern Dancer. Hunter has also published the award-winning fiction stories "The Passing of the Torch" and "The Foundation," both prizewinners in the *Thoroughbred Times* Biennial Fiction Contest, and regularly writes pedigree articles for *The Blood-Horse, MarketWatch,* and *Owner-Breeder International.*

A former Air Force officer, Hunter is a graduate of Vanderbilt University (BA, psychology) and Southern Illinois University at Edwardsville (MA, clinical psychology) and has worked as a mental health professional since 1993. She lives in Florida with her husband and two children.